LIMBANG REBELLION

EILEEN CHANIN is a Sydney-based author and historian. She received the Royal Marines Historical Society Literary Award in 2014, which marked the 350th anniversary of the formation of the Royal Marines. She is the first woman to be awarded the literary prize in its 48 year history. The prize is one among several awarded to her books. Her most recent book is *Capital Designs, Australia House and Visions of an Imperial London*. She is an Associate of the Australian National University and a Visiting Fellow of King's College London.

LIMBANG

7 DAYS IN DECEMBER 1962

REBELLION

EILEEN CHANIN

NEWSOUTH

First published in Australia in 2013 by New South Publishing,
University of New South Wales Press Ltd
Sydney NSW 2052

Reprinted in 2014 and reprinted in this format in 2021 by
PEN & SWORD MILITARY
An imprint of
Pen & Sword Books Ltd
47 Church Street
Barnsley, South Yorkshire
S70 2AS

ISBN 978 1 52679 698 1

A CIP catalogue record for this book is
available from the British Library

Printed and bound in England
By CPI Group (UK) Ltd, Croydon, CR0 4YY

Pen & Sword Books Ltd incorporates the Imprints of Aviation, Atlas,
Family History, Fiction, Maritime, Military, Discovery, Politics, History,
Archaeology, Select, Wharncliffe Local History, Wharncliffe True Crime,
Military Classics, Wharncliffe Transport, Leo Cooper, The Praetorian Press,
Remember When, Seaforth Publishing and Frontline Publishing

For a complete list of Pen & Sword titles please contact
PEN & SWORD BOOKS LIMITED
47 Church Street, Barnsley, South Yorkshire, S70 2AS, England
E-mail: enquiries@pen-and-sword.co.uk
Website: www.pen-and-sword.co.uk

CONTENTS

ABBREVIATIONS

ADC	Assistant District Commissioner; also, Aide-de-camp
ADO	Assistant District Officer
AIF	Australian Imperial Force
BBCAU	British Borneo Civil Administration Unit
BOAC	British Overseas Airways Corporation
Cdo	Commando Unit
Coy	Company
CQ	Company Quartermaster
CSM	Company Sergeant Major
DO	District Officer
FARELF	Far Eastern Land Force
GHQ	General Headquarters
GPMG	general purpose machine gun
HQ	Headquarters
IS	internal security
LMG	light machine gun
LPH	Landing Platform Helicopter
MAS	Malaysian Airways System
MC	Military Cross

MMGs	medium machine guns
MOA	Marine Officer's Attendant
NCO	Non-Commissioned Officer
'O' Group	Operations Group Meeting
PERINTREP	Periodic Intelligence Report
PRB	Parti Rakyat Brunei (People's Party of Brunei)
SITREP	Situation Report
SLR	self-loading rifle
SNCO	Senior Non-Commissioned Officer
SP	Special Purpose
TNKU	*Tentera Nasional Kalimantan Utara* (North Kalimantan National Army)
VAD	Voluntary Aid Detachment
VSO	Voluntary Service Overseas

GLOSSARY

Abang/Awang	traditionally a title for aristocrats, now a courteous form of address equivalent to the English 'Mr'
Apai	father
Astana/Istana	a palace
Attap house	traditional Kampong housing, made of attap palm (commonly known as the nippa palm) that grows widely in estuarine areas
Ayer	water
Bedara	make offering and sacrifice to accompany prayer
Belian	Borneo ironwood
Bibi	'dear/loved one', term of endearment derived from the Arabic *habib*, 'beloved'
Bilek	room, bedroom family space in longhouse
Bin	son of
Bruang	Malayan sun bear, bear
Bujang	young man, bachelor
Council Negri	Sarawak State Legislative Council
Dato	a title of honour
Dayang	a courteous form of address to women (the feminine of *Awang*)

Duku	sword, weapon; hunting knife with blade of around two feet (0.6 m) in length
Emergency	the State of Emergency throughout Malaya, 1948–60
Ganesha	Hindu elephant-deity, remover of obstacles
Hadj	pilgrimage to Mecca
Jalan	road
Jamban	toilet
Kalimantan	Borneo
Kampong	a Malay village
Kris	traditional Malay dagger
Ladang	clearing
Ngajat	Iban dance
Padang	field
Parang	bush-knife
Penghulu	district or village headman
Perentah	government
Pulau	island
Rakyat	the people
Ruai	gallery, verandah, commonly shared space of longhouse
Sais	driver
Sangar	fortified position above ground built with sandbags etc., with overhead cover to protect against shrapnel etc.

Sirat	man's loincloth
Songkok	Malay male headdress, cap
Sungei	a river, stream
Tabek	greeting, salute
Tuak	rice wine
Tuan	sir
Tuhan	Almighty, God
Ulu	upriver
Utara	north

ACKNOWLEDGMENTS

This book has been many years in the making. The story and many of those who have been part of it have been also a part of my life. Some of the people whom I would like to thank have sadly passed away, including my parents-in-law Dick and Dorothy Morris; Major General Sir Jeremy Moore KCB, OBE, MC & Bar; Tun Jugah; Professor William R Geddes; Alastair Morrison MBE; Wan Ali Ibrahim and Wan Alwi bin Tuanku Ibrahim.

There are many to whom I owe great personal debts that I have accumulated in researching and writing this book. I am sincerely grateful to them for their generosity in sharing their thoughts and records, and for discussing at length what has been a significant experience in their lives. Captain Derek Oakley MBE, RM has been unstintingly generous with his encouragement, time and hospitality. Lady Veryan Moore and Helen Arthy have given me much help. Major General Julian Thompson CB, OBE gave me his time and valuable insights.

Over the years, I have been privileged to meet many of the Royal Marines. Their spirit and courage are inspirational. Generous help has been given to me for this book by retired Royal Marines Mike Bell, Tony Daker, Brian Downey, David Greenhough, Colonel Ian Moore, Corporal Bob Rawlinson MM, Lieutenant Ricky Targett Adams and Colonel Bengie Walden MBE. From the Royal Navy, special thanks go to Lieutenant Peter Down.

Thaine H Allison, Jr has been a life-long friend of Malaysia since his days there with the Peace Corps and my thanks go to him for his help with the history of those early days.

In Sarawak, I would particularly like to thank Deanna Ibrahim; Dr Peter M Kedit, Kuching; Tan Sri Amar Leonard Linggi Jugah, Chairman of the Tun Jugah Foundation; Janet Rata Noel, Curator and Librarian, The Tun Jugah Foundation, Kuching; Heidi Munan, Kuching.

Richard Woolcott AC, Dr Alison Broinowski, and Peter Church OAM have long been friends of South-East Asia. They have always been most generous with their time and thoughts.

Scholars and writers to whom I am indebted are Professor Bee Chen Goh, Southern Cross University; Dr Jeffrey Goh and Dr Julitta Lim, Kuching; Richard CT Gregory for his maps; Dato Dr Erik Jensen; Emeritus Professor Clive Kessler, University of New South Wales; Amitava Kumar and fellow writers at the Norman Mailer Writers Center, Provincetown; Emeritus Professor Robert Reece, Murdoch University.

I am grateful to librarians and archivists who opened up material that was otherwise difficult to access. They include Anthony Richards and Richard McDonough, Imperial War Museum, London; Matthew Little, Librarian and Archivist, Ian Maine, Curator, Alison Firth, Curator of Images, and Anna Cummins at the Royal Marines Museum, Eastney; Fr Tom O'Brien, Mill Hill Missionaries Central Archive, London, and Fr Terry Burke, Mill Hill Missionaries, East Malaysia; Richard Groocock, Public Service Manager, Document Services, The National Archives, Kew; Jason McGregor, Volunteer Committee Member, and Sir-anne Hose, Library Volunteer, both at Fort Queenscliff Museum, Geelong; the librarians and staff of the Oral History Centre of the National Archives of Singapore; National Library of Singapore; Mitchell Library, Sydney; and the University of New South Wales Library.

Research in Sarawak was undertaken over several visits, most recently in 2007, and in England, most recently in 2012. I would like to thank the many friends who have helped me during these trips.

I am grateful to Phillipa McGuinness, Publishing Director, UNSW Press, for appreciating forgotten history. Likewise to Charles Hewitt, Managing Director, Pen & Sword Books, and Peter Schoppert, Director, National University of Singapore Press.

My helper with printing and photocopying, Sharon Kelly, has made my task easier.

Great appreciation goes to my sister-in-law Geraldine Bull and her family, and most of all to my son Roland Chanin-Morris, and husband, Adrian Morris, foremost critic, who was always there.

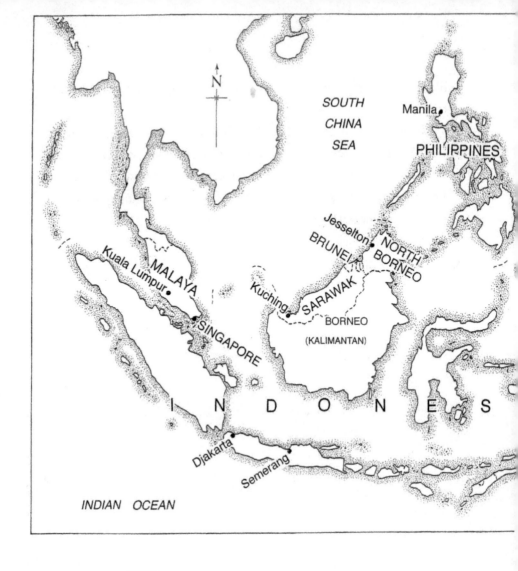

N

SOUTH
CHINA
SEA

Manila •

PHILIPPINES

Jesselton • NORTH
BRUNEI • BORNEO

Kuala Lumpur • MALAYA

Kuching • SARAWAK

BORNEO

SINGAPORE

(KALIMANTAN)

I N D O N E S

Djakarta •

Semerang

INDIAN OCEAN

SOUTH EAST
ASIA

0   1000 km

A

BRITISH
TERRITORIES
OF
BORNEO

N

SULU SEA

○ Jesselton

BRUNEI
Brunei Town

NORTH
BORNEO

● Tawau

SARAWAK

● Long Jawi

Biawak ●
● Kuching
Betong ●
● Simanggang
Tebedu ●

(KALIMANTAN)

INDONESIA

0   300 km

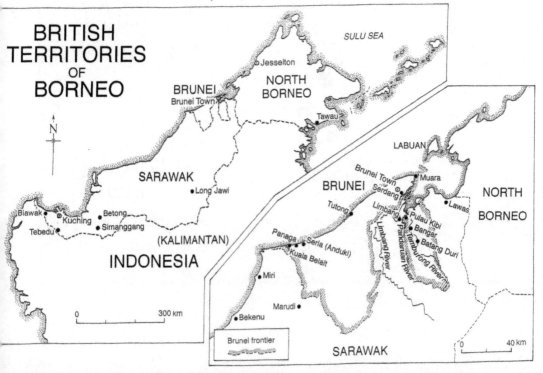

LABUAN

Brunei Town
Serdang ●

BRUNEI

● Muara

Limbang
● Lawas

Tutong ●

Pulau Kibi
Bangar
Batang Duri

NORTH
BORNEO

Limbang River
Pandaruan River
Temburong River

Panaga ●
Seria (Anduki) ●
Kuala Belait ●

● Miri

Marudi ●
● Bekenu

Brunei frontier

SARAWAK

0   40 km

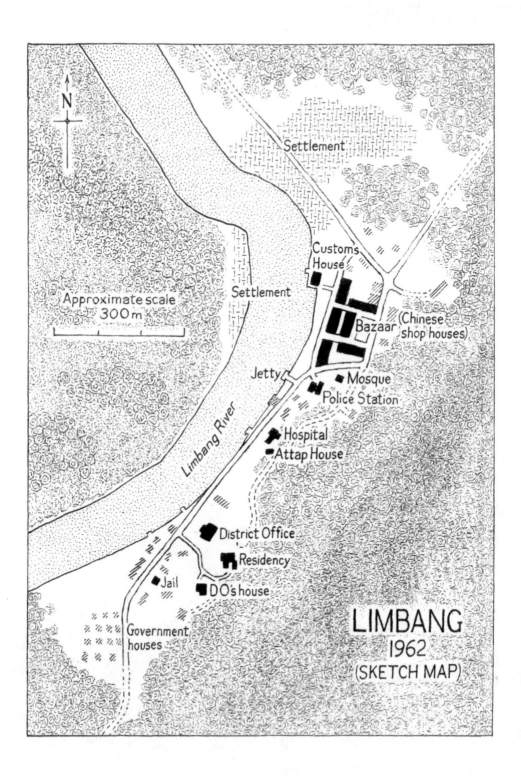

N

Settlement

Customs House

Settlement

Approximate scale
300 m

Bazaar (Chinese shop houses)

Jetty

Mosque

Police Station

Limbang River

Hospital

Attap House

District Office

Residency

Jail

DO's house

Government houses

LIMBANG
1962
(SKETCH MAP)

FOREWORD

I am delighted to welcome the publication of *Limbang Rebellion: 7 days in December 1962* by Eileen Chanin. It is an important contribution to the story of the historic changes that were underway in South-East Asia in the 1960s.

I was Australian Commissioner in Singapore in 1963–64, having served as Deputy to the High Commissioner in Malaya in 1961–62. In Singapore my area of responsibility included Sarawak, North Borneo (Sabah) and Brunei, a British protectorate ruled by its hereditary sultan.

This was an interesting and at times exciting period that would change the map of South-East Asia. Colonialism was drawing to a close and the enlarged Federation of Malaysia was being negotiated. The rest of the large island of Borneo – east, west, and central Kalimantan – was already part of an independent Indonesia, which strongly opposed the inclusion of Sarawak and Sabah in Malaysia.

This book focuses on the Brunei Revolt in December 1962 when Dick Morris was taken hostage, along with his wife Dorothy, by the Brunei rebels. At the time, Dick was Resident of the Fifth Division of Sarawak neighbouring Brunei, and stationed in the small river town of Limbang. I visited Sarawak and Brunei in May 1963. In Kuching I met Dick and Dorothy Morris. I spent many hours with Dick discussing the situation following the Brunei Revolt, the Cobbold Commission, and the progress towards the formation of Malaysia. Dick had a deep knowledge of the region, especially Sarawak and Brunei. He also had a good sense of humour and an understanding of the currents of change underway in the region.

I believe this book, based on Dick's knowledge of the situation, will make a special contribution to understanding the great changes that were underway in South-East Asia, including those in the north of the island of Borneo. The fall of Malaya and Singapore to Japan presaged the reality that Britain's Imperial outreach in South-East Asia was over, and the post-WWII colonial tide was receding.

I benefited greatly from Dick Morris's knowledge, as I am sure will the readers of this book.

Richard Woolcott, AC
Sydney

INTRODUCTION

Here is the story of a remarkable event in world history, told through the eyes of some of the key players. The centrepiece in Eileen Chanin's skilfully crafted book is the dramatic early-morning rescue of hostages held in the remote town of Limbang, in what was then British North Borneo. Two of the hostages – Dick Morris, the British Resident Commissioner, and his wife Dorothy – became Eileen Chanin's parents-in-law some years later.

Before focusing on the events that led up to the rescue, Eileen Chanin provides an excellent account of the geopolitical background to what became known as the Brunei Revolt of 1962 – except for Limbang most, but by no means all, of the action in the immediate aftermath of the revolt took place in the Sultanate of Brunei. The British in the Far East, having initially been taken by surprise, reacted fast and effectively. Fortunately, the senior commanders were experienced soldiers, and not the types to hang about dithering. At all levels there was much initiative displayed, and making do as you went along. Nowhere was this more apparent than in the Limbang Raid by L Company under the command of Captain Jeremy Moore. The morning after his arrival in Brunei, he was told to prepare a plan to rescue the British Resident and his wife and left to work out how to do it.

Meanwhile, Dorothy Morris tells how she and Dick, having been hustled from their bungalow still in their nightwear, were held for hours in the jungle fringes, bitten by hordes of mosquitoes. Later in the day they were incarcerated in the Limbang police station, where Dick overheard the rebels planning to hang them.

The story cuts back and forth between the fate of the hostages, told mainly through Dorothy Morris's eyes, and Moore planning the rescue. Others chip in with their accounts, from officers such as Derek Oakley, to marines like machine-gunner Tony Daker.

Moore faced a number of problems. He first had to work out how to reach Limbang; without helicopters, the options were on foot or by boat. He discarded the former as it would take too long and as the only route was bound to be defended, any fighting to clear the opposition would give the rebels time to kill the hostages. The river was the only way, but at first no suitable boats could be found. Eventually, thanks to Derek Oakley, two Z lighters were located – flat-bottomed and low-sided, they were the nearest thing to a landing craft available. By an amazing coincidence these particular Z lighters had been obtained by Dick Morris during a previous tour of duty in Brunei, to carry stores to the more inaccessible parts of the country. Moore now had craft, but no charts of the river up as far as Limbang, and no maps either. Captain Muton, the Brunei harbourmaster, offered his services as a pilot, although he had never travelled the route. Moore was told that Limbang was held by 30 rebels; the correct number was more like 400. Moore's company was a mere 89 strong, plus some invaluable Vickers machine gunners.

The pre-battle tension and doubts among the young men of L Company is well depicted both by some of the participants and by Eileen Chanin, an experienced writer and historian. She skilfully weaves text and oral history to tell the story of the raid; we get a clear picture of what was actually chaos and confusion, like most battles.

The battle for Limbang cost L Company five dead and six wounded, of whom all but two wounded were from just one troop of 30 men. L Company found fifteen rebel dead and took 50 prisoners. The remainder fled into the jungle, taking some of their walking wounded with them. The Limbang raid was only the beginning for the Royal Marines, as Eileen Chanin points out; the campaign initiated by President Sukarno of Indonesia, called 'Konfrontasi' (Confrontation), was to encompass the whole of North Borneo for another four years.

Limbang Rebellion is a great story, beautifully told. Eileen Chanin's pen-pictures of Dick Morris's life as British Resident Commissioner introduce the reader to a world now long gone. Both Dick and Dorothy Morris loved their life in Borneo and Brunei. Dick was never happier than when visiting an Iban long-house. He would sometimes act out the part of a head hunter, to the vast amusement of the Ibans, themselves head hunters in the very recent past. The regard with which the Morrises were held by the majority of the local population was made clear after the rebellion, when the Ibans who had captured some fugitive rebels brought them down river to Limbang, Union flags flying from their craft.

Major General Julian Thompson, CB, OBE
London

'We aren't all born with courage, but it is latent in all of us and can and should be pulled out whenever the occasion rises.'

Lady Laura Troubridge

.

'What we have within us is called out by what goes on around us, and if what goes on around us is too predictable, too safe, too known, then those of us who are not exceptional but ordinary may never find the opportunity to stretch our human nature.'

Mora Dickson

PROLOGUE

Between 8 and 12 December of 1962, world attention fixed on a surprise rebel uprising that sprang up in northern Borneo.

Britain at that time was engaged in an 'end-of-empire' exercise of state-building, when the forces of indigenous nationalism, which had mushroomed after the Second World War, erupted. Britain and the Malayan Prime Minister aimed to create a federation of Malaysia by combining British dependencies in Borneo and the island state of Singapore with already-independent Malaya. Opposition to this course came from Brunei Malay politician Sheikh AM Azahari. The self-styled Prime Minister of a 'united' North Borneo mounted an anti-Malaysia insurrection which took hostages and cost lives. This uprising became known as the Brunei Revolt.

The small river town of Limbang, administrative centre of the Fifth (and most northern) Division of the British Crown colony of Sarawak, was the pivot of the confrontation, which British Prime Minister Harold Macmillan told United States President John F Kennedy was as dangerous a situation in South-East Asia as the Western Allies had seen since the Second World War. An amphibious dawn assault at Limbang on 12 December by L Company of 42 Commando British Royal Marines liberated hostages whom Azahari's rebel forces were preparing to execute.

The extent and strength of the revolt caught all unprepared. All concerned – Azahari's rebels, the defenders, the hostages and their liberators, as well as observers in Borneo and beyond – were caught up in the intense and testing experience of these events.

The Brunei Revolt was the prelude to the diplomatic and military conflict between Indonesia and Malaysia known as Confrontation ('Konfrontasi'). This involved coercive diplomacy and military measures between 1963 and 1966 that stopped just short of all-out war. The highly permeable jungle border between Indonesia and the northern Borneo states became the site of sensitive cross-border conflict and counter-insurgency which tested international relations in the heated part of the world that was 1960s South-East Asia.

The revolt featured both force and farce. Azahari's uprising was abortive. The Limbang attack by 89 Royal Marines is recognised as the archetypal commando raid.

This book looks at what it was like to be thrown into this sudden, intense and unexpected conflict. What is it like to be caught up suddenly in such a life-and-death situation – to face execution? Where do extraordinary courage and noble behaviour come from?

Limbang drew from those who were there remarkable qualities of bravery, devotion to duty, friendship and loyalty. While terrifying, Limbang was also a life-affirming experience and forged lifelong bonds. Appreciation of this comes from walking in the shoes of the people caught up in the events. This history draws on the contemporary accounts of those involved and narrates their hour-by-hour experiences. Quotations contain material from letters, diaries, memoirs and other historical documents. The intention of this book is to reflect the experiences of those who in Limbang showed courage, resilience and dignity. It is to allow them to tell the story as they saw and lived it. Personal, eyewitness accounts take us to the heart of the action.

In the Brunei Revolt the British suffered seven fatalities and 28 wounded, many of them during action at Limbang, where British forces faced heavy resistance and a fierce fire-fight.

Since 1962, December 12 – the 'double-twelfth' – has been of special significance to people and their families, around the globe, whose lives became linked to what happened then at a far-flung outpost of an empire in its closing days. Limbang is a town whose name has a soft start and sharp end. It is where a seemingly quiet way of life exploded violently.

From the turmoil that disrupted the peace of the British Borneo territories in the first two weeks of December emerged acts of both individual and collective courage, heroism and loyalty, brought here into public view.

I first met Dick and Dorothy Morris ten years after their ordeal in Limbang. I have lived with their story since then, when they became my parents-in-law. I have known many of the people who shared their story. However, one's familiarity with a tale does not always bring with it an appreciation of the circumstances which put the tale in its proper context. I had to discover and draw out the many parts of the narrative to fully understand the story of Limbang and what it represents.

Until recently, the Brunei Revolt has received passing mentions in secondary sources on the history of Confrontation. Limbang is mentioned in one paragraph in JAC Mackie's *Konfrontasi: The Indonesia–Malaysia Dispute, 1963–1966* (1974), considered the leading work in the field based on open sources. Martin Spirit and Nick van der Bijl, BEM filmed recollections about Limbang in their film *Return to Limbang* (2006). With Harun Abdul Majid's *Rebellion in Brunei: The 1962 Revolt, Imperialism, Confrontation and Oil* (2007) came a comprehensive history of the Brunei Revolt that considered the implications of the revolt in terms of international relations. Forces at play at the time need to be considered in order to understand the revolt in North Borneo. Most recently Keat Gin Ooi's *Borneo in the Cold War, 1950-1990* (2020) offers a richer understanding of events throughout Borneo against the background of the global Cold War.

One reason why the history of Limbang has not been written is the difficulty of accessing primary sources. I have largely drawn on those that exist in Britain. Since writing the book, the Foreign and Commonwealth Office released previously concealed sensitive records of colonial administrations prior to decolonisation. Unfortunately these 'Migrated Archives' confirmed concerns that records dating from towards the "end of empire", holding material of a sensitive nature covering policy, security, intelligence and other issues that 'might compromise sources of intelligence information' or embarrass 'members of the police, military forces, public servants or others eg. police informers' – let alone 'Her Majesty's governments' – were destroyed at that time. Britain's engagement with insurgency in North Borneo was necessarily covert in the jungle located on the permeable boundary between Indonesia and the North Borneo states of Sabah and Sarawak. Britain was engaged in winning hearts and minds in an undeclared war. To date, no 42 Commando unit diaries for December 1962 have been traced. I drew as widely as I could on sources that were available to me when writing the book.

Fundamentally, the human stories about what happened amid the wider events should not be overlooked. It will soon be sixty years since the action at Limbang took place. This book was written to remember the courage of those who were there.

Eileen Chanin,
Sydney, March 2021

1

1962: COUNTDOWN TO EMERGENCY

Straddling the equator, Borneo is the world's third largest island. It is situated strategically, at the centre of South-East Asia's maritime region and main sea routes, and has been a crossroads for centuries.[1]

Long commercial rivalry between the Dutch and English led to colonial territories in Borneo, and eventually saw the island divided. What was Dutch Borneo, occupying the southern part of the island, is now Kalimantan, since 1945 part of the Republic of Indonesia. In the northwest of the island, two former British colonies are now the states of Sabah and Sarawak, which since 1963 have been member states of the Federation of Malaysia.

Set between Sabah and Sarawak is the small Malay sultanate of Brunei. The island's name, 'Borneo', is a Portuguese mispronunciation of Brunei, from when the centuries-old sultanate became known to Europeans in the 16th century.[2] The name 'Brunei' may be derived from the Sanskrit word for 'land'.[3] In the 19th century, Brunei became the smallest of the British protectorates in Borneo.

The Dayak people of Borneo's Sarawak call the jungle interior *ulu*, the end of the world. That is how, at the start of the 1960s, most people outside Borneo generally looked upon the island. Distance from major world centres, and the difficulty of getting through its uncharted jungle, meant that the world remained largely ignorant about and indifferent to Borneo. It generally overlooked the pivotal position, for centuries, that Borneo held in the region's trade routes. It overlooked the remarkable ways in which a Stone Age culture and the modern world came together in Borneo. It overlooked the fact that, like so much in the post-war era, Borneo was on the cusp of change. The colonial world and the jet age met in Borneo and, inevitably, tradition and development collided.

The Federation of Malaya achieved independence in 1957, and its Prime Minister, Tunku Abdul Rahman, proposed in 1961 that a larger federated state of Malaysia be formed, embracing Singapore, Sarawak, Brunei and North Borneo. The creation of an independent Malaysian federation caused considerable dissension and unrest in Brunei and Sarawak. It was immediately opposed by Indonesia, which did not want Sarawak, Brunei or Sabah to join the new nation.

Four main actors were caught up in the post-colonial drama that unfolded. They mirror aspects of the changes that were then sweeping across northern Borneo as the forces at play pulled between tradition and development, diplomacy and war, empire and nationhood, colonial paternalism and political self-determination.

From the circumstances of these four men we can gain insights into the issues that form the backdrop and feature in the story of the assault on Limbang.

In 1962 Sir Omar Ali Saifuddin III ruled the minute Malay sultanate of Brunei. The seventh of ten children, his elder brother's sudden death saw him proclaimed Sultan in June 1950, at the age of 36. Up to then he had enjoyed a courtly upbringing, and lived a largely sheltered life.

He ruled over the remnant of a sultanate, from his palace in Brunei Town (today's Bandar Seri Begawan). The sultanate, at its height in the 15th to 17th centuries, encompassed all of Borneo and parts of the Philippines, including the island of Luzon. In 1962 Brunei was a sparsely populated, British-protected mini-state of 83 000 people. It covered a total area of 5765 square kilometres (2226 square miles) that consisted almost entirely of dense equatorial rainforest. It was a fraction of its past size, but rich in oil and natural gas. Extraction of these reserves was only begun in the first half of the 20th century.

In the course of the 19th century, Brunei's empire had been eroded down to a tiny enclave under British protection. In 1846, Brunei still covered most of West Borneo from Jesselton to Kuching and Labuan Island, but the territorial aspirations of the White Rajahs of Sarawak during the latter half of the century swallowed up most of this. Brunei became separated physically into two distinct parts, split by a finger of Sarawak, about 6 kilometres wide at the coast, jutting into Brunei Bay. The enclave of Temburong, with its capital in Bangar, encompassing the entire eastern portion of Brunei, was separated from the rest of the country. Brunei split into its two distinct portions when the Sultan of Brunei ceded the intervening Limbang district to the White Rajahs. Limbang is now a part of Malaysia, a point which Brunei disputed until recently.[4]

The key challenges facing the new Sultan were to modernise his sultanate and manage the process of decolonisation. He came to a sultanate that had little infrastructure, a largely coastal-dwelling Malay population (of whom just over 22 per cent were literate) and no defence force, yet held the then fifth greatest oilfield in the British Commonwealth.[5]

He set about rebuilding Brunei into the Abode of Peace. In 1953 he instituted the first of a series of National Development Plans. He set in train a wide-ranging development program, funded by burgeoning oil revenues. Communications that were developed – roads, an airport, a radio station – ended Brunei's extreme isolation.

Britain encouraged the Sultan to introduce democratic reforms. He began a process that opened Brunei to constitutional change, while stalling its implementation. He prolonged negotiations towards a written constitution. When this was introduced in September 1959, the post of British Resident was abolished, removing Whitehall's interference in Brunei's internal affairs. The Sultan established a legislature with half its members nominated and half elected. The constitution strengthened the position of the Malay language and of the Islamic religion. It enshrined the dominant role of the monarchy while making vague promises on 'democratisation'. Britain remained responsible for defence and foreign affairs.

Bruneians today hail Sir Omar Ali Saifuddin III as the Architect of Modern Brunei. In reality, he was very good at forestalling democratic advances. He kept up Brunei's protected status with the British for as long as possible, while consolidating an absolute monarchy. He has been described as 'a political activist without a peer among the royalty of the Malay world in that era'.[6]

The Brunei royal house could trace an unbroken line of descent as far back as the late seventh century. The Sultan's first marriage was childless. His second marriage, in 1941 to a distant cousin ten years younger, produced ten children. Four sons who survived into adulthood ensured the dynasty.[7]

A pious Muslim, the Sultan performed the pilgrimage to Mecca in September 1951 and in May 1962. He instituted a religious affairs department (1954) and an Islamic religious council

(1955), appointed a government mufti (1962), and expanded religious education. His traditional upbringing and religious values gave him a conservative outlook.

He had a sincere concern for his people, but his iron will would not bend to British persuasions to introduce a measure of democracy. Nor would he heed the quickening political consciousness of his subjects. Japanese occupation during the Second World War had left Bruneians with a diminished view of British rule. A nationalist movement arose and in 1956 this saw widespread support go to the Brunei People's Party (the Parti Rakyat Brunei, or PRB). When the PRB won a landslide election victory in August 1962, the Sultan delayed convening the Legislative Council.

He rejected the PRB's nationalist project for Brunei and cemented feelings of common interest with the hereditary elite, appealing to their fears about the popularity of Sheikh Azahari, the PRB leader, and the advance of communism in the region. While Azahari and his supporters saw the Sultan as Brunei's constitutional monarch, he dismayed them by playing along with Brunei's merger with Malaysia. He would not accept democracy or independence.

He played interests off against each other. He played off the British, with their gradual approach to decolonisation, against the PRB, with their left-leaning but constitutional approach. He invoked British principles of self-determination to the Colonial Office, but frustrated their efforts to lead him to constitutionalism. He achieved absolute power under the self-governing Constitution of 1959, without losing Britain's defence support to protect Brunei from internal or external threats.

Negotiations at the time signalled potential threats. Between 1959 and 1962, the United Kingdom, Malaya, Singapore, Sabah and Sarawak were involved in negotiations to form a new Malaysian Federation. The unexpected proposal by Malaya's Prime Minister Tunku Abdul Rahman in May 1961 for a new state, hailed as a 'Greater Malaysia' plan, caused alarm in Brunei. It was hoped that the merger would take place in 1963, but the Philippines and Indonesia opposed any move towards unifying North Borneo and Sarawak with the new federation. The PRB favoured joining Malaysia in a North Borneo Federation with Brunei's Sultan installed as constitutional monarch of the North Borneo Federation so as to resist domination by peninsular Malay states or Singapore. Widespread anti-Federation sentiment existed in Sarawak and Brunei, where an unprecedented growth of political activity was seen during 1962 as a reaction to the 'Malaysia' proposal. Ethnic groups faced questions about what it meant for them in the future. Both support for and opposition to the proposal gained momentum.

Brunei's new-found wealth complicated the Sultan's position. It promised prosperity for its people but, in light of Brunei's history, it also suggested insecurity unless guarded. Offshore oil could sustain Brunei in a separate existence. However, protection of the resource was essential, whether from Kuala Lumpur, British interests or nearer neighbours. The Sultan founded the Brunei Malay Regiment, but it would take time to develop into a well-rounded fighting force.

In the early 1960s climate of nationalism and nation-building, the Sultan would steer Brunei on its own nation-building course. Brunei would achieve independence on its own terms. This would not be as part of a Malay Federation; nor as part of the North Kalimantan (*Kalimantan Utara*) proposal as the PRB wanted, and as was favoured by local opposition against the Malaysian Federation plan; nor as Greater Indonesia (*Indonesia Raja*), as envisaged by President Sukarno. Brunei would recover its history as an independent sultanate, based on its oil wealth. In his unwillingness to be subjected to peninsular Malaya's political domination, the Sultan was at one with his people. Brunei would be the only independent sultanate on the island of Borneo.

If the Sultan expected an untroubled passage, without criticism in Brunei of his strategy to court British and peninsular Malay interests while engineering absolute monarchy, he was confronted by the eminent Sheikh Ahmad M Azahari bin Sheikh Mahmud, the charismatic Brunei Malay nationalist leader of Brunei's Parti Rakyat.

Both leaders were after the same thing: reviving their country. They were close, Azahari being a high-caste Malay whose uncle accompanied the Sultan on the *hadj* to Mecca.[8] The Sultan personally nominated Azahari to the Legislative Council. Yet the two of them could not have been more unalike. Nor could their visions of Brunei's future have been more different. The Sultan was short in stature, moustached, with a high forehead, and slicked-back hair. He wore large-framed spectacles, which gave him an owlish appearance, and bow ties. He was softly spoken (which some, among the British, thought was a deliberate ploy to hold attention). The novelist Anthony Burgess, then living in Brunei, described him as 'a grave withdrawn figure'.[9] Azahari was taller, with a broad nose, wore a more thinly clipped moustache and dressed casually. He was persuasive, a riveting speaker, who his followers saw as a 'prophet'.[10]

In 1958 Burgess was teaching at the Sultan Omar Ali Saifuddin College in Brunei Town. He lived opposite Azahari, whom Burgess found 'wished to make the growing oil-wealth serve a modern state, not a traditional sultanate'.[11] Writing in 1987, Burgess described Azahari as hospitable, 'a civilized man who only accepted riot as a device of political reform', although he found

Azahari's project unrealistic.[12] You get the sense that Burgess found (and remembered) Azahari, if quixotic, as being likeable, unlike the Sultan.

Whereas the Sultan was autocratic, Azahari believed in the democratic process. The Sultan's traditionalist views were at odds with Azahari's belief that hereditary rule was undemocratic and that democracy could not be stopped. Azahari formed the Brunei People's Party in 1956, modelling it on Malaya's left-leaning Parti Rakyat Malaya. Independence for Brunei was its main aim. It did not favour dissolution of the sultanate, but sought to democratise the government by shifting the national leadership from the palace to the *rakyat* (people) through democratisation in the government. In 1961, the PRB's membership of 26 000 people represented more than a quarter of Brunei's population.

Azahari and the PRB rejected Tunku Abdul Rahman's idea of Malaysian Federation. Although the Sultan at the time appeared open to Brunei joining the proposed federation, the PRB maintained that joining Malaysia would end any revival of Brunei's predominance in the region and result in Brunei losing its unique identity. Azahari ran the Malay-medium newspaper, and harshly criticised Brunei's reportedly proposed arrangements with the Federation as a 'back door' negotiation without reference to the people of Brunei, who might well not like the idea of sharing their oil wealth with, and being governed by, the peninsular Malays. In the estimation of British expatriate Geoffrey Daniels, working for the Brunei Shell Petroleum Company from 1960, it must have been almost without precedent that a Sultan was criticised so publicly.[13]

Alarm at Brunei's possible incorporation within the Federation saw the PRB gain strength as it voiced popular dread of the proposal. The 33-year-old Azahari was a powerful public speaker. He drew ready listeners among Brunei Malays, who were more aware than before of the world beyond and who were living in what was now a rich country.[14] The PRB became a magnet for dissidents among the truculent Brunei Malays and disaffected Kedayans, who felt they enjoyed little share of Brunei's new-found wealth.

Hopes for change grew when the PRB won a landslide victory at the general election of August 1962, winning all 16 of the elected seats in the 33-seat Legislative Council. But they could not form the government as the 17 government nominees outnumbered them.

The first meeting of the Legislative Council was scheduled for 5 December. Azahari put forward three motions for the meeting: first, to reject the proposal of a Malaysian Federation; second, to request the restoration of Brunei's sovereignty over Sarawak and North Borneo, and the installation of the Sultan as constitutional monarch of the North Borneo Federation; and, third, a request to the British to grant independence to Brunei not later than 1963.

The Speaker of the Legislative Council disallowed the motions because the issues fell within the purview of the British Government under the 1959 British-Brunei Agreement. The Sultan rejected the proposed resolution and postponed the opening of the Legislative Council to 19 December 1962.

Before the PRB's electoral success, a military wing of the party had emerged. The North Kalimantan National Army (*Tentera Nasional Kalimantan Utara*, abbreviated as TNKU) saw itself as an anti-colonialist liberation organisation. Its sympathies lay with Indonesia, which was seen as having better 'liberationist' credentials than Malaya and Singapore. Azahari was closely tied to Indonesia, where he had fought with the Indonesian Army in the Independence War against the Dutch. He was in touch with Indonesian intelligence agents, when the Indonesians organised underground agents to foster subversion (as they did in Singapore, to disturb internal security).[15] By late 1962, the TNKU had a force of about 1000 armed men and could assemble a force of about 15 000 men.[16]

Whereas the Sultan was lucky with his timing – favoured by the massive oil revenues that were pouring into Brunei – Azahari was unlucky. It was a poor time to be cast as a freedom fighter. Azahari was under surveillance by Special Branch in Brunei and in Singapore. The Malayan Emergency had just ended in 1960, the Vietnam War was in its opening days, and images of the Sharpeville massacre were vivid.

Rebellion had a long history in this region of Borneo. In 1841, Sir James Brooke, a British adventurer and former military officer of the East India Company, assisted the Sultan of Brunei to suppress a rebellion. He was made Rajah of Sarawak and rewarded with land which remained in his family until it was ceded to Britain in 1946.

By 1962, to the superficial eye, it might have seemed that things had changed very little from the days of the Rajahs. Yet Sarawak had been shaken by the war and Japanese occupation, and the pace of change quickened there from the late 1950s.

Australian-born Richard Holywell Morris had experienced the changes of regime. He first arrived in Borneo with the Australian Imperial Force (AIF). In 1945 he was attached to the British Army and a year later was appointed as an Officer in Rajah Sir Charles Vyner Brooke's Sarawak Civil Service. Later, in 1946, when Rajah Brooke ceded his sovereignty to Britain, and Crown rule replaced Brooke family rule in Sarawak, the Colonial Office became directly responsible for Sarawak.

At the age of 47, Richard Morris, known as Dick, was in his 16th year in the Colonial Administrative Service and his 17th year in the service of Sarawak. He had worked in all of the five administrative divisions that made up Sarawak. While extensive in area, just under the land size of Greece, Sarawak's population in mid-1962 was just under 800 000.

As the Resident in one of Sarawak's administrative divisions, Dick was responsible for overseeing the civil administration of the division. He worked closely with the police and magistracy.

The changes occurring in the course of the post-war recovery brought variety to his career, which saw him working also on secondment in the British Protectorate of Brunei. Much to the ire of many Bruneians, their administration was shared with Sarawak, and the Governor of Sarawak was also High Commissioner of Brunei.

In Sarawak the Brooke administration promoted education and welfare. Brooke rule left a legacy of benevolence that most Sarawakians did not want to lose. Yet from the 1950s, the British were reluctant colonialists. Wanting to extract themselves from the Far East, the British encouraged self-sufficiency within their Borneo dependencies. Britain wanted out – but most Sarawakians wanted the status quo preserved. Sarawakians were nervous about political change because they were uncertain about how a Malay Federation would accommodate their country's diverse ethnic mix, particularly the Chinese. The Malayan dollar was introduced in Sarawak in 1953, a move that declared British policy in regard to Malaya and Borneo.[17]

As a civil servant in the service of the Crown, Dick Morris was deeply engaged in the decolonising process that was under way. He had played a part in regime change before, in 1945 when the military handed administration back to the Rajah, and in 1946 when the Rajah ceded to the British Crown. He began work-ing in Borneo anticipating that independence would come. In 1962, he knew that he was living at a turning point in the region's history.

The Brookes believed in the efficacy of personal rule and rapport between rulers and ruled. Brooke rule had established a tradition of consultative administration and of listening and holding discussion among the people.

Consequently, Dick was closely engaged with the people whom he strove to serve: the Ibans, the largest ethnic group in Sarawak; the Malays, largely found in the First Division; the Chinese, the second largest community in Sarawak; the mainly Christian Bidayuhs, kampong-dwelling farmers; the mostly coastal-dwelling Melanaus, thought originally to be of Balinese origin; the Orang Ulu, 'upriver people' found in the interior, and respected for their skilful artistry. The Brookes and the British encouraged local ability, and many Ibans elevated to positions of administrative authority and civil responsibility were strongly loyal to British rule. The region was notable for harmonious relations and dealings between its varied races and ethnic groups.

Dick was Assistant-Resident in Brunei from October 1954 to January 1956.[18] He served as Brunei's Acting State Treasurer (1956) while a Member of the State Council of Brunei and Chairman of the Brunei Finance Committee. The following year, he became Brunei's Acting Commissioner for Development and Controller of Civil Aviation. More recently, from 1958, he held a senior post in Brunei as Secretary for Economic Development. There was little he did not know about the workings of govern-ment at the centre and on the ground.

In the starched white uniform and regalia of the Colonial Civil Service, worn for formal occasions, Dick could be an imposing figure. He stood a little under six feet tall and was of trim build and fit. Blue-eyed and fair-skinned with dark brown hair and a short-clipped moustache, he appeared compact, self-contained. He stood before a camera impassively, with a stony face. This made him look somewhat stern and austere, belying his essentially warm personality. He was a naturally gracious man, with a cheerful and caring disposition.

He possessed an abiding affection for the many friends he made easily among the people in both Sarawak and Brunei, and deeply respected their customs and traditions. Mindful of others, he was a stickler for courtesy and good manners.

Up to the early 1950s, little infrastructure existed in Brunei, leaving most Bruneians remote from the wider world. Brunei itself, wrote Anthony Burgess, was a kind of prison, walled in by sea and jungle.[19] Yet oilfield riches meant that the country had no public debt and enjoyed revenue three to four times greater than its expenditure. In the 1950s, this revenue helped to fund the post-war recovery that Brunei needed.

Public works were Brunei's chief item of expenditure. Dick enjoyed the Sultan's trust, being closely engaged with the Sultan's infrastructure program over which Dick had charge. It would transform the town. Part of the building program was the new Saifuddin Mosque and Brunei Airport, both under Dick's purview. Political development is difficult in a country that is mostly without roads. When he was Commissioner for Development, Dick oversaw the construction by Australian engineers of the Brunei Town to Seria Trunk Road. Air connections were significant in a pre-television age, when letters and radio were the main means of communication. The Brunei Airport Terminal, which the Sultan opened in May 1957, helped end the remove of Brunei from the world.

Other airfields were being opened in the region at the time. By 1960, Sarawak aimed to have 16 airfields in operational use. Developing the internal air services in the three territories of British North Borneo mattered because internal air communications, an *ulu* air service, would facilitate the development of the region, and help solve the problem of communications that its geography and equatorial jungle imposed. It would bring medical and agricultural services within closer and easier reach of the people.

Borneo Airways Limited used two Twin Pioneer aircraft. They bore the insignia of the crests of the three Borneo governments superimposed on a pair of white wings, seen as 'almost symbolising a herald of a "United Borneo"'.[20] The governments of Sarawak, North Borneo and Brunei purchased the aircraft jointly for the expansion of the internal air services of the three territories. Twin Pioneers were ideal for the undeveloped conditions of North Borneo's hinterland. Their remarkable ability to take off and land in under 375 yards (342 metres) made possible commercial air communications to remote mountainous areas that could not previously be reached. By being able to land on small hinterland airstrips, these aircraft freed communities cut off by the region's mountainous terrain and heavy jungle from days or even weeks of hard and wearisome travel.

The idea of a united Borneo was aired many times in the 1950s, despite the Sultan of Brunei's nervousness about a three-colony union. In a broadcast over Radio Sarawak, the Governor, Sir Anthony Abell, argued that closer association would advantage the three territories.[21] His view was in line with that taken by Alan Lennox-Boyd, Britain's Colonial Secretary from 1954, who favoured a federation of Britain's territories in South-East Asia.[22] By 1961, Greater Malaysia Union was being urged by Tunku Abdul Rahman.

The Colonial Office held as commonplace that political development must be prepared and planned for, otherwise chaos might occur. Political change was thought to be all the more difficult in multiracial societies, such as Sarawak and North Borneo. Many in Sarawak were wary of a Malaysian Union. Opposition to cession by the Brookes inspired the assassination of the second British Governor of Sarawak, Duncan Stewart CMG, in late 1949, an attack that shocked the country.

A warning against the premature introduction of political parties in Sarawak was given by the Governor in 1959, only a few weeks before the Sarawak United Peoples' Party was founded.

> It is ... essential that party politics should not cause further
> divisions in our community but should have a unifying
> and binding effect. If a party tends to be dominated by
> one race or class ... it may have a disintegrating effect on
> our community ... I frankly doubt if political parties at the
> present stage of development will spell faster progress in this
> small country.[23]

These misgivings were echoed from North Borneo, by its Governor, some six months later. 'People of like taste or like purpose are all too probably of like race, and nothing could promise greater disaster for this country than its division on communal lines.' He knew of no multiracial society in the world 'where as yet there has been evolved a satisfactory, stable or easy working form of fully representative Government'. Nearly four years later, the next Governor of North Borneo warned of the danger of 'mounting the tiger of political parties prematurely'. The formation of parties at this stage 'carried the greatest danger of communal strife'. There was disquiet among Sarawakians about how Malaysian Federation might upset the harmonious relations that were maintained among Sarawak's different ethnic groups under British rule.[24]

In Brunei, the Sultan introduced a far-reaching social service program instituting free schools, universal free medical care and old age pensions for all Brunei citizens. However, critics asked 'but what do you do if you are not sick, or old?' They argued that little of the estimated $US40 million in annual royalties paid into the Sultan's treasury by the Brunei Shell Petroleum Company went to the town in cash. Most Bruneians lived a hand-to-mouth existence by fishing, farming and unskilled labour, crying 'we are poor in a rich country'.[25] The poverty of Bruneians, living in small wooden houses built on piles at Kampong Ayer in the Brunei River, contrasted starkly with the $US3 million mosque, newly built in the town, and one of Asia's largest.[26] The mosque, with 20 minarets and a 165-foot (50-metre) high tower, and its great golden dome, was as splendid as Kampong Ayer was humble.[27] More than 60 per cent of the town of Brunei lived in Kampong Ayer. They ignored resettlement schemes proposed by the Sultan and on which Dick had worked.[28] Many of these sea-dwellers had rarely set foot on land, which was regarded as the abode of evil.

Among the forces at the ready that Britain maintained, to deal with trouble spots in parts of the world over which Britain still held jurisdiction, was 3 Commando Brigade of the Royal Marines. During 1962, Royal Marine troops were converted to a new Commando organisation, in an extensive strengthening and stabilising of the Commandos, wherever they served. At this time, 45 Commando was serving in Aden and 41 and 43 Commandos were serving in the United Kingdom. 40 Commando was re-deploying from Malta to the Far East, and 42 Commando was serving in Singapore. Royal Marine troops were reorganised from the Second World War troop organisation of five rifle troops of 65 men each, into a company organisation of three rifle companies of 100 plus Marines.

In November 1962, Captain Jeremy Moore MC was the newly appointed Company Commander of L Company 42 Commando (also known as Lima Company). It was his first command of a rifle troop in the brigade. He saw himself as primarily a front-line soldier, and had felt the lack of experience commanding a rifle troop in a commando brigade up to then.[29] He and his company of 120 men were at Kota Belud, in North Borneo, at an established training area used by the British and Malaysian armies. Over six weeks he trained his company in the new organisation, which required learning new tactics to handle different formations. As one of the company's Marines remembers it, they were training 'with our own commanders, our own NCOs, as a unit, teaching us how to move and fend for ourselves'.[30] Training exercises like these were an essential part of soldiering, drilling the men to stay cool under fire and take the correct steps so as to keep alive when in action.

After finishing his initial commando training, Moore joined the Commando Brigade in the Far East in late 1950. He joined 40 Commando in the Malayan jungle, where he was among the British forces who in the years 1948–59 succeeded, with the help of the local population, in putting an end to communist-inspired terrorism. In 1948 peace in Malaya was threatened by Chinese communists who wanted to seize part of the country and set up their own government. These terrorists, trained by the British to fight the Japanese during the Second World War, wrought havoc on the rubber plantations to achieve their aim. British forces, including Royal Marine Commandos, were engaged to help the Malay police restore order. Skilful use of jungle patrols defeated the terrorists. Success depended on good intelligence and communications to direct patrols operating deep in the jungle for days on end. These tactics paid off and by 1960 the terrorist threat in Malaya was effectively brought to an end.

During his time in Malaya, Moore saw intense fighting against the highly skilled communist insurgents. During their stint in Malaya, 3 Commando Brigade killed or captured 221 Chinese communist guerrillas at a cost of 30 commandos killed. Lasting from 1948 to 1960, this politico-military campaign in support of Malayan nation-building is often cited as a model of its kind.[31]

Moore distinguished himself in a jungle patrol ambush for which he was awarded the Military Cross when 24. He was the third generation of his family to be awarded the MC.

After Malaya, Moore was engaged in operations against Greek-sympathising Eoka guerrillas during the Cyprus emergency, and had been adjutant of 45 Commando in the Near East. He would become a distinguished Royal Marine and serve 'more than 36 years of mainly fighting service around Britain's colonial hotspots'.[32]

His career would be marked by leading his troops 'with bravery, care and skill to victory on the ground against all the odds'.[33] He would most famously demonstrate this when confronted by the Falklands challenge in April 1982. He would be Commander of the Land Forces during the Falklands War to whom Argentina surrendered, thus becoming 'the most famous military commander in Britain'.[34] In 1982, he would be knighted Sir Jeremy Moore.

At 34, Moore was of slight build and medium height. Under the Marine's green beret he was boyish-looking with a wide grin and a hint of mischief in his eye. He bore a slight resemblance to the American Marine Corps pilot and matinee idol Tyrone Power and himself had a thespian streak. Moore was a man of great character, 'a kindly, thoughtful man with a boyish enthusiasm for soldiering'.[35] A keen reader of military history, his determined lips and jaw gave him a disciplined appearance that matched his insistence on proper behaviour.[36] He would come to be known 'to throw convention aside' and 'to be as upbeat as possible within the constraints of veracity … while giving his subordinates their missions and letting them get on with it'.[37]

When Moore joined the Corps, older men within it had served in the Second World War or in useful occupations in support of the war effort. He came from a military background with both grandfathers, uncles and his father all in the services. Therefore, as a young man, joining the Royal Marines seemed a natural thing to do. 'Because there had been the war', he explained, 'everybody thought in terms, to some extent, of duty towards the nation. That was what the war years had been all about. So, that was just an accepted part of the background'.[38]

By the mid-1950s, new technology was bringing changes to the way the services operated. Since the Second World War, Commandos had been employed in internal security and counter-insurgency duties in Hong Kong, Palestine, Malaya, Egypt, Cyprus and Aden. In addition, 41 Commando had fought in Korea from 1950 to 1951, and 3 Commando Brigade landed at Suez in 1956 from conventional landing craft and by helicopter in the first-ever amphibious helicopter assault in history. The deterrent value in having forces like the Royal Marines stationed off the coast of troublesome spots, which could be reached quickly, and as needed, by helicopter, was being recognised. The carrier HMS *Bulwark* was converted to an amphibious assault ship in 1959 and commissioned in 1960 as the first Commando Ship. Later designated a Landing Platform Helicopter (LPH), the ship could carry a Commando group to land them by helicopter or assault craft, and keep them supplied in the field. HMS *Albion* was likewise refitted as an LPH in 1961 and was the companion carrier to *Bulwark*. The first operation from the LPH was by 42 Commando landing from HMS *Bulwark* in Kuwait in August 1961, deterring an invasion by Iraq.

While the role of the Royal Marines was being looked at anew, Moore's men were among the troops kept in the Far East, with 42 Commando based in Singapore from 1960. Battalions in Singapore were known as airportable battalions because they were responsible for designated areas in the world and were prepared with maps and operational instructions to fly to those countries as necessary. From its Commando carriers, 3 Commando Brigade was employed in internal security and policing duties in Egypt, Cyprus, Palestine, Hong Kong and Malaya.

The Colonial Office was apprehensive about Indonesian moves in the Borneo region. It was expecting that the Indonesian Government would distract attention from serious domestic problems by launching 'claim' to neighbouring territory, as, for example, in New Guinea. Indonesia's economic difficulties, particularly food shortages in Java, had already given rise to considerable popular discontent, and it was thought not improbable that the Indonesian Government may accordingly consider that a fresh offshore distraction was needed. The Colonial Office, concerned by Indonesia's military capability and Sukarno's unpredictability, attempted to anticipate Indonesia's moves. Britain's Navy was in the region because it was feared that Indonesia might also seek to develop its naval and air strength to a point at which it could profit by its geographical position to block, at will, the passage between the Indian and Pacific Oceans.

Moore was enthusiastic about his command. 'Most people see command of one's own regiment as the peak of the role of an officer', he would say.[39] He took pride in his company being a very professional commando.

I believe that I had a standard of training in which I could particularly rely on my company commanders using their initiative and understanding the way that I thought, and operated, and wanted things to happen. Nelson had developed this understanding in the days of sail, when things were different, by spending a great deal of time with his captains, discussing how they would operate, so they thoroughly understood his way of thinking. It is said that at Trafalgar as Nelson hoisted his famous signal, one of his captains remarked 'What is he raising the signal for now? We all know what he requires of us.' I believe that one of the things I was able to do was to develop among my people that sort of, to a lesser degree than Nelson of course, but hopefully, that understanding. I felt they knew my mind, and I knew them and their characters, and how their company could perform. I could give them the role that they were going to be suitable for and could rely on them. That is, above all, the sort of way that one would hope a commando would behave. So, I think we were particularly good operationally at that sort of thing.[40]

Wrapping up at Kota Belud, with Lima Company returning to base at Singapore in early December 1962, Moore said of it: 'Everybody was a trained marine. They all had a green beret. They knew they were God's gift to soldiery because they'd passed the commando course and they were all qualified. I reckon the company were bloody good'.

2

FRIDAY, 7 DECEMBER: COUNTING THE DAYS

Limbang town in Sarawak lies approximately 12 miles (19 kilometres) south of Brunei up the Sungei Limbang. In 1962 the town occupied a narrow strip of land, at most several hundred yards wide and a little more than half a mile long from end to end. A single straight road ran parallel to the steep river bank. Limbang perched, somewhat tenuously, between river and rainforest, as if either might engulf its few buildings.

A prospering centre, the town with its adjacent villages was home to no more than about 2000 people. At its northern end sat the commercial centre or bazaar. It had been razed to the ground during the Second World War and since rebuilt. The bazaar was a modest collection of buildings arranged in two blocks, one closer to the customs house by the river, and the other a triangle of some 50 two-storey shop-houses facing an open square. Produce was brought to it from outlying districts.

Several buildings made up the town's administrative quarter, located at its southern end where, close by the river, stood the old fort, one of a series built around the country from the 1860s to protect strategic points and guard against native insurgents. An abrupt hill rose behind the fort. Halfway up the hill, reached by a steep path, was the District Office, the administrative centre for the region. Above this, and crowning the hill, was the Residency.

It was from here that Dick Morris oversaw the country's Fifth Division (or province), as Resident (chief government administrator) for the Government of Sarawak.

The system of Government Residents could be traced to the early 1870s when Malay chiefs in peninsular Malaya signed an 'engagement' with the British to protect their states against internal and external enemies. The British agreed to provide security. A British Resident would be installed in Malay territory with authority over all matters other than those touching Islamic religion and its customs. Collection and controlling of all revenue and the general administration of the country were regulated under the advice of these Residents.

The Resident system was successful from the outset. The tact and patience that early Residents exercised in dealing with the Sultans and their subjects, combining firmness with friendliness and dignity with deference, enabled the successful working of this system of indirect rule.

From 1926, administrative training for colonial service was formalised in courses at Cambridge and Oxford. Britain's unified Colonial Administrative Service emerged six years later. Once the Colonial Office had recruited and trained an administrator, he became the responsibility of 'his' Colonial government, until he either was transferred to another territory (usually in the context of promotion) or he retired at the age of between 45 and 55. Thereafter he came into the care of the Crown Agents for the Colonies for the payment of his pension.

Typically a career progressed up the ranks from Cadet, Assistant District Officer (ADO) or Assistant District Commissioner (ADC), District Officer (DO) or District Commissioner (DC), to the ranks of Senior DO/DC, and Resident or Provincial Commissioner after 15 to 25 years' service.

As Dick explained:

the basis of Administration in Sarawak from the beginning
of Brooke Rule was 'Travelling'. This meant that the
DO visited the people in their own villages, longhouses,
kampongs or bazaars and there considered their requests;
settled 'Native Court' cases; saw for himself their state of
health, prosperity, or otherwise; and explained Government's
policy and efforts on their behalf.[1]

District Officers worked closely with the local people and travelled
extensively within the district they were administering, listening
to complaints, mediating disputes, maintaining a census of people
and guns, and supplying medicine. District officers maintained
law, order and health, and oversaw public works. Dick continued,
'It was simply a case of taking Government to the people and of
finding out for oneself the attitudes and the general welfare of the
population'.

This method suited him, coming from a family background of
movement, in search of a better life. His 19th-century forebears
left Wales for Canada before reaching Australia, where his father
roamed Western Australia, prospecting unsuccessfully for miner-
als. Dick was ideally suited for going to the *ulu* (the equivalent of
going bush in Australia). He was happiest amongst the *ulu* peoples of Sarawak.

His Australian-born wife, Dorothy, shared his preference for
living in the more remote outstations. She had been reared in
country towns in New South Wales, where her father was a bank
manager. She valued the special bonds that develop in close-knit,
outlying communities.

Dorothy Morris was the same age, and nearly the same height,
as her husband, although owing to her sunny personality and
self-assurance (or through being slender) she could appear taller.
She was warm-hearted with a ready, wide smile. She was lively

and quick to laugh. The natural wave of her dark blond hair, worn short, crowned her unaffected, easy manner. She was active in local communities, running workshops to teach girls essential health care and domestic skills like sewing. She shared Dick's belief that female education was the best hope for the future of their children. She managed bazaars and social events to benefit the Red Cross for which she was a life-long volunteer. She served as President of the Division of the British Red Cross Society in her previous posting at the river town of Simanggang, in the Second Division. A skilful office manager, she helped with vetting the recruitment of Secretary Typists for the Government of Sarawak. She also sold air travel for British Overseas Airways Corporation (BOAC). The airline was keen to demonstrate to expatriates the advantages of then still novel air travel. These activities were in addition to her role as wife of the Tuan Resident, with the many calls which that brought.

The Morrises enjoyed their engagement in the many spheres that life in Borneo provided. They had been together in Sarawak and Brunei for 16 years and both loved the life. They genuinely loved the people there, and being part of their lives, especially away from the large towns. Postings in the smaller outstations, where they had lived, tested their adaptability and resourcefulness. They were enterprising and dedicated to serving their community.

Both relished their close engagement with local community life. Dick noted:

> In Sarawak, the District Officer did not stay in a Resthouse
> or establish his own camp as was the case in some Colonies;
> he stayed with the people in their own community, sharing
> the 'Ruais' with the dogs, the fighting cocks, and the
> bachelors. He bathed in the river with the people and he ate
> either in the 'bilek' or on the 'ruai'.[2]

More often than not, Dick's family was with him.

Dick loved best the *ulu* longhouse-living Ibans. His impish sense of humour could best be at play among them. For them he could be prevailed upon to perform a form of mime dance called a *ngajat*. After the communal evening meal, late-night storytelling and a little rice beer, called *tuak*, Dick would allow himself, with feigned reluctance, to be taken away and then return clad only in the *sirat*, a form of buttock-baring loincloth worn by the *ulu* men, and at his waist a decorated *duku* or short sword. Dick would then act the part of a young headhunting Iban, stalking through the jungle, seeking an enemy for the purpose of taking his head. The climax was a great whoop as he sprang upon the hapless victim and removed his head, which he then bore triumphantly back to his longhouse. The audience in the *ruai* would rock with mirth and admiration. Hanging in the rafters above them were likely to be dusty skulls from long and not so long ago. Some of the older men still bore tattoos reserved for those who had taken heads. While eliminated during Brooke rule, the practice saw a revival during Japanese occupation among the anti-Japanese Ibans, who were loyal to British rule.

Dick did not take himself too seriously, but he deeply respected local culture. In 1960 John Gorton, future Australian Prime Minister, and his wife Bettina made an official visit to Sarawak. Dick drew up their eight-day program, beginning what became a life-long friendship between the Gortons and the Morrises. At the time Senator Gorton was the minister assisting Paul Hasluck as Minister for External Affairs, and Bettina Gorton was on her first trip to South-East Asia.

Dick told Bettina, 'It is not possible to work in Sarawak without learning Malay'. He added, 'It is not very difficult to learn'.

He taught her a prayer in the language of the Sea Dayaks so that this could be chanted at the longhouse of Penghulu Jugah.

Tun Jugah was a prominent Iban chief, the Iban leader of the Upper Rejang. At the time, he had recently returned from Australia, where he had been a guest of the Commonwealth Government. His longhouse was a communal dwelling on stilts hung with ancient skulls and housing 150 people.

The Gortons cheerfully took part in the '*bedara*' ceremony, each invoking blessings on the occupants by waving a live cockerel over every head present while chanting the prayer. 'This caused a sensation – it was the first time any overseas visitor had taken the trouble to learn the prayer', said Dick.[3] Bettina Gorton would later help to edit an English–Malay dictionary compiled at the Australian National University.

Living in Borneo, with its diverse ethnographies, also met Dick's liking for cosmopolitanism. He disliked the growing insularity that he observed in post-war Australia. It was a time when the nation, he felt, was beset by anxiety about being invaded – the enemy being communism, not only beyond its own borders in South-East Asia, but also within Australia.

The Morrises appreciated that living so much in the outstations meant that they were generally spared the large gatherings and round of receptions that were a feature of expatriate life in the Sarawak capital of Kuching. These could become oppressive. Sunday curry lunch in Kuching meant for some expatriates 'assembling at midday with people you see too much anyway and drinking beer, pink gin and brandy ginger ale until well into the afternoon'.[4] When living in Brunei, Dick would go sailing to escape the hardened torpor of late-afternoon Sundays.

Living in outstations meant always receiving guests, and the Morrises were notably genial hosts. Government officials would stay with them while travelling on inspecting tours. Close friends were made from among the ever-rotating parade of officers and their spouses moving between placements in Sarawak, or to postings beyond, and ultimately retirement around the world. Their friends were part of a large extended family of like-minded souls, whose experience of Sarawak bound them together. These 'Sarawakians' were always eager for the latest news of each other.

The Morrises relished the specialised knowledge that came from work in Borneo. Close friends were the authors on British Borneo, Bill Geddes and Bill Smythies. The notable anthropologist Professor WR Geddes introduced the Land Dayaks to many in his book *Nine Dayak Nights*, published by Oxford University Press in 1957. BE Smythies was acclaimed for his magisterial work on the birds of Borneo that appeared in 1960. Other close friends were Tun Bujang bin Tunku Othman, future Governor of Sarawak (from 1969), and the great Iban leader Tun Jugah.

The Morrises were animated conversationalists. Dick's sonorous voice could always be heard at the centre of conversation. It was known that 'Dick's memory is phenomenal'.[5] He had a deep, inexhaustible memory for detail. He liked nothing more than debate over history or the exact meaning of a word from the English language. In Borneo, he could engage in his love of languages, and the background that came with each culture. He was fluent in Malay and Iban, was comfortable in Cantonese, and passed examinations in written Arabic.

Dorothy, who spoke Malay and Iban, was a ready listener and inveterate letter-writer. She exchanged among her many close women friends solutions to overcome the shortages that often came with outstation living. She shared remedies for medical ailments, recipes for limited food supplies, and the little delights (like clothes) that could offset the hardships that women often endured.

The Morrises never requested a posting beyond Sarawak. They were wedded to the country and its people and traditions. They were among the European Officers in the Borneo Territories who envisaged staying on after the changes that would come with the anticipated formation of Malaysia.

News of their posting to Limbang reached them while they were on leave, spent with their children in Europe and in Australia. The previous Resident wrote to Dick. He was unconcerned about meeting for the hand-over.

> If you like we can meet in Kuching or alternatively have a
> gunpowder plot in Limbang. But you know this end of the
> country pretty well so even if we don't meet at all you will
> soon be at home. I must say we have found the 5th Division
> jolly nice to work in and I am sure you will like it here.[6]

Dick's approach to Limbang was far from casual. Before leaving Australia, he wrote to a friend that he was 'returning to "I don't know what headaches" in Sarawak'.[7] The Fifth Division shared borders with Brunei, Sabah and Indonesia. It extended over some 8000 square kilometres, with a population speaking five different languages. The Division's administrative centre and chief town, Limbang, was only accessible by river from Brunei. No land communication between the Division and the rest of Sarawak existed except by means of long and difficult journeys through the hinterland. In May that year there were reports of underground movements in the Brunei Territory of Temburong, which adjoins Limbang and nearby Lawas districts. Gun-stealing had been reported in the area.

The Morrises were old hands at moves into the government residences. These were usually colonial buildings, 'rubber regulation' bungalows raised on piers. Customarily they occupied an elevated position overlooking the town. This brought the advantage of breezes that could offer some relief from the heat and humidity of Sarawak's rainforest climate.

The Residency in Limbang was different. It was a relatively new single-storey house with large windows. With a close-cropped lawn immediately around it, the house had a modern appearance, much like a suburban home of the time in Sydney's North Shore. It opened at one end to a deep open porch that overlooked the river, and the nearby District Office, lower down the hill. This was the only outlook that the house had, as it backed onto the impenetrable green wall of jungle.

The previous Resident's letter told them that they could expect their new home to be reasonably well furnished. 'We have put curtains in all the rooms and a complete set of cushion covers. It was decorated from top to bottom at the beginning of the year but in neutral shades so that almost any furnishings will do.'[8] The Morrises thought this might save them some of the effort they had gone to in earlier assignments where it had been necessary for Dorothy to be canny with her sewing so as to furnish them with a small degree of simple comfort beyond what was provided.

The letter noted some quirks they might expect. 'There are numerous irritating things which you will soon find out about. The main one being that you can't get water in more than one tap at a time and sometimes not even in one.' They shrugged their shoulders: it would not be Sarawak without such quirks. Every move brought some difficulties to be overcome.

Dorothy was used to coping with the characteristics of colonial service. Frequent moves, adjusting to new environments, establishing new households, finding and training staff to help in meeting official obligations in the tropical conditions: this was all part of being in Sarawak. However, their arrival in Limbang had been so full of incident that they had been given little time to attend to their settling in. Dorothy now busied herself with this. She took a tally of the Residency's linen, mindful that this would be passed on to the next Resident. Doing this she thought that it was essential to regularly air clothing and linen to offset the damp and mould. Flour and rice had to be cleared of weevils, and books from mould. Nothing had been aired from their camphorwood chests since April that year. December was the wet season and she was eager for a hot, sunny, airy day.

The Morrises were looking forward to the arrival of their children. Geraldine, known as 'Bibi', aged 15, and Adrian, known as 'Bujang', aged 13, were coming to them from boarding school in Australia for Christmas and their long summer holidays. Geraldine was in her Intermediate year at Ascham, Edgecliff, and Adrian was at Shore, North Sydney. Dick farewelled his son the day before he left Sydney. Dick had planned to see Bujang again before departing, but school timetables intervened. The following day, Dick wrote:

> My dear Bujang, I was terribly sorry we were not able to see you again yesterday afternoon. Perhaps it was just as well as goodbyes are not the most pleasant thing. Until 15 Dec, we shall be counting the days. Take good care of yourself and work as hard as you can, until December auf wiedersehn. Apai.[9]

Before their arrival, Dorothy was appointed President of the Limbang Group of the Red Cross. The group had lapsed for lack of support and funds. Her task was to revive it. This meant taking overall charge and responsibility, and giving the lead in Limbang to local people willing to participate. To kickstart this, she had called a meeting in the town's Recreation Club, which was well attended.

Needs, owing to limited medical support, were stressed at that meeting. Dorothy said that the town needed 'to have a Red Cross HQ building of some sort, to serve as a centre for our activities, such as training Junior Links, hopefully Cadets and finally a VAD [Voluntary Aid Detachment]'.[10]

Response from the town was heartening. Dorothy described this: 'The Chinese community in the bazaar and others in the timber and sawmilling business volunteered to provide building materials and labour. An English ex-nurse, Mrs Kathleen Brake, living in the town with her husband Harry, a Public Works Department supervisor, volunteered to give First Aid and Home Nursing classes'.

Dorothy counted this first meeting as a success. 'We were able to elect a small ad hoc committee to get things going and felt greatly encouraged over the local response.'[11] A local headman and town dignitary, Abang Omar bin Abang Samaudin, Limbang's postman, volunteered to assist and his daughter Dayang Achen binte Abang Omar was appointed cadet officer. The interest and enthusiasm shown at the meeting reassured Dorothy; to her mind, Limbang looked promising. She could not have imagined how important this would prove to be.

Accommodation for visitors to the town was also limited, without a Government Rest House. Shortly after they had arrived, the Morrises received their first house guest.

Sir John Martin came from London, where he was a distinguished servant of Whitehall. From 1941, he had been Churchill's Principal Private Secretary. Martin was a perceptive observer, present at almost every summit meeting that Churchill attended. Now 58, Martin was, from 1956, the Deputy Under Secretary of State, at the Colonial Office. He arrived via Jesselton, some 120 miles (190 kilometres) to the north, just after the Morrises reached Limbang and were still unpacking.

Martin's visit was urgent. He was involved in decolonisation. He believed that Britain's post-war purpose was to lead territories for which it was responsible forward to independence, and that Britain should exit countries that became independent by agreement. He was concerned that the imminent formation of Malaysia be achieved peacefully. He believed that Britain should contribute to maintaining peace in the Far East. In November 1962, the Prime Minister of Malaya, Tunku Abdul Rahman, paid a visit to Sarawak. It was becoming apparent that there was little consensus of opinion in Borneo on the idea of 'Malaysia'. People questioned the proposal for union. Some viewed the proposed merger as offering some security in communist-threatened South-East Asia, whereas others viewed the proposal as a 'neo-colonialist' device. Elections to be held in Sarawak in June 1963 would measure true sentiment. Meanwhile an Inter-Governmental Committee under the British Minister of State for the Colonies was appointed to consider the timing of the scheme and deliver its findings early in 1963. Martin was after intelligence.

After staying in Limbang, he wrote to Dorothy. His letter revealed some of his concerns. He told her that his visit was well timed 'for getting in focus a picture which, unfortunately, may be on the screen in coming months. The 5th Division may not be a popular posting but it obviously lacks neither interest nor attractions and I hope you are going to have a happy tour'.[12]

Martin's visit reflected recognition that there was more to Limbang than the town's seemingly placid appearance suggested. It sat within a region with particular sensitivities. As Martin saw it, the Morrises were well posted there. Martin served briefly in the Malayan Civil Service in the early 1930s, so he appreciated the complex ethnographic and potentially explosive cultural mix that existed in Malaya and Borneo.

His stay had been cordial, such that Martin wrote again to

them, addressing them informally, and starting his letter by saying 'I am so addressing you in the hope that in future you and Dick will no longer think of me as Sir John'. He thanked them for their welcome: 'Many thanks for giving me such a very enjoyable time and also for giving me the chance of meeting the local community on Sunday evening'. He was genuinely grateful; not only had he enjoyed the weekend with them, but he left Limbang feeling confident about affairs there. He told Dorothy, 'At the risk of sounding patronising, I was tremendously impressed by the way in which Dick has taken a grip of the situation in such a short time. I think he really enjoys having a tricky situation to grip!'[13] Dick was clearly posted to Limbang due to his background in Brunei's affairs.

Dick was well aware that Borneo was not immune to ideas nor to change. He possessed a keen sense of history and therefore knew that, while Borneo was portrayed as being remote and unchanged, it was connected historically to its surrounding world and that beyond, through ethnic and trading and religious links. He was aware of the links developed through the Haj, which the Dutch scholar of Oriental cultures and languages Snouck Hurgronje wrote about earlier in 1916 and 1931.[14] The Japanese and British were simply one of the many links which the area enjoyed with the world beyond.

Dick's experiences in Borneo in the closing days of the Second World War made him acutely familiar with the profound changes occurring on the island. He had worked then in the British Borneo Civil Administration Unit (BBCAU), whose task was to provide a civil administration to the British Borneo colonies following the Japanese surrender, as the pre-war administration had either left or been interned by the Japanese, and many had died during their internment.

He would say that 'to really understand the post 1945 changes one needs to study the effect of the Japanese occupation and the Japanese Military administration of the occupied territories'. To Dick, 'Whether one is a serious student or merely an interested dilettante, the war in the Western Pacific was the precursor of fundamental political and social changes throughout East and South-East Asia'.[15]

Rebellion had a long history in Borneo. Dick recalled too how, even in Sarawak where a legacy of the Brooke Rajahs was strong loyalty to the British, some had turned their allegiance to the deeply unpopular Japanese. He said, 'As one of my old Sarawak friends smilingly confessed, "One finds it difficult, Tuan, not to collaborate when the Kempeitai show you the alternatives"'.[16] It was not inconceivable that the same could occur again, as with a turn to supporting communist insurgents, as had happened in peninsular Malaya during the Emergency.

The Limbang area was much contested. This contest had its origins in the 1880s when British North Borneo and Sarawak were intriguing against each other to gain possession of the remains of the once-powerful Sultanate of Brunei. The area around Limbang was the last parcel of land that Brunei lost. The district of Limbang was incorporated into Sarawak in 1890 after Britain's protectorate had been established. It divided Bruneians geographically. They were separated by the Limbang–Lawas district, a finger of Sarawak, poking into Brunei Bay. Since that time, the problem of Limbang smouldered continually. Until recently, Brunei remained in dispute with Malaysia in its claim to the Limbang River and district.[17]

Dick recognised that this dispute engendered disaffection towards the Sarawak Government. Tensions ran high over the government's slowness, or failure (as some thought), in its responsibilities in the vital areas of land reform and secondary and advanced education. Most arable land was tied up by traditional native ownership, obliging many Chinese to farm illegally and leaving the native people unable to capitalise on their ownership. Serious re-examination of the land system was only begun in 1961 and the hard decisions had not been made.

Many in the Chinese community were disgruntled. This could be destabilising. Threats of communist organisation in Sarawak began to surface in the Chinese secondary schools in the early 1950s. Radical thinking was developing among these young educated Chinese, who were frustrated in their efforts to find employment. This led to education department and police warnings of 'Communists behind every bush'.

Within Limbang town was found the mix of racial groups that characterised Sarawak. This could be seen among the civil servants, some with their wives and families – Iban policemen, Chinese engineers, a Malay postmaster, a British schoolteacher. Some of the few Europeans there were volunteers assisting with essential services, like the priests of the Roman Catholic mission, and a young American from the United States Government volunteer program, the Peace Corps. In December 1962, he too had only just arrived in the town.

Hints of brewing trouble came in early November when the Resident ahead of Dick received some intelligence about planning for insurrection. Information came to him from his officers, civil servants working in the field, like his District Officer who reported on his travels in the Division. Dick explained how such reports were relied on. 'The "Travelling Report" one wrote and sent to one's Resident on return from "Travelling" kept him informed and enabled him to influence the formulation of policy.'[18]

Rumours circulated about lost weapons and shortages of green cloth. Added to this were rumours from Brunei Town about young men disappearing into the jungle. Special Branch police from Kuching visited Limbang and found some uniforms with badges of the TNKU or North Kalimantan National Army. Little was then known about the TNKU.

The Morrises' arrival in Limbang coincided with the visit of a delegation from Malaya as part of the moves towards the Federation of Malaysia. Heading the delegation was Ismail bin Yusof, Minister of Information in Kuala Lumpur and adviser to the Federation representatives on the Malaysia Inter-Governmental Committee. He was touring remote areas in Sarawak to speak to the 'people who formed the backbone of the country'. It was, he said, important to understand them and find out their attitude to Malaysia. After ten days in Sarawak, he concluded that 'the people of Sarawak like to see North Borneo join Malaysia rather than the Philippines'.[19] They were indifferent to the Philippines' claim to North Borneo.

In late November, Dick heard that an insurrection was planned for Brunei, but not before 19 December (when Brunei's Legislative Council was due to meet). Claude Fenner, the Inspector General of the Malayan Police, flew to Sarawak to investigate but found insufficient evidence to be alarmed. Such reports and rumours of rebellion were not new. Similar rumours that had circulated earlier were found to be false alarms. The Chief of Staff in the British Far East Headquarters in Singapore reviewed and updated the contingency plan, Pale Ale, for Brunei. However, the risk was assessed as low. The British Far East Land, Sea and Air Commanders-in-Chief were away from Singapore. The operational commander of land forces, Major General Walter Walker, was on leave.

On 6 December, Dick heard that a rebellion would start in two days' time. The next day, similar information reached John Fisher OBE, Walker's brother-in-law and the Resident of Sarawak's Fourth Division, based in Miri, 75 miles (120 kilometres) southwest of Limbang and 20 miles (32 kilometres) southwest of Brunei. As a result, police were put on full alert throughout Brunei, North Borneo and Sarawak, and Police Field Force reinforcements were flown from Kuching to Miri.

Dick submitted to the Chief Secretary in Kuching proposals about how to rehabilitate the area in the event of any uprising. This expressed his concern about the safety of the civil servants in the district and that of their families. The police force was dedicated, but small and generally under-resourced. The police station in Limbang was centrally located; it faced the river in the middle of the narrow town. However, given Limbang's topography and isolated location, the police could not expect back-up support to reach them quickly should an outbreak become violent.

If uneasy, Dick accepted the official opinion that there was no certainty of trouble. He concluded, 'I was not by any means certain that an attack would be made, despite reports which had been received from Limbang and from Miri'.[20]

He took comfort in the fact that this was also the attitude of the Commissioner for Police in Brunei. This was Alan Outram, appointed in December 1959. Dick and Outram shared views about their concern. 'And we agreed', Dick confirmed, 'that the Police should be placed in a state of alert but that no further action should be taken'.[21]

Yet, Dick thought it might be best to be cautious. He phoned the Secretariat in Kuching in the afternoon of 6 December and spoke with Chief Secretary F Derek Jakeway CMG, OBE. Dick had reservations about Jakeway's judgment. Jakeway was new to Sarawak. He arrived in 1959, after 22 years in Colonial Administrative Service, largely in Nigeria. Dick disliked the stuffy attitudes which characterised many former 'Africans'. They stood on ceremony unnecessarily, as far as old hands in Sarawak like Dick were concerned. He did not want to see a return to the days of the Rajah when tension between regulation-wielding Kuching bureaucrats and semi-autonomous outstation officers was the norm. Informality was a feature of Sarawak, a legacy of Brooke rule, and of getting to know and mix with locals. 'Europeans mingled with local people', said a close friend of Dorothy's, Daphne Richards. She described how this familiarity astonished a visiting Indonesian officer. He told her he had never seen anything like it. 'He had never sat down with the Dutch!'[22]

Jakeway's visit to Limbang in late May 1962 sparked off a demonstration by about 3000 local residents (the majority of the people of Limbang district) demanding the return of Limbang to Brunei.[23] Jakeway and Dick knew disaffection was about. After speaking with Jakeway, Dick walked around the town.

> I carried out a reconnaissance of the Limbang Town area
> to see if there was any area which could be turned into
> a defended locality capable of being held by the forces
> available, and in which it would be possible to accommodate
> the wives and families of civil servants and those civil
> servants who were not capable of bearing arms. There
> was no such area, and I therefore decided not to issue
> any warnings or to take any action which might cause
> despondency or alarm to the civil population.[24]

3

SATURDAY, 8 DECEMBER: BLACK SATURDAY

People in Sydney woke to the news of the deadly smog that was paralysing Britain, and closed London airport for the fourth successive day. The festive season was getting into its momentum and, with 16 shopping days to Christmas, the newspapers were filled with '100 suggestions for Christmas' and details of the Christmas tree erected in the city's Martin Place.

All were oblivious to the fact that in Brunei at 2 am local time that morning, coordinated armed attacks were unleashed and that during the next three hours, shooting had been heard near police stations all over Brunei.

The armed insurgents were members of the TNKU, the armed wing of Sheikh Azahari's Brunei People's Party (PRB).

The rebels began coordinated attacks on police stations and government facilities around the protectorate and in the oil town of Seria (targeting the Brunei Shell oil installations). They seized Radio Station Brunei and the airport at coastal Kuala Belait, Brunei's second largest town. Hostages were taken at Seria. The rebels attempted to seize power.

The attacks were well timed, to happen simultaneously across the country. This showed that the revolt was undeniably well planned and well organised. It was later learned they were led by Yasin Affandy bin Abdul Rahman, TNKU Military Commander for the Borneo Territories, the Secretary-General of Parti Rakyat and a close confidant of Azahari.[1] Azahari himself was not in Brunei. Earlier in the year, he invoked the United Nations Declaration on the Granting of Independence to Colonial Countries and Peoples, adopted by the General Assembly on 14 December 1960, and sought to put Brunei's case before the UN's Special Committee for Trusteeship and Information from Non-Self-Governing Territories, which was scheduled to meet in December.[2]

A teacher at the Sultan Omar Ali Saifuddin College in Brunei Town witnessed the revolt in the centre of Brunei Town.

> At 2 am I heard the sound of firing. I looked out of my
> window and saw troops in military uniform moving about.
> They were converging on the power station. Suddenly all
> the lights went out and I realized that something unusual
> was happening. Then I saw them moving towards the
> civic centre, which is opposite the main police station. The
> troops, dressed in berets and jungle green, suddenly opened
> fire on the police station and I realised then that they were
> rebels.[3]

John Muda, a Sarawak Council Negri (State Council) member, was also in Brunei Town at the time. He thanked his 'lucky stars' that he escaped miraculously, being only a few hundred yards from the shooting. 'The rebels, dressed in jungle-green with red and white *songkoks*, were yelling and whooping amidst the cracking of shot-guns and punctuating sounds of machine-guns which lasted till 4 am.'[4]

Officials heard word that at Temburong, 17 miles (27 kilometres) away, the District Officer, Pengiran Haji Besar bin Pengiran Haji Kula, and a few others from Brunei security forces, and a number of civilians, were executed for refusing to join in the rebellion. The Brunei police remained loyal to the Sultan and his government. Many among them that day became unsung heroes, refusing to abandon their posts.[5]

This was undeclared war against Sultan Sir Omar Ali Saifuddin, his government and loyal subjects. After meeting with the Deputy Chief Minister, the Sultan made a public radio broadcast in which he condemned the TNKU for treason.

Signals from Brunei to British Far East Headquarters in Singapore reported rebel attacks in Brunei Town on police stations and the Sultan's Istana. The electricity supply was cut off. Another rebel force was rumoured to be approaching the capital by water.

At this stage it was not known that rebels had also attacked police stations elsewhere throughout Brunei, in the Fifth Division of Sarawak, and on the western edge of North Borneo. The situation was most serious in Seria, where the rebels had captured the police station and were threatening the oilfields. Miri was still in government hands, but Limbang had been taken by the rebels.

General Sir Nigel Poett was Commander-in-Chief of the Far East Land Forces (1961–63). Now 55, he had been part of decisive actions during the Second World War, when he had commanded the 5th Parachute Brigade. This brigade consisted principally of battalions formed up from volunteers, when parachuting was still a novelty. Brigadier Poett inspired them to throw themselves into making ready for a crucial role in the forthcoming assault into France. He dropped himself with the reconnaissance and *coup de main* parties and shared the perils of the men whom he led to the war's end. He was respected as much for his physical courage as for his military talent.[6]

Up to mid-1946, Poett was in Dutch Borneo, where he was sent to maintain internal security between the Dutch colonial authorities and Sukarno's nationalist forces in Semarang. This task called for as much political judgment as military sense.

More recently, he had been deeply disappointed at being unable to press for a quick military response to the blocking of the Suez Canal in 1956. Formerly Director of Military Operations at the War Office in 1954, he believed that a parachute brigade and Royal Marine commandos should have been engaged at once instead of waiting months for the arrival of a British corps. He favoured the decisive military solution over political negotiation, which could fail, as he thought Suez did, 'all due to being over-awed by the opposition'.[7]

In late 1962, Poett visited Indonesia. Britain was grappling with the question of how to reconcile strategic interests with rising popular nationalism and the views of neighbouring governments. Singapore was of strategic importance as Britain's principal naval base in the Far East. Chiefs of Staff believed this strategic position was likely to increase in importance in the years ahead and be vital for the security of the whole region. Poett would have to have been aware of Indonesia's concern, as the largest regional power, over the continued British military presence close to Indonesian territory, and of Indonesia's desire to be consulted on matters of regional political development. Poett found Sukarno in Indonesia 'at his most relaxed and affable'.[8]

So when the Brunei uprising started, Poett did not want to lose the potential advantages of surprise and speed. He was advised that a major force would be needed to suppress the rebels. But such a force would take two or three months to assemble. He lacked a close reserve.

Poett was assisted in his resolve by fellow Second World War veteran, Admiral Sir David Luce, the first Commander in Chief Far East. Through the year both had been involved in proposals for a unified command for the Far East.[9] The Ministry of Defence regarded a unified command as the logical development of the increased interdependence of the three services. The unified command organisation was outlined in the 1962 Defence White Paper and was set in train formally with Luce's appointment. With the outbreak in Brunei, combined operations swung into action under their command.

Of similar cast to Poett were two men who would immediately be brought in to manage the Brunei crisis, and who would work together. They were Brigadier JBA Glennie DSO and Major General (later Sir) Walter Walker DSO, CBE.

Like Poett, both men had distinguished themselves during the Second World War. Glennie served in North Africa and at Monte Cassino. After the war, he served in Korea. Walker developed his mastery of unconventional warfare when engaged against the Japanese in Burma and northeast India, as a member of the Forgotten Army, as British soldiers wryly referred to such jungle action of 1942–45. Glennie was serving as Brigadier, General Staff, Far East Land Forces in Singapore, when Brunei's revolt began. Walker was commander of the 17th Gurkha division in Malaya.

A striking figure, erect and immaculate, Walker would accept nothing but victory. His precepts were 'lie hard, fight hard, die hard'.[10] He was a stickler for detail because he refused to have his men killed by slipshod methods. He recognised early the importance of the lessons learned in Burma, of jungle warfare techniques, while NATO and the Russians, and conventional warfare, held the attention of his military colleagues. Walker risked the displeasure of the Ministry of Defence by pressing home his view that preparedness for a different enemy, in the Far East, was essential, and that the Gurkhas could lead in handling worldwide threats of another kind. To him, the primary task of the defence force should be more than being a purely continental force. It should be able to move quickly, wherever there may be confrontation in the Far East, and 'the person who will win will be the person who can get there the quickest with the mostest'.[11] He had faith in the ability of his men, so that 'it sometimes seemed that Walker thought that there was no military problem that could not be solved by a battalion of Gurkhas'.[12]

Walker was in Nepal visiting his Gurkha pensioners when he heard on 8 December that a revolt had broken out in Brunei. Before going to Nepal, he had checked carefully with General Headquarters (GHQ) that nothing untoward was expected.

> I was very surprised when they said that the coast was clear, because my intelligence said the exact opposite. So I had a good wireless set with my ADC and he was listening to the news one morning, and at the same time frying an egg, and heard that the Brunei Revolt had broken out, and the Divisional Commander – me – was five days away from the nearest airfield in Nepal.[13]

When he reached Singapore, Walker would at once be appointed director of operations in Borneo. As he recalled, 'The Commander-in-Chief said to me "see you in three months." And I said "Three years." He just looked at me: I could see him thinking to himself that Walker is riding his hobby horse as usual!'[14]

From his headquarters in Brunei, then later on Labuan Island in Brunei Bay, and as British, Gurkha and Malayan reinforcements were flown in from Singapore, he would formulate his plan for an aggressive defence. This would be necessary because, although the initial revolt in Brunei would be contained, and the British would quickly rout Azahari's supporters, aggression would grow along the 1000-mile (1600-kilometre) frontier with Indonesian Borneo. Walker knew straightaway that the trouble was Indonesian inspired. 'I knew even then that Sukarno wasn't using his regular troops', he said. 'The powers that be were underestimating the operation.'[15]

As Walker was hurrying back, a commander and staff were taken from Poett's own headquarters to back a fighting core of Gurkhas, who were based in Singapore. Far East Headquarters ordered a force of two Gurkha infantry companies on 48 hours' notice to move. Two companies of 1/2 Gurkha Rifles moved to the RAF airfields at Changi and Seletar to fly to Labuan. Only a year before, most of the 800-strong Gurkha Battalion had been in Kuala Belait for training.

From the Anglo-Nepalese War back in 1814–16, Gurkha heroics in battle with the British and British Indian Armies inspired fear around the world. The word 'Gurkha' derives from the Hindu warrior-saint Gutu Gorakhnath, who gave his name to the region of Nepal from which the Gurkhas hail. Field Marshal Sam Manekshaw, a former chief of staff of the Indian Army, once said, 'If a man says he is not afraid of dying, he is either lying or he is a Gurkha'.[16]

Their embarkation went slowly because the RAF was following normal peacetime procedures at the time and was unprepared for urgent military action. The vagaries of air travel, of flight schedules and turnarounds, with delays at both Aden and Singapore where troops were stationed, impeded a rapid response.

The Gurkhas were flown to Labuan Island in a Bristol Britannia and three Blackburn Beverleys, each able to carry around 80 men. The Beverleys were diverted mid-flight from Labuan to Brunei airfield when it was learned that this was not in rebel hands.[17] That night, at about 10 pm, just under 24 hours after the rebellion started, their planes landed, and the Gurkhas advanced in the darkness into Brunei Town. In the resistance they met, two Gurkhas were killed.

Reinforcements following by sea from Singapore would arrive after two days' sailing.

The Sultan was rescued by a small detachment of Gurkhas

led by Captain Digby Willoughby. Educated at Blundells and the Royal Military Academy Sandhurst, he was commissioned into the 2nd Gurkha Rifles and joined the 1st Battalion in Malaya in 1955. Willoughby was fearless: a champion bobsledder, his two-man team broke the world record on the St Moritz bobsleigh run the year before. Exploits of men such as he caught public attention in reports of the Brunei Revolt. The bravery of the Malay police, who had robustly defended their posts to the end, was largely unnoticed.

Unknown to Dick and Dorothy Morris, Limbang was to become the focus of rebel action.

Their ordeal began when they were woken from sleep. Their dog, Spatter, became restless; the name tag on his collar was clinking. The phone was ringing. It was 2 am. At the same time, heavy firing broke out in the town area.

They also heard sounds outside the house, close to them.

'Seeing a number of armed men in front of the Residency', said Dorothy, 'we tried to escape from the back but ran into an armed party and were taken prisoner'.

They were ambushed and seized at gunpoint.

The attack in Limbang was led by a 30-year-old Limbang local, Salleh bin Sambas.[18] Salleh being a common name among the rebels, Sambas was known as Salleh Jangut or 'Salleh the bearded one' (describing his appearance).[19] He was a former member of the Sarawak Field Force, a jungle-trained paramilitary-type force. British-trained in Kuching, his mastery of the Bren gun saw him become known as 'Father Bren'. On orders from Yassin Affandy, the TNKU Military Commander, Sambas had his men positioned at all of the key points in and around

Limbang, such as the police station, the prison and the Resident's house, poised ready for the 2 am attack. Sambas saw himself as a freedom fighter, like Rosli bin Dobhi, the 17-year-old Malay nationalist who assassinated Sarawak's Governor in 1949.[20] Now a turncoat, he was aggressive.

The Morrises were pushed back into the Residency, which filled with armed men. They were fierce looking, if mostly young. Dick tried to exercise his authority. He addressed them in Malay. He reminded them that detaining the civilian authority was an offence. They were deaf to him. They tied his hands together and pinned his arms. The suddenness of their ambush left Dorothy feeling unable to think quickly enough. She wanted to help her husband.

She remarked, 'Dick was fairly savagely bound with nylon fishing cord, but my hands were free'.

Not that this gave her much comfort as both were manhandled. To Dorothy's discomfort, a *kris* was pointed unpleasantly close to the middle of Dick's back.

Dick was the prize catch. He would learn that this was due to the resistance shown to the rebels by the police in the town.

With their arms gripped by rebels, the Morrises were marched out of the Residency into the dark, and shoved down the steep lead-up to the house, towards the river. They were moved to dense jungle, just above a section of the river with very steep banks, and held there. It was pitch dark. The vegetation was dense, tangled and damp.

'Two decidedly halitosical little thugs squatted unpleasantly and unnecessarily close on either side of me', said Dorothy, 'each clutching an arm'.

While unnerved, Dorothy's good-natured sense prevailed through her shock at their predicament.

In an attempt to impress on them how unlikely would be any attempted break for freedom by either Dick or myself, I tried indulging in light drawing-room conversation, telling them how my brother had been among the Australian soldiers who had rescued them and their parents and others from the Japanese in Limbang not so many years ago, enquiring whether they were married, what children they had, stressed the importance of sending them to school regularly, concluding with vehement assertions that I was old enough to be the grandmother of their children, and capping this with the ghastly truth of my own age.[21]

She hoped they might free her, or loosen their grip on her arms. The reply that she received to her banter did not match the response she hoped for. 'Followed a whispered conclave between the two of them', she said, 'and one produced a match, struck it, held it close to my face, and from the pair of them there issued a prolonged groan, expressing a mixture of disappointment, disgust, resignation, and – I like to think – disbelief'.

They were being held while resistance to the TNKU attack continued in the town. In the dark, and without information, Dick could not assess what he later came to know. Resisting police were putting up a determined fight. A policeman on guard at the telephone exchange in the early hours killed one rebel. This policeman, most likely by way of alarm, made the call to the Residency which woke them. Dick later learned that the shots that they heard came from the police station. Five rebels died in their attack on the station; a number were badly wounded. Resistance too came from the District Office. Dick would discover that the constable on duty at the District Office shot and killed one rebel before he was overpowered and captured by a force of approximately 30 rebels, some of whom were armed with shotguns. Like elsewhere across Brunei, the TNKU attack was directed at the offices and quarters of the government and its security forces.

The sound of gunfire, coming from the town, punctuated the noises of the jungle around them. 'We sat there', said Dorothy, 'with every form of biting night-life assailing us, Dick clad only in underpants, jockey type without much seat in them and the inevitable perished elastic band at the top and *no* safety pins'.

Dorothy explained, 'Having had certain security measures to take before quitting the house, he couldn't spare the time in the dark to locate more dignified clothing'. When invaded, Dick's first reaction was to ensure that government files with him were concealed. There had been no time for him to dress. As the rebel party moved into the Residency, Dick had quickly hidden the files.

Dorothy continued, 'I had had the extra minute or so in which to fumble about and dress more adequately'. She had been able to find some heavy shoes. They might insulate her from the jaws of leeches.

A large number of armed rebels, wearing assorted uniforms, filed past. Some inspected them in the dark. Dick couldn't tell how many there were but estimated there were up to a 100, if not more: the size of a company. Their intent was clear and this concerned him. From what he could see, they were armed with an assortment of weapons. Besides firearms, many carried swords and parangs, traditional sharp-bladed weapons which he had seen many times before used with skill, force and accuracy.

By this time, the Morrises were shouted at to move again. Dorothy recalled, 'It was with some relief an hour or so later that we were ordered to blunder up the slope again, to a clearing above the Residency and thence down a very ill-defined path with cobble stones and irregular steps'.

The darkness was disorientating, making them unsteady, as did being shoved about on the slippery, uneven ground. Dorothy's unsteadiness on the irregular terrain gained her some relief from the closeness of her guards.

> As my hands were still free I was firmly held by a tough on each arm, but threw them off half way down, by the simple if unplanned expedient of losing my footing on a flight of seven old-world steps and slithering down to the bottom and earning a really worth-while bruise from hip to shin.

The guards were thrown off by her fall. 'After that they let me walk unaided to the District Office.'

The Morrises were moved to the District Office, adjacent to and just below the Residency. Once there, Dick was yanked away from Dorothy. He was interrogated in his own office.

Dick looked sternly at the men around him. It was awkward to maintain dignity in underpants, but he kept his composure. He held to his authority as the Resident, and the Sarawak Government's representative. He had little to tell them. They rummaged through his office. He hoped that maintaining dignity might protect him against assault. Anxiety about Dorothy gripped him. He feared for her well-being when alone, and wanted to get back to her. Their time apart seemed an eternity.

Dorothy tried to keep up her banter, with the guards holding her. Like Dick, she was trying to throw off the apprehension which she felt creeping over her. Armed rebels leered at her. One attempted to spit in her face. His aim was poor and he missed her. Their hostility was confronting. It was new to her experience of Sarawak. Her spirits lifted when she sighted Dick once more. He was still bound and, like her, he was under heavy guard.

Firing continued in the town.

It remained dark, although dawn would soon be approaching. The Morrises were pushed to a building located diagonally opposite the District Office. This was the jail, which sat behind the old fort. Dorothy described it. 'This is a square wooden building of four cells, divided by a central passage. Built on piles it is not remarkable for lighting or ventilation, nor are the bathroom and toilet block at the back remarkable for sanitation.' Cells were intended only for short detention. They were small, airless, claustrophobic. They were pushed into Cell No. 1. Power in the town was cut off, so the cell was pitch black.

The small jail held eight prisoners at the time. The rebels released them ahead of moving their hostages into the jail. They also took as hostage the policemen on night duty, Inspector Abang Zain bin Abang Latif and Inspector Latif bin Basah.[22] They were locked into one of the cells. Inspector Latif was wounded. He had been shot in the arm.

The Morrises barely had time to take stock of their situation when Dick was hauled away again. His hands remained tied with fishing cord. Guns were pointed at his back.

Finding it hard to grasp the reality of what was happening, Dorothy was again left with her fear about what might become of them.

She learned later what he had endured. 'When day broke', she said, 'Dick and Inspector Zain were taken out to the police station. The small police detachment had put up a very stout struggle but the rebels had already infiltrated into the police compound.'

The rebels intended to make Dick and Inspector Zain persuade the police to surrender. Both were used as a 'human shield' to stop resistance from the local police.

Their arms upraised, they were marched forward, 300 yards down the road, towards the police station, to face the resisting police, and possible death. Prodded with guns, each yard they walked seemed a mile.

Nearing the station, heavy firing broke out. Dick and Inspector Zain were caught in the cross-fire and dived to the ground.

Dick was ordered to tell the police to surrender. He did so, knowing there was no way that help could arrive in the town in time to save the resisting police, who could not possibly hold out.

At that moment, the police station was finally overwhelmed. Firing stopped.

Looking around him, in the early morning light, Dick could observe the rebels more closely. Of those whom he could see, he noted, 'approximately half the rebels were armed with shotguns and the remainder with swords, parangs or daggers'. It was about 6.45 am.

Later, thinking back on her experience, Dorothy noted:

My story is one of 'highs' and 'lows'. It is these which, naturally enough, come most vividly to mind in looking back over the events of five rather dramatic and, let's face it, anxious days. These are the events which have not yet faded into the blurred picture of the general suspense, the waiting, the listening, the discomforts, the nagging worry of 'I wonder what happened to so-and-so', and of 'I wonder what's going to happen to us'.

She continued, 'The highest of the "highs" was Dick's reappearance at the door of our cell, not his usual healthy colour, still of course bare-footed and wearing his dejected underpants, but alive and uninjured'.

Upon learning about what he had just been through, she was shaken. 'This event', she said, 'probably provided the lowest of all the "lows" for us both'. Speaking about it later, she described this event as 'one we still prefer to "slither over" in our recollections'.

The grimness of their situation was relieved momentarily. 'What followed', Dorothy explained, 'we like to think, could only happen in Sarawak'.

One of the prisoners released from the jail, showed them a kind-heartedness that gave them hope.

> One young Dayak was most loath to accept his release.
> He was changing from his prison garb of canvas-like shirt
> and draw-string pants into his own civvies when we were
> admitted, and while Dick had been down the road facing
> the music at the police station, had produced two small but
> very welcome khaki pillows, his own sleeping mat, and a cup
> of coffee. On Dick's reappearance he assisted the now rather
> grey-faced Resident into his own discarded prison pants.

As she remembered it, 'The poor young lad was in tears at our plight and even asked the "authorities" if he might stay on to help look after us. This was of course denied him.'

This was one of many acts of kindness and goodwill they would receive in the coming days.

Dick did not know the extent of rebellion, and could only speculate what this might be. He made calculations based on the rumours that he had heard earlier. He was remorseful that he had not avoided endangering Dorothy.

> We were in quite serious trouble and if I had been permitted
> to do so I would have sent for the Royal Marines – or
> anybody else – to get us out of it; as it was we just had to
> hope – and pray – that someone, somewhere would do
> something about it, and quickly.

In early 1945, while on leave in Sydney from serving in New

Guinea, Dick had come to know a couple of Royal Marine officers.

> Over the next few days we saw quite a lot of each other,
> drank more than we should have, had far too little sleep and
> became pretty good friends. There was, of course, a good
> deal of 'bull' in much of our conversation but I do remember
> the last party we had together when one of them said, 'Well
> if you ever get into trouble send for the Royal Marines.'[23]

About a mile from Limbang, 18-year-old American Fritz Klattenhoff thought that the noise he heard from his bed was a Chinese wedding. 'I heard shooting at 2 o'clock', he said. 'I lay there – oh, must have been ten or fifteen minutes. I thought, "Those crazy fools, so late at night." I went back to sleep. It was 2.30 when I woke up again. Then I heard a Bren gun and a machine gun.'[24]

Fritz was brought up on a dairy farm in Washington state in the Pacific northwest region of the United States. A burly 15 stone (95 kg), he stood just over six feet (1.8 m), with sandy hair, a freckled face, and an easy-going manner. It was his third month in Limbang. Six months earlier, he had graduated from high school. He was in Limbang because he had rallied to the call from President John F Kennedy, who challenged America's youth to contribute part of their lives to their country by serving for a year or two abroad. In November 1960, Kennedy called on 'talented young men and women, willing and able to serve their country' who wished to serve the cause of freedom to join a volunteer corps.[25] They were to be ambassadors of peace. The Peace Corps was created in March 1961.

The idea for the Peace Corps was inspired by voluntary organisations such as Voluntary Service Overseas (VSO), which was established in 1958 by a British couple, Alec and Mora Dickson, following a visit they made to Sarawak.[26] When the VSO was established, to provide contributions from youthful volunteers to developing countries as they emerged into independence, three of its first eight recruits went to Sarawak. They were among the many young people who were attracted by the faith in humanity and the power of trust that organisations like the VSO and the Peace Corps represented. Kennedy's challenge saw a quick uptake: within six months, just over 1000 volunteers were at work in 17 nations.[27] Malaysia was among the four host countries in South-East Asia which welcomed volunteers from 1962. It provided the Peace Corps with some of its most remote assignments.

Fritz was the first Peace Corps volunteer in Limbang. He was there to help with the setting up of regional agricultural development schemes. He worked at an agricultural station, to teach basic agriculture and technical skills, and with children to create 4-H clubs, engaging them in hands-on learning. At both, he taught English. Peace Corps workers only went to countries where they were invited. They served under local supervisors and worked with host-country co-workers, as active participants in projects. In Limbang he lived on the same level with his co-workers. And, as with many young volunteers overseas, he was unprepared for what awaited him.

In the early morning, a Malay acquaintance came to the two-roomed hut in which Fritz lived. He told Fritz that rebels had captured the town, and warned him to stay hidden.

Not far beyond the northern end of Limbang, Abang Omar took note of the firing that he heard in his kampong. A Malay, he was Limbang's postmaster. Recently he had attended the meeting that

Dorothy held to revive the Red Cross in Limbang, and had volunteered his services.

He adds to the picture of that morning. 'Two armed revolutionary troops came to my house', he later wrote, 'about 1½ miles from the government offices in Limbang town. They asked me for my daughter, Dayang Delima Asaf, who is a nurse, to come down to the hospital to carry out her duty for wounded men'.[28]

At the time she was not with him, being in another kampong about a mile away. 'So in this case', said Omar, 'I must go with them to fetch my daughter'.

They were driven to the hospital, located mid-way between the District Office and the police station. When they arrived at the hospital, they found two nurses working on the wounded. He continued, 'So my daughter and myself work together for the wounded men with calm. Within a few minutes nine wounded revolutionary troops are dressed and we put them in the ward.' They were unable to save a policeman. Bujang bin Muhammed was a sturdily built Malay with a pleasant cheerful countenance who had been second in charge of the police at the station.

Afterward, Omar went to the police station. There he found a policeman lying dead in the front of the building and another lying dead inside.

I carry out my duty. I asked the Rebel troops to remove
the men to the mosque for burying purposes. When all the
dead men in the police station were taken to the mosque, I
asked the Rebel troop if any more dead men were not taken
to the mosque. So one then told me there was one more
at the back of the government general office. I go with the
rebels in a Land Rover to the place and took the body to
the mosque to be buried by the mosque's official staff. On
my way, returning to the hospital, I saw the District Officer

Abang Zainudin being guarded by armed guards. I told them to take care of the DO properly, the same as they treated me.

By then the rebels were done with Omar, and told him to go home.

Omar was someone who would not be cowed. He came from noble descent, as his name and that of his daughter suggests. In Brunei and Sarawak a *Dayang* is a female descendant of a noble state dignitary known as an *Awang* or *Abang*.[29] Omar's great-grandfather was Abang Fatah, whom Spenser St John, the British Consul-General in Brunei in 1856, described as 'a warm friend to English rule'.[30] St John described Fatah as one of the Rajah's most trusty and trusted followers. 'He was one of the best of the Malay chiefs, frank, loyal, honest, brave as a lion … He subsequently lost his life in gallantly defending the Rajah's Government.' Omar spoke of his great-grandfather with pride. 'He led the Band of Abang Fatah, while the White Rajah was attacked by the revolutionary forces of Chinese from Tarado, Bau (upper river Sarawak), and my great-grandfather recaptured the "Astana" from the hand of Chinese forces, and saved the life of the 1st Rajah of Sarawak.'

Omar was taken as a prisoner of war when the Japanese occupied Limbang. They moved him to Brunei, where he insinuated his way to gaining influence so that he would be returned to Limbang together with some of the Japanese forces. Then he used his local knowledge to trick the Japanese and help some missionaries and Europeans, who were trapped in the region of the upper Limbang River, to escape.

Now, with Limbang in rebel hands, he was again ready for action. 'It is easy for me', he resolved, 'to carry out the SIP for the life of Her Majesty the Queen's subjects'.[31] He had a Strategy and Implementation Plan.

The Morrises' small cell was bare beyond the pillows and sleeping mat they had been given. The cell floor was hard. Their guards stared at them constantly. Dick, with his hands tightly bound, found it difficult to hold a single position for long.

Relief from their confinement came when they were returned briefly, heavily guarded, to the Residency. A number of rebels now occupied the house. Dick was struck by their aggressive mien.

Though Dick's hands were still bound, the Morrises could wash, collect some clothes and get food under armed guard. Dorothy was uninterested in food but felt a surge of strength when, 'while in the kitchen we heard the tremendously exciting and reassuring sound of an aircraft swooping low over the Residency. We guessed from the expression of our guards that it was one of "ours".'

This heartened them, as did scooping up some personal items.

Before being escorted back to the jail, we requested permission to take a few things with us. This was granted, and we rapidly assembled some bits and pieces including a comb, a small bronze 'ganesha' (which we had been persuaded to buy in Old Delhi a few months before, on the grounds of its special care for travellers), a bottle of Entero-Vioform, photographs of our two children, a Bible, a bottle of Alka-Seltzers and a package from a Sydney bookseller. This latter I had assumed to be a Christmas present and had put it aside. On this occasion I decided to break the inflexible family rule regarding Christmas presents.

Returned to the jail, she turned to the unopened package that she had grabbed.

Opening it up in our cell I found myself faced with Lady Troubridge's *The Book of Etiquette*, which I had ordered at the request of a Chinese friend some eight months before but which had been out of print. Dick had gathered up from a bedside table Latta and MacBeath's *Elements of Logic*.[32]

They found it hard to read. 'Our cell was so ill-lit, however', said Dorothy, 'that we couldn't take the opportunity to improve either our manners or our minds'.

4

SUNDAY, 9 DECEMBER: 'HIGHS' AND 'LOWS'

When word of the rebellion first got to Singapore, where British Naval and Royal Marine forces were based, the signals received from Brunei were not taken too seriously.

It was the weekend, and not long before Christmas. Among the troops in Singapore, thoughts were turning to the holidays ahead, and to making contact with loved ones at home, over 7000 miles (11 000 kilometres) away. Married servicemen were enjoying the opportunity to spend time with their wives and families who were quartered in Singapore.

On Saturday, 8 December, Lieutenant Colonel Robin Bridges, Commanding Officer of 42 Commando Royal Marines, was briefed that a situation was developing in Brunei which might require the unit to move at short notice. No action appeared to be required at the time, but precautions were taken to ensure key personnel could be readily obtained.[1]

It had been a busy past few months for the men in 42 Commando. One, writing in the Commando Journal, noted: 'I suppose the last two months of 1962 were among the busiest and most disrupted since 1956. It has been highlighted by exercises, cancelled and rewritten; moves from the Far East to the Middle East, back, again, and then some more.'[2] Unsurprisingly, the men were enjoying the respite in Singapore. Most had only been on the island for a week; on 1 December, some had arrived in Singapore from exercises in Aden. They were eager for time to sort out equipment and prepare for the festive season, besides enjoying Singapore's 'exciting strangeness … [where] everyone, irrespective of rank, could live it up a little'.[3]

Groups of them gathered the night before to enjoy a screening of the blockbuster war epic *The Longest Day*. The action and star-studded cast in the Darryl F Zanuck film about the Normandy landings on D-Day appealed to the men. They appreciated the fact that the film portrayed actual participants in the action, just short of 18 years earlier, who had advised on the film's production.[4] Moreover, in October 1961, 62 men from the Marine Corps took part in the filming on the Île de Ré. They enacted wet landings through the Atlantic rollers, and were variously part of the US Invasion Force and the British Commandos, in scenes with Peter Lawford, Kenneth More, Ron Randell, and Mike Medwin.[5] Royal Marine Tony Daker, just turned 20, was picked to be Peter Lawford's bodyguard, 'he playing the part of Lord Lovat, who always had a bodyguard and a personal piper'.[6] Daker appeared on the screen next to Peter Lawford in several scenes.

Many of the Marines formed parties to dine together after the screening, and quench their thirst. It was a relaxed night.

L Company of 42 Commando in Singapore quickly became involved in the events in Brunei. Royal Marine David Greenhough explained why. 'As it happened we were Duty Company', he said. 'One company was on duty throughout the army units that were on the island in the event of any emergency arising. We had just taken over as Duty Company, when we heard that the uprising in Malaya and Borneo had started, and we were stood by.'

Being ready was familiar procedure for the men, who were consequently generally indifferent to this news. Greenhough continued, 'We had been stood by occasionally beforehand so it was nothing new to us'. The men were expecting to be sent to Hong Kong, which was popular with them.[7] However, these plans were put aside. 'A certain Mr Azahari put paid to that notion', said a Royal Marine.[8] Instead, as Greenhough said, Brunei 'got a little bit more serious. We were all brought back from ashore, kitted up, and put on 12 hours standby to move.' News of the revolt in Borneo and being given the task to restore law and order in Brunei shattered their hopes for Christmas.[9]

With the men preparing to carry out operations, the general thought among them was that they had no sooner arrived back in Singapore, trying to return to a normal day-to-day routine, than they were moving again. As one put it, 'We have hardly had time to sit back and take a deep breath, before plunging into something new'.[10]

At 1 pm on Sunday, the Commando was brought to four hours' notice. Operation 'Round Up' was put into action. The whole Commando was equipped and ready to move, and concentrated at Sembawang in the north of Singapore island.

Thoughts similar to those expressed by one Royal Marine are likely to have crossed their minds. 'It is extraordinary', he remarked, 'how people with a rebellious nature always seem to show their hands during November–December: Suez, Hungary and now Brunei'.[11] Another reflected on how 'almost every contingency since the war has found some unit of the Commando Brigade ready at hand and among the first troops to be on the spot'.[12]

At 5 pm Bridges held an 'O' Group (Operations Group Meeting) and prepared the unit to move by air and sea to Brunei, on light scales of ammunition, including 3-inch mortars and medium machine guns (MMGs), for an IS (internal security) 'Shooting War'. Brigadier Billy Barton, in 'Birdcage' block of 3 Commando Brigade Headquarters in Sembawang, despatched 42 Commando to Brunei.

The logistics of reaching Brunei rapidly were problematic. The Far East Command was caught without a commando ship, because HMS *Bulwark*, with Brigade HQ and 40 Commando embarked, was at Aden, exercising with her relief, HMS *Albion*. There were few landing strips in Brunei capable of receiving fixed-wing military aircraft, and it was two days' sailing away from Singapore. At this stage, it appeared that landing by air was only possible at Brunei Town airport, which the rebels may have taken, and at Labuan Island. Added to this was the number of men to move, and the ordnance and supplies they might require. The difficulty of getting troops to Brunei becomes apparent when one appreciates the size and strength of a Commando.

In 3 Commando Brigade Royal Marines at the time there were two Royal Marine Commandos, 40 and 42 Commando, each of around 700 men, equivalent to the strength of a British Army infantry battalion, and commanded by a lieutenant colonel. In addition, the brigade included a commando light regiment Royal Artillery with 105-mm pack howitzers. The brigade was commanded by a brigadier along with appropriate staff, and communications and logistic support sub-units. The three other Royal Marine Commandos were deployed elsewhere: in Aden and the United Kingdom.

Three elements made up a typical Commando. Each arm dealt with separate aspects of Commando activity: administrative and regimental organisation; fighting; specialist support. This was reflected in Commando organisation. First there was HQ Company, which provided administrative, logistic and communications support to the Commando (commanded by a senior captain or major). Second, there were the Rifle Companies; three of these made up the fighting sub-units of a Commando. In 42 Commando, these were K, L, and M Companies. Commanded by a major or a captain, with a further four officers (second-in-command and three troop commanders), the full strength complement of a company was 120 Marines. Every rifle company included three rifle troops with 35 Marines (commanded by a second lieutenant or lieutenant; a sergeant was usually second-in-command). Each rifle troop was made up of three sections, each consisting of nine Marines (including their commanders, a corporal and a lance corporal who was generally second-in-command). Third, there was the Support Company. This sub-unit was normally commanded by a captain or occasionally a major. It provided specialist support in the form of a mortar troop (3-inch mortars), a machine-gun troop (Vickers .303-inch medium machine guns), a reconnaissance troop and an assault engineer troop.

42 Commando Royal Marines were deployed with other troops, the 1/2nd Gurkhas and the Queen's Own Highlanders, to crush the rebellion.

Orders were to get to Brunei, 750 miles (1200 kilometres) away, as fast as possible.

Getting from Singapore to Brunei, by air and by sea, would take several days to achieve. Few were clear as to where they were heading or why. Among the men, knowledge of Borneo was limited. Some of the troops may have recalled the publicity that accompanied a Royal Tour three years earlier. The Royal Yacht *Britannia* brought the Duke of Edinburgh, Captain General of the Royal Marines from 1953, to Borneo for visits to Sarawak in early 1959. In Brunei he visited the Seria oilfields, which gave Brunei its consolidated revenue of £605 million that year.[13]

By now there were five more hostages confined to the jail in Limbang. Put into the cell with Dick and Dorothy was Iban Police Constable Max Bisop Kunjan. From him they learned of the bravery of the policemen who had refused to submit to the rebel attack.

As the town magistrate, Dick knew the policemen well. Most senior of the four was Corporal Kim Huat, of mixed Land Dayak and Chinese parentage, and nearing 40. He, and his offsider, Constable Bujang, had been in Limbang for the past year, after serving in many stations, particularly in the Fourth Division. Dick knew both had children. The younger two were in their mid-20s. One of them, Constable Insoll Anak Chundang, was a Sea Dayak from the small town of Betong, a posting that the Morrises remembered warmly.

Besides Inspectors Abang Zain and Latif, imprisoned in the adjacent cell was Joseph King Shih Fan, the Hong Kong-born Chinese Divisional Engineer of the Public Works Department. Being Hong Kong-born he was also British, and therefore an 'enemy'.

The fifth policeman who had held out at the police station, Constable Essa bin Meratim, avoided capture by climbing into the roof of the police station, where he hid, with five rounds in his rifle, and with no food and little water for the next four days.

The Morrises later found out that other Europeans in the town were also being held. As Dorothy said, 'A number of other Government officers including the District Officer, Abang Zainuddin bin Adi, were placed under house arrest'. The government housing area at the south end near the Residency and the Roman Catholic Mission at the other end of the town were surrounded. The rebels had Limbang covered.

Lying low in his hut at the agricultural station, Fritz Klattenhoff was pleased to see a Chinese-Malay acquaintance in his doorway.

He came to tell Fritz that he had joined the rebellion, and that Fritz would not be harmed. At this news, Fritz set out to feed the animals under his care.

Suddenly, he heard shouts. 'Stop! Stop or you die!'

About half a dozen men on foot ran at him with shotguns, 'with the man who had previously told me I would be all right'.[14] At that there appeared two Land Rovers and a truck carrying about 40 rebels, armed with shotguns. They surrounded him.

'The Chinese-Malay stuck a shotgun in my belly and kept pushing me back', said Fritz. He was shoved into one of the Land Rovers. He was taken to the police station and to Salleh bin Sambas.

'I showed him my Peace Corps identity card and I told him I was an American, and that if he bothered me, America would cause big trouble.' In British Borneo, real awareness of the United States was slight. Few had personal impressions of Americans based on direct contact. United States aid reached the area through British channels. The replacement of British by American power in the world scene meant British authorities had little interest in building up American prestige in Borneo. Attention given to the United States in Bornean newspapers tended to be critical. Peace Corps volunteers were required to learn the language of their host country, although fluency was not essential. They had no diplomatic privileges or immunities. They were goodwill ambassadors. As President Kennedy said, 'Our Peace Corps is not designed as an instrument of diplomacy or propaganda or ideological conflict … [but] to permit our people to exercise more fully their responsibilities in the great common cause of world development'.[15]

Fritz was locked into an eight-by-four-foot cell. In an adjacent cell were three Roman Catholic priests, and an official of the Public Works Department.

Dorothy adopted a brave front during 'the initial period of our capture when conditions were very tense'. The first 24 hours were difficult. She and Dick were cramped in the cell, uncertain about what might happen to them next, anxious about their children, and under constant surveillance.

'One of the most unsettling aspects of our incarceration', said Dorothy, 'was the very distasteful business of being stared at and glared at by our guards through the bars of our only window, which looked onto the short passage between the cells'.

'Expressions varied, but even when one turned one's back to the window', she explained, 'it took great strength of will not to turn round and glare back when a new guard took over and the scrutiny was more prolonged'.

'The guards on the first few days were fairly cocky', Dorothy added, 'and the reciprocal glares were a mixture of triumph and dislike on their parts and of assumed indifference on ours'.[16]

The privilege of being allowed to return to the Residency was stopped. They did not know it then, but guarding 'enemy' government officers and Europeans – 14 hostages by now – scattered in locations across the town, was stretching rebel resources.

The strain of their confinement was wearing on the Morrises. They were particularly anxious about their children, concerned that they would not arrive as planned, and worried about how they would be cared for. Dorothy tried hard to suppress her apprehensions.

Although I didn't speak of it to Dick at the time, on Sunday night my spirits and hopes hit a record 'low'. During the night I had heard whispered discussions in Malay between the guards sitting just outside our cell-door. Although I only heard snatches, there was frequent mention of prisoners, sunrise and shooting. I will never know, nor do I really want to know now, whether it was just my overtaxed imagination, or wishful thinking on the part of our guards, but I do know that I took a good whack of codeine tablets about midnight, prayed as I'd never prayed before that we would all be given courage to face bravely whatever lay ahead, and then I prayed for our children.[17]

The previous night, frantic activity had occurred at the home of Limbang's Postmaster, Abang Omar. He had decided to take the 'restoration' of the local Group of the British Red Cross (over which Dorothy presided) into his own hands, as a matter of extreme urgency, in order to get any assistance possible to the hostages either in the police station or the jail.

He assumed the 'authority' of the Red Cross, and enlisted 'staff' supporters, who volunteered to help him.

As Dorothy recounts the story, 'His wife and his daughters prepared Red Cross "uniforms" of their own design. Crosses of red cloth were sewn onto shirt sleeves, pockets, and very large ones to the back of white shirts'.

Omar was thus attired in the morning.

Dorothy continued, 'He completed the effect with a "Red Cross" Cadet's beret, which had belonged to one of his daughters when schooling in Kuching and a member of her school's Cadet Group'.

Omar's helpers were similarly dressed. There was Inche Kasim, an anti-malarial sprayer; another was the Malay hospital orderly.[18] Their headgear consisted of white rag hats with the cloth red crosses stitched to the crowns.

Omar also enlisted the Senior Hospital Assistant, Mohammed Edin bin Abdullah, by drawing him into his plans. By Sunday morning, Omar was ready. 'On the second day, I make discussion with Mohammed Edin to release all the civilian patients, so this is also carried out.'

Dressed in his 'Red Cross uniform', Omar put his plan into action. Dorothy said that:

> he presented himself to the rebel leader, Salleh bin Sambas, and demanded permission to visit the prisoners to inspect their conditions and enquire into their needs, under the rules of the World Red Cross Conventions on the treatment of prisoners of war. The rebel leaders were suitably impressed and granted permission for these visits.

Omar also declared that Kathleen Brake, who with her husband had been ordered into house arrest, should accompany him.

Granted both requests, the postmaster gathered his group of Red Cross 'workers' in their makeshift uniforms. He and Kathleen Brake appeared at the jail to tend to the wounded, and bring food and comfort to those captured. They defied the rebels to interfere with their brave and humane work.

Their arrival lifted Dorothy to another 'high'. Both Omar and Brake had offered their support at the Red Cross meeting that Dorothy had convened. Then, her intention had been to foster the delivery of humanitarian assistance from Limbang. She never expected that she would be on the receiving end of Red Cross 'aid'.

'They arranged for us to be brought food and supplies', she said. 'Our spirits rose considerably when members of the hastily reconstituted Limbang Red Cross appeared with coffee, rice, towels, codeine, bandages and ointment for the wounded Police Inspector in the next cell – and friendly smiling faces.'[19]

Their arrival brought hope to all in the jail.

'These tireless brave and devoted few', continued Dorothy,

'did more than they will ever know for the morale, as well as for the comfort, of all of us behind the bars'.

However, contact was limited. TNKU guards, armed with shotguns, parangs and other weapons, kept watch in the narrow corridor between the cells.

Dorothy explained:

These Red Cross visits to the jail were not occasions for idle chatter, we were only permitted to speak in Malay, but there were certainly welcoming smiles and warmth between hostages and our brave visitors, albeit through the prison bars. They were not permitted to enter our cell, but were allowed to pass to us some bottles of drinking water, rice and a big soft blanket which Mrs Brake had brought from her bungalow – a welcome softener between us and the very hard *belian* wooden floor. She also brought some English magazines which we were able to peruse when daylight was sufficient. The Limbang power station was out of action for lack of an operator and none of the rebels had the necessary skills to get it functioning again. The usual operator had 'gone missing' and there was indeed no light nor power.[20]

Most importantly, they were able to dress the wounds of the wounded Police Inspector. Locked in an adjacent cell, Inspector Latif remained defiant. Dorothy said that 'the call to his guard each morning would be "*Minta escort pergi jamban*", which interpreted meant "I request an escort to go to the toilet", but his tone suggested "Take me to the *jamban* or else"'.

Dick and I would request our escort and be led by a guard (always armed) together to the small *jamban* and adjoining bathroom which consisted of a concrete floor and large jar ('tong') of rainwater in a small detached building some 20 yards behind the jail. The *jamban* (a 'squatter' job of normal local design) had within a short period of use by the rebels become blocked solid. However there was no alternative plumbing, and at least the tong of water was a useful, and our only, means of hand-washing.

All the while Dick's hands were tied.

No attempt was made 'to feed or water' them. The hostages had to depend on rations brought to the jail by 'gracious' permission of the guards.

Again, Dorothy was moved by the kindness that she received.

The wives of the police were allowed to bring basic food such as rice to the jail where the guards took delivery and in due course handed it to the inmates. Our fellow police hostage would share his rations with us, and on a later occasion an elderly Chinese friend who owned a rubber garden and sawmill in the outskirts of Limbang arranged for one of his family to deliver bread, rice, cigarettes and even cigars to us.

This was Law Ah Kaw, whom Dick later thanked for more than his gifts of food and kindness. He wrote, 'Your cheerfulness was of tremendous assistance to us and did much to keep up our spirits during that unhappy time'.[21]

It was essential to keep drinking to counteract their sweating in the near 100 per cent humidity. 'Our greatest need was always for good safe drinking water', said Dorothy, 'as our appetites were not very keen, and this was brought to us regularly by Omar or one of his new "recruits". This was at the time when "they" – the rebels – were reading the signs and aware that all was not going well for their campaign.'

Dick weighed up their position. He was certain that they would be delivered from their captors. 'I did a reasonably leisurely appreciation of the situation and came to the conclusion that we could expect something to happen on either the evening of the 11th or the morning of the 12th December.' At this point there was no knowing how large the rebel force was which held Limbang. So, as Dick said, 'Most of the bases of my appreciation were wrong, but that doesn't matter because I did get the right answer'.

Had Omar been able to give the Morrises information about what was going on in the world outside, he could have passed on some cheering news. 'For the rebels', as Dick later learned and recounted, 'the news was not so cheering, for Radio Sarawak had broadcast reports that the 1/2 Gurkha Rifles had driven the Rebels out of Brunei Town and had rescued the Sultan and his family from the besieged Astana'. The rebels clearly heard this news, because their attitude changed markedly for the worse. No conversation was allowed when Omar returned later in the day.

The TNKU rebel force in Limbang was later found to number approximately 400, perhaps more. Of this, just over half belonged to two companies of the TNKU which had been raised in Limbang, and the remainder, mobilised shortly before the rebellion, were attached to these companies or to the special force charged with capturing the Residency.[22]

What concerned Dick was 'how to avoid getting shot by our friends'. He had to ensure they would not be caught in crossfire. He would have to signal to them where they were being held. 'Obviously we would have to devise some means of communication and that's how the verse that we sang came to be written.'

'They'll be wearing dark green bonnets when they come,
when they come
They'll be wearing dark green bonnets when they come,
They'll be wearing dark green bonnets but they won't be singing
sonnets
They'll be wearing dark green bonnets when they come.'

Unbeknown to Dick at that time, Yassin Affandy, the tall, heavily built military chief of the rebels, passed through Limbang on his way to Temburong District, already realising his cause was lost in Brunei with the coming of the British forces.[23]

5

MONDAY, 10 DECEMBER: STANDING FAST

Until now news from Borneo was too meagre to yield a clear picture of what was happening. Speculation was rife. That the situation was hard to read is evident from a letter to the Morrises from one old Sarawak hand, Justice (later Sir) Geoffrey Briggs, by then in Honiara in the Solomon Islands where he was Chief Justice of the High Court of the Western Pacific.

'Merry Christmas to you', he wrote on 10 December. 'But are you SAFE? My news comes ex Australia and is full of inaccuracies. I note that the Sheik is safe in the Philippines and Shell are confident. But what passes through the minds of the British soldiery when asked to prop up that Morguey Fox grey Sultanate?'[1]

By now, it was becoming clearer that the insurrection raised some serious questions. That it was a complete surprise was disquieting. Where did security intelligence fail? Why had the intelligence services failed to get wind of the rebellion? Why were precautions not taken? 'The authorities were as sound asleep in their beds on Friday night as their predecessors were on December 8, twenty-two years earlier to the very day and hour', charged Malaya's *Straits Times*.[2]

Sir Dennis White, British High Commissioner in Brunei, was in Britain on sick leave. When news of the revolt broke, he rushed from his hospital bed to return to Brunei. At the same time,

Lord Selkirk, Commissioner-General for the United Kingdom in South-East Asia, based in Singapore, flew to Brunei. He met with the Sultan at midday. The Colonial Office and Whitehall were anxious to receive Selkirk's reading of events.

Selkirk gave London this picture.

> As I anticipated it was much too early to form any
> conclusions on the political situation following the revolt.
> Brunei Town is on twenty-four hour curfew completely
> controlled by Gurkhas. There is, therefore, no contact with
> the people as such. The Sultan is living in the Government
> administration block with his senior officials. He is very
> apologetic about what has happened. We had some
> discussion about public relations and he has quite a story
> to tell about the welfare services of Brunei compared with
> other South East Asian countries.[3]

Britain was concerned about how the revolt would affect progress towards Malaysia. Selkirk reflected on how the revolt could upset the political sensitivities which already existed. 'The Sultan has not declared his view in regard to Malaysia.' Sir Omar discussed Brunei's internal security. Selkirk reported:

> I said he would be quite justified in suspending the
> Constitution until order had been properly reasserted.
> Pressure has not been brought to bear by him or anyone else
> on the people of Brunei to enter Malaysia. The Sultan has
> subsequently declared the Party Rakyat is associated with
> the TNKU and declared the party an illegal organization.

The Sultan was aggrieved that his leadership in Brunei should be contested. Selkirk continued, 'He left me in no doubt of his contempt of Azahari and all he stands for, root and branch'. The Sultan offered rewards to anyone who gave information which would lead to the arrest of the revolutionaries.

Knowing that Sir Dennis White would soon touch down in Brunei, Selkirk returned to Singapore, poised to give White any assistance as the situation developed.

British forces were on the move to Brunei, by air and by sea.

Activity at Changi and Seletar over the previous 24 hours indicated that the revolt was on a bigger scale than at first thought. The size of the force being deployed was growing hourly. As the British airlift to Brunei grew, the drone of aircraft, loaded with Gurkha and British troops, indicated that the emergency in Brunei was by now regarded as critical.

Captain Derek Oakley, the 3 Commando Brigade's Intelligence Officer, was despatched to Brunei as the brigade's liaison officer with 42 Commando. Oakley arrived in Labuan on 10 December. He was among the troops that made the rough passage in HMS *Cavalier*, a 2500-ton destroyer with a ship's complement of about 180. The ship's maximum speed was over 31 knots, the fastest in its class. They sailed in poor weather, with a typhoon blowing up in the South China Sea.

The passage was rough in the stormy conditions. Many, like other troops deployed to Labuan, arrived unfit for immediate action. Bruce Jackman, a 22-year-old English subaltern with the Gurkhas who crossed to Brunei by sea, described the 'motley crew assembled on the quay with towels around their heads, wretched, looking ill, feeling ill, hardly in the state to arrive into a war zone'.[4]

'That morning', said Oakley, 'Labuan was chaotic, with troops arriving by sea and air, and sleeping bodies strewn everywhere'.[5] Reinforcements flowing into Labuan still had to get to Brunei Town.

The rebels made the mistake of not taking Brunei Airport.

Consequently, four companies of the 1/2 Gurkha Rifles were already in Brunei. However, further reinforcements were called for and the 1/2 Gurkhas were brought up to battalion strength. Brigadier AG (Pat) Patterson, Commander 99th Gurkha Infantry Brigade, arrived to take overall command. On 10 December, about 400 men of the Far East 'spearhead battalion', the Queen's Own Highlanders, began arriving in Brunei as part of the 'follow up force'. Ground troops of the Royal Air Force Regiment were flown in to guard airfields and installations. It was hoped that by darkness a total of two battalions of British and Gurkha troops would be in Brunei.

Lieutenant Colonel Robin Bridges was with the Royal Marines who were on the move. 'The first to move, by air in the early morning on Monday, 10th December, was L Company Group', he said, 'which included a Section MMG and Mortar [from Support Company] … I myself flew with the Recce Group at 2100 hours from Changi with the balance of Support Company'.[6] Being flown to operations was new to some of the men because the Royal Marines are associated with the Royal Navy, which usually transported them. The RAF had no plane for them: some filled a civilian Britannia. Most were despatched to Brunei by sea: M & K Companies of 42 Commando Unit travelled in HMS *Alert* and HMS *Woodbridge Haven*; and Commando Headquarters and HQ Company and the remainder of S Coy travelled in HMS *Tiger*.[7]

Logistical difficulties saw parts of units conveyed in different ways and by different routes. This added to the confusion, yet order prevailed. Bridges gives an example. 'On arrival at Labuan at midnight I heard that I could not fly until 0630 hours to Brunei, and spent the remainder of the night organising the onward routing of the remainder of the Unit to Brunei.' Some would fly to Jesselton, where they joined two offshore minesweepers that would take them to Brunei. Some, like Bridges, would fly into Brunei airport. While his Commando CO was stranded in Labuan, the Section Commander of 6 Section in 5 Troop of L Company, Corporal Mervyn Jones, found himself and his men on Brunei Airport fully 'booted and spurred', ready for their task.[8]

From their arrival in Brunei Town, the 1/2 Gurkha Rifles quickly established their authority. This was maintained by an around-the-clock curfew. Armed forces went in to suppress the rebellion, by search and patrol. They were ordered to use minimum force. Any rank could arrest anyone suspected of possessing weapons. Firearms, ammunition or explosives were banned, as was consorting with or harbouring anyone whose manner prejudiced public security. All ranks were given wide powers of search, to seize any weapon and to arrest anyone suspected of threatening the Preservation of Public Order.[9]

Captain Jeremy Moore, Company Commander of L Company 42 Commando Royal Marines, touched down onto the tarmac of Brunei Airfield just before dark with some of his company. It was the last plane for the day.

He went in to the airport lounge and rang up the HQ in Brunei Town to say that they had arrived. 'L Company 42 Commando is here.'[10] Some of them anyway; some of the commando were coming over by sea.

The major to whom he spoke said:

Ah, good. I do not want you to move tonight, because it is pretty chaotic. There is the danger of your trying to come into the town and, with the Gurkhas not knowing who it is in the dark, getting a blue on blue (battle between our own side). Stay in the airport. In the morning, I want you to go down to the British Resident's house and take over the guarding of it.

'I have not just brought the best trained rifle company in the British forces in the Far East to go and do a police job!' exploded Moore. 'You give me a proper job for the best rifle company you're going to get.'

Moore and his company spent the night in the airport lounge. He lay on the floor behind the bar to ensure that the bar was not drunk dry, thinking to himself that in the morning he must face the major, one rank above him, and say to him, 'Now look come on'.

Sydney's *Daily Mirror* reported that the Brunei Revolt was near collapse.

In Manila, 800 miles (1300 kilometres) away from Brunei, Sheikh Azahari gave Britain a one-week ultimatum to accept his demands for independence of the three Borneo territories. 'If they do not accept our right to self-determination then I will go into the Borneo jungles and lead the fight until my death', he said. He proclaimed himself Prime Minister of the revolutionary state of Kalimantan Utara (North Borneo). He declared that the rebellion was only directed against the British. 'I am sure this fight will continue for even 20 years', he said. 'Borneo will never be a peaceful territory again unless our proclaimed Government is recognized by Britain.' [11]

Crossing the Indian Ocean on HMS *Albion* were 40 Commando Royal Marines. They had been on exercise north of Mombasa when they were called to Brunei. The ship increased speed on 9 December, having been ordered to proceed with all speed to the

Borneo area. After four days' sailing, they would reach Singapore on 13 December, stopping only for four hours to pick up more Commandos and stores. HMS *Albion* would become colloquially known by Radio Australia as 'the Grey Ghost of Borneo', as its contingent would support the operations in Sarawak.[12]

With operations occurring on the ground, the initiative was taken as well to suppress the rebellion over the radio. In Sarawak, over the previous 36 hours government statements released details of the grave events in Brunei and their incidence in neighbouring territory, where action centred on Limbang. Outside contact with Limbang had been lost soon after the insurrection started. Aerial reconnaissance indicated the probability of the town having been overrun. This was the plane which Dorothy heard when she was allowed to return to the Residency. No precise news had been received, said the Governor of Sarawak, Sir Alexander Waddell, in a broadcast over Radio Sarawak. 'A contingent of the Field Force has been endeavouring to penetrate to Limbang but without success.'[13]

He affirmed over the radio that political parties and leaders in Sarawak firmly and unequivocally condemned the insurrection. 'Sarawak repudiates Azahari and his henchmen and has no intention whatever of submitting to domination by Brunei or elsewhere.' Waddell sought from listeners their fullest cooperation in restoring law and order wherever it had broken down and in preserving it where it had not.

In Limbang, the rebels were preparing to make a stand and fight. They believed in their superiority in numbers, and that the natural cover from the jungle would be sufficient defence.

Waddell would learn that rebel forces converged on Limbang. Dick Morris would later report on this.

On 10 December there was a considerable increase in the number of TNKU rebels in the Limbang area: their strength may have been as high as 600. The increase was the result of conscription from kampongs close to Limbang, and it is believed that the intention may have been to reinforce the TNKU rebels in the Brunei area, leaving Limbang to be held by a few hard-core rebels and a larger number of conscripts.[14]

However, at this point in Limbang, it became clear that this force was divided. 'Some of these pressed men managed to slip away on the following day and did not take part in any of the TNKU activities', Dick continued. 'On the other hand, quite a number were willing volunteers and they included a number of Malays, Bisayas, some Muruts and a few Ibans. The rebels came almost entirely from the Limbang District, but there were some people from the Temburong District of Brunei.' Noticeably, there were no Chinese among them.

A number in the town, like Omar, were unhappy about the insurrection. Malays, like Omar, resented being shanghaied, and disliked their kampongs being 'terrorised'. The Chinese hid behind the locked shutters of their shops, fearing looting or worse. No one felt safe.

The codeine that Dorothy had taken worked effectively. It was long past sunrise when she woke. 'Dick and our other cell-mate, Constable Bisop, were both very alive and whole, and there were the usual greetings being called from cell to cell, and even – to add to all this – a familiar whuffling and chinking under the jail. Our dog "Spatter" had found us!'[15]

Spatter was the Morris family dog. Part spaniel and part setter, he was given to their son as a pup six years before when their daughter first left for boarding school. It was thought that the dog would be a companion to their son, so he would not feel lonely. With a roving eye and a libertine spirit, the black-and-white dog became well known in the communities in which they lived, leaving his bountiful progeny behind each time they moved.

The Morrises were delighted at being reunited. 'Spatter – the Indestructible, whom we were fairly sure had been shot on the night of the 7th/8th, after helping to give the alarm that our compound was being surrounded', said Dorothy.

> However, being an old and a wise dog he had presumably headed for the jungle when the firing came too close, and bided his time before emerging to see how the new regime was acquitting itself. Finding no joy at the Residency where twenty-six rebels were making themselves at home, he had continued his search and finally smelt us out.

Having the familiar nearby was comforting, as it was obvious to the Morrises that their guards were on edge and hostile.

The dog's irrepressible excitement quietened Dorothy's apprehensions about a firing squad. 'We received a tremendous welcome when we emerged for our early morning escorted stroll to the "loo", and from then on he never left the premises', continued Dorothy. The dog also seemed to disarm the stern-faced guards.

> Some of our guards were actually feeding him with rice, and he was soon allowed to sit at the head of the steps [to the jail corridor]. So possessive did he become that on several occasions he even baled up the incoming new guard, and we would have to shout to him to lie down before he got shot – the clot.

Some disaffection among the TNKU troops became apparent to their hostages. Dick observed that 'they spoke to one another very quietly or in whispers and it was clear that they were uneasy. Late in the afternoon the regular guards were replaced by others who seemed to have been newly conscripted'. Dick thought that, in contrast to the hard core of long-haired tough individuals who had first guarded them, many of the rebels now appeared bewildered and with little heart in the uprising.

'By Monday with each change of guard there appeared at our window more of the older men, of less aggressive mien, and including some who appeared to be genuinely distressed at the turn of events and even ashamed of the role they were being forced to play', said Dorothy.

> Many of these had, in fact, been beaten up and threatened
> with harm to their families and homes, if they refused to
> join the cause. With these the photos of our children were
> always a talking point, and many of them echoed our own
> heart-felt relief that Geraldine and Adrian had not yet
> arrived in Limbang for their Christmas holidays.

From conversations among the guard that Dick overheard, he deduced that their situation was changing. 'The tougher, more dedicated elements had been despatched to the outskirts and upriver as rumours spread of Dayaks coming down to "do over" the TNKU. We had suggested when we could that they should see that their wives, children and homes were adequately protected in this event.' The indigenous Sea Dayaks, the Ibans, who predominated among the mixed ethnic population of Sarawak, were happy with British rule. Progressive Iban leaders participated in colonial government and resisted any federation because they feared Malay assumptions of power.

The local members of the Red Cross, dressed in their contrived Red Cross uniforms, broke the gloom in the jail with their visits, bringing coffee, rice, towels and water. As before, they were accompanied by guards who kept them under surveillance and allowed them to speak only in Malay.

Desire to help the detainees was emboldening some townsfolk. Perhaps Omar and Ah Kaw had a hand in this. Omar's Red Cross group grew to now include more than ten members. Ah Kaw had a number of the Chinese businessmen of Limbang offering him food for the hostages.

As the self-appointed Dato of the Red Cross Branch in Limbang, Omar's 'authority' was accepted by the TNKU command. They asked him to move their wounded in the morning. He said, 'We sent all wounded revolutionary troops to their kampong at Batu (8 miles [13 kilometres] from Limbang) as requested by them'. However, he was prevented by the ever-present guards from conveying news to the Resident. Omar decided that he would have to devise a way to do so.

In his cell at the police station, Fritz Klattenhoff fought off sleep. He did not dare to sleep, for fear that he might be shot. 'I would rather be shot looking at the gun than sound asleep', he said later.

Fritz was the only Peace Corps volunteer in Limbang. He knew two volunteers in North Borneo. Thaine H Allison, Jr and his wife trained with Fritz Klattenhoff and were doing similar work to Fritz, in agriculture. 'I trained for three months in Hawaii with Fritz', said Allison.[16] 'Most of us were quite young, Fritz was only 18 and had not gone to college, and was naive.'

Fritz was four days out of high school when he joined the Peace Corps. The idea of the Peace Corps was to promote world peace and friendship by Americans 'willing to serve, under conditions of hardship if necessary'.[17] Up to now Fritz had found, like Allison did, that the hardest part of his job was building trust. Each day was filled with learning the language, building trust with the farmers and demonstrating with small tasks that he was someone with the ability to help solve problems. He knew nothing about the underlying tensions in North Borneo and Sarawak and was unprepared for what he now faced.

Fritz and the four European hostages in the cell next to his were kept standing. One of the three priests, 35-year-old Father Daniel Cronin, had come to Limbang during 1962 to teach at the primary school. He was a sociable Irishman with curly brown hair. Like Fritz, he was tall and hefty. They had stood for the past 24 hours and were forced to remain standing.[18]

Dick's hands, still bound, lost feeling. His wrists were lacerated by the fishing cord used to tie them. His arms and shoulders ached. Omar's insistence that the detainees be properly treated broke the resistance of the guards. Dick's hands were untied.

In his childhood, Dick had learned early to be resilient. His mother was a proud woman of English stock and his father was Welsh and a rolling stone by temperament, forever starting anew, from Australia to England and back again. Dick was their only child. Crisis marked his early years, as their marriage broke down. Despatched to a boarding school, aged six, he is photographed sitting among his fellow boarders, the youngest among them, arms crossed, resigned, stoic. Later, shifted through a number of schools, as his parents' finances fluctuated, he received a patchy education.[19] He learned to be a sharp observer, and became largely self-educated and self-reliant. His family were his mainstay.

Dorothy drew strength from him. She later told him, 'I don't think I'll ever be able to tell you how proud I am of the way you behaved during all that horrible time, and for the tremendous strength and comfort you were to me. I could certainly not have come through unscathed mentally or physically without you.'[20]

6

TUESDAY, 11 DECEMBER: PLANS IN ACTION

The insurrection, if doomed, was not yet over. Brunei and the adjacent small areas of Sarawak and North Borneo over which the insurgents established control on the previous Saturday are difficult terrain. Subversive forces could take advantage of this. Small bands of men could, and would, continue to give trouble there for some time longer. The British flag flew over the former PRB headquarters in Brunei Town, but the British Command knew there was more work ahead.

The problem for the British was they did not yet know a lot about the enemy they were fighting. Police sources said there was a known rebel strength of 400 armed men in Sarawak and reports from Brunei put the rebel force 'in the thousands'.[1] Uniforms worn by the dead or captured rebels bore the Buffalo Head insignia of the now illegal PRB; it symbolised 'heroism, bravery and the "never to surrender" attitude', said Ahmad Zaini, the PRB's first organising secretary.[2] Azahari hinted at having an army of 30 000 men. The difficulty magnified if suspicions proved correct that he was receiving foreign assistance, perhaps support from Indonesia.

'Britain can pour all her armed might into Borneo to suppress the revolt but the fight will continue and we shall not lay down our arms until the last British coloniser is driven out and an independent Kalimantan firmly established', declared Azahari.

'Britain can be assured we will not take a single cent of British investments, which will be safe throughout the Territories, if we were given Government authority.' He added: 'We are still willing to sit down with the British. We are not anti-British. We are anti-colonialism.'[3]

The rebels killed in Brunei were found to be fighting with shotguns and rifles. It appeared at this stage that superior fire power came from the weaponry carried by British soldiers. John Fisher broadcast a plea to the people of the Fourth Division who were with the rebels not to continue with the insurrection. He announced the failure of the uprising in Brunei, and emphasised that order in Sarawak would be restored. 'For you to continue this insurrection in Sarawak can only have one end. To fight as civilians with shotguns against professional soldiers with machine guns is sheer madness.'[4] Fisher also announced that government canoes, carrying hollow bamboo sticks with red feathers – a traditional call for help – were sent upriver to the native Kayan and Kenyah tribesmen. These tribes were thought to have originated from the Indonesian part of Borneo. He said of the tribesmen:

> These people are fiercely loyal to the British and we have
> always had the warmest personal relationships with them.
> You can take it that if there is anything they can do to help
> us at any time they will do it instantly and willingly, even
> though there is personal danger.

As many as 3000 were expected to answer the call for help.

Support came from hundreds of Dayaks from the interior of northern Sarawak who made their way through the jungle to police and military centres to volunteer to fight against the rebels. They would not have their sovereignty dictated to. A prominent Dayak leader said that subversive elements would soon discover that in Sarawak the jungle is not neutral. 'The Ulu peoples will see to that', he said.[5]

There was still no contact with Limbang. Fears were held for the safety of the Europeans there and also for Mr James Wong, a Council Negri member. A Limbang son who began his political career as a member of the Limbang District Council, Wong backed the idea of Malaysia from its early stages and supported Sarawak joining the proposed Federation. He played an instrumental role in its formation, as a member of the Sarawak delegation in the Malaysia Solidarity Consultative Committee in 1962, a precursor to the Inter-Governmental Committee that led to the federation's birth a year later. He later admitted that the rebels were after him for this, and he had to hide in the jungle to avoid them.[6]

With Seria taken, Shell announced from London the death of a hostage, an oilfield radio operator who was shot while being used as a human shield.[7]

In Kuala Lumpur, Parliament members read the revolt as a lesson to government which they urged ought 'not to be lulled into a false sense of security'. To them, the outbreak of violence was inexcusable because there existed the constitutional means to effect political changes in the state.

'Brunei was not governed by a military autocratic dictatorship or by a totalitarian system of Government', said one member. 'Hence it was possible to use constitutional means for the purpose of effecting political changes', he declared.

He continued that the government should be grateful to Azahari and the Opposition for providing insight into the way they were thinking. 'They have lifted the veil from our eyes so that we can see things for what they are. This rebellion might prove to be a blessing in disguise if it reinforces our conviction that enemies within can sometimes be more dangerous than enemies without.'[8]

Anduki Airfield, which the rebels held, was strategically important because it served the oil town of Seria. The Queen's Own Highlanders flew into action to recover Anduki's airstrip in a two-pronged attack. At Panaga golf course, 5 miles (8 kilometres) west of the airstrip, five RAF Pioneers with a short landing run, although only able to carry up to 13 troops at a time, landed one after the other soon after 1 pm on rough ground never meant for an aircraft. Before each Pioneer had pulled to a stop, the soldiers jumped out and the plane took off, to be followed immediately by the next. Fifteen minutes later, a giant Beverley carrying up to 80 troops landed at Anduki. The rebels were taken by surprise. The only injuries from rebel gunfire were bullet holes in the Beverley tail; they did not prevent it from taking off. Further similar flights landed between 600 and 800 troops. The airfield was soon in government hands.

Asked at his press conference if he believed the rebels would try to use Europeans held in Seria as hostages, the overall force commander in Brunei, Brigadier Jack Glennie, said, 'I think we have been too quick for them – let's hope so'.[9] However, he was proven wrong. The rebels held 48 Europeans hostage, although women and children were released.

Nor could the British do otherwise than respond rapidly, when it did not look impossible that British service chiefs had bungled in failing to prevent the armed aggression. Vigorous action could make amends.

From Jesselton, another prominent political leader, the Honourable Donald Stephens, the leader of the Sabah Alliance Party, denounced Azahari and his London School of Economics educated deputy, Zaini. 'These two self-proclaimed heroes of the revolution are nothing but cowards. Acts committed by many of their colleagues, like the killing of hostages, are nothing but the action of murderous cowards.'[10] While expressing outrage at the

TNKU's methods, this condemnation by Stephens also represented a change from his previous stance of communication with Azahari and with Ong Kee Hui, the Malaysian Chinese leader and founder of the Sarawak United People's Party, established in mid-1959.[11]

Stephens continued:

> Azahari resorted to violence thinking that he had enough supporters in all three territories to gain control and make himself self-proclaimed Prime Minister of Kalimantan Utara which was to comprise the States of Sabah, Brunei and Sarawak. It is true that he had enough supporters in Brunei to allow his so-called Tenetera Nasional Kalimantan Utara to gain initial advantage because of the surprise element in attack by his gang of murderers. But his claim that he had a large following both in Sabah and Sarawak has been proved to be completely false. In Sabah the only people who took to rebellion at his command were a small number of uneducated and misguided men who had been led into believing that Azahari would win and in winning would see that they got rich rewards.

Azahari's claim to speak for Sarawak and North Borneo was repudiated. Two days later, motions condemning the rebellion and 'barefaced lies' of Azahari would be passed unanimously in the North Borneo Legislative Council and the Sarawak Council Negri.

On all sides, anger and indignation were expressed that the intrigue of a bunch of Brunei politicians brought about the emergency. Members were angered that 'Azahari and his gang of conspirators had managed to infiltrate our country' and 'aimed at overthrowing the lawful government by force'. In Jesselton members said, 'We condemn Azahari's action and wish the whole world to know that we are extremely angry with him and regard him as the arch enemy of Sabah'.[12] In their view, Azahari's men had desecrated Sabah's soil.

'But where was this brave and mighty leader Azahari when the rebellion took place?' asked Stephens.

> He was safely ensconced in a very comfortable hotel in
> Manila and with him was his so-called deputy Zaini. They
> had got as far away as possible after giving their final orders
> in Brunei. Not for them shooting which is dangerous, and
> there is always the chance of being at the receiving end of
> the firing. Their excuse was that they had to present the
> case of the rebels to the United Nations. They are nothing
> but cowards, and the killing of hostages is the action of
> murderous scoundrels.

Stephens then suggested that the Philippines were supporting Azahari in the rebellion and also that the Parti Kommunis Indonesia had taken part in the rebellion, although he added, 'I prefer to believe that much of what happened was unknown to Djakarta'. He urged that North Borneo give Brunei and Sarawak all the help possible. 'Let us show the world how big a liar Azahari is.'

By now, the emergency was causing international repercussions on the political and diplomatic stage. Moscow issued a statement condemning the creation of Malaysia as 'a normal Colonialist manoeuvre' designed to 'perpetuate the regime of slavery in the form of independent Federation which existed in Malaya'.[13] Britain had to assure the Pakistanis that Russian assertions were false.[14] In the Philippines, Diosdado Macapagal had just finished his first year in the presidency, and his non-committal position over Brunei caused diplomatic anxiety owing to a Philippine claim over parts of Borneo.[15] New Zealand offered

Britain troops to serve in the three Borneo territories.[16] Canberra looked on nervously.

Far removed from the chancelleries, the military continued their operations. Airlifting of troops to Borneo took approximately five days to complete.[17]

At first light on 11 December, Captain Moore was in the Brunei airport lounge shaving when his Marine Officer's Attendant (MOA) came in and said, 'There is a Brigadier outside who wants to see you'. Moore thought he was to be court-martialled for his impertinence the night before. He cleaned off his shaving soap and went out. Sitting on the bonnet of a jeep was Brigadier AG Patterson, commander of the 99th Gurkha Infantry Brigade and now in command of operations.

Pat Patterson was a tough, inspirational leader with a stern, purposeful look, hooded eyebrows and dark, short-clipped moustache. Between 1959 and 1961, Patterson commanded the 2nd Battalion 6th Gurkha Rifles in the jungle of the Malayan–Thai border where his troops eliminated some of the last communist terrorist gangs. He was dismissive of anyone whom he found not to be straightforward and trying to do their best.[18]

'Good morning, Jeremy.'
'Good morning, Sir.'
'I think you had a bit of an altercation with headquarters down the way last night, didn't you?'
'Yes, I did actually, Brigadier.'
'Well, I have now arrived and taken over command of the operations. This is what I want you to do. Go down into Brunei Town. Go to the headquarters and get what

information they've got on a town called Limbang. Commandeer transport. Road transport. Boat transport. Find a hotel. Take it over to accommodate your commando when it arrives. This town called Limbang is occupied by the rebels who have hostages, some British. It is an important centre which needs to be cleared. When your commanding officer arrives, you are to hand the task to him. If he doesn't, you are to do it.'

Moore thought, 'Great! We've got the sort of job we ought to be doing, and this is commanding a company for real!'[19]

Moore then had only 56 men of L Company, including a section of Medium Machine Guns, at Brunei Airport. The other half of the company were still making their way to Brunei.[20]

He had little information on which to plan the Limbang operation, but his mission was crystal clear.

> Brigadier Patterson told me (my Commanding Officer did not arrive in Brunei until two or three hours later) that the Resident and his wife and a number of other people, it was thought about half a dozen, had been taken as hostages when the rebels had attacked and secured the police station and town three days before. L Company was to rescue the hostages. I do not think that any task I have had to perform has ever been clearer in my mind.

Intelligence was of vital importance. 'A decision', said Moore, 'on the best way to set about the task was naturally dependent on information and [he found] this was hard to come by'. Moore searched for detail that could be relied on for their looming mission. Little existed. He was at a terrible disadvantage in terms of information.[21]

'Maps were scarce and small scale', Moore said. 'Limbang was all of a millimetre across on the map I had.' The 1:253 440 scale map showed Limbang as a little red spot, about the size of a pin-head, beside the river. Marked on the map with a pecked line, was an indifferent track which some people thought was motor-able to arrive on the Brunei bank of the Limbang River, opposite Limbang. 'There were dwellings along the west side of the river opposite the town. No bridges cross either of the rivers.'

An aerial photograph of part of Limbang showed the police station and the government buildings (hospital, jail, district officer's house, residency), but not the bazaar, the main part of the town. 'Some buildings, important as it turned out, were not built when this was taken', Moore divulged. The photograph was ten years old. Much of Sarawak territory, which sat under the almost continuous presence of heavy cloud, was not yet covered by aerial photography.

The intelligence regarding the rebels in Limbang was sketchy. There had been no communication with the town since the day the rebellion started. During that Saturday, a lightly armed police launch went up the river to investigate but was fired on as it approached Limbang. The police returned to Brunei, knowing that the town was occupied. Moore spoke to them, but found they could not really tell him very much. 'They found they knew that the Resident was there with his wife and would therefore have been captured, but didn't really know how many hostages there were. They thought there might be six or seven. They didn't know how many policemen were still alive.' It was understood that Limbang's police station stored a quantity of rifles and auto-matic weapons; it was presumed to have been overrun, with the armoury held in rebel hands. 'The rebels were thought other-wise to be armed with shotguns – most effective weapons at close quarters.'

Within a couple of hours of Patterson's briefing, Moore's commanding officer, Lieutenant Colonel Robin Bridges, arrived at Brunei airport. He was met and briefed by Patterson. 'He briefed me quickly that Brunei was now in our hands', said Bridges, 'that the situation was still confused on the coast but that we were gaining control, and that my task was to take Limbang as quickly as possible'.[22]

To gain more information, Bridges and Lieutenant Bengie Walden flew over Limbang in an Auster. Rebel leaders, recognising the light observation aircraft, told their troops to stay under cover so the town would look deserted. Through a break in the low and heavy cloud cover, Bridges and Walden were able to confirm the position of the hospital and other buildings, but as an intelligence-gathering operation their flight did not contribute much. The urgent need to get to the hostages fast meant that they had to rely upon information that was at hand without any major reconnaissance or information gathering. As the day progressed it became evident that Limbang, surrounded by jungle, with no major road, and mountainous areas immediately behind it, was only approachable by river. Moore favoured heading straight for the enemy's headquarters, presumed to be in the police station, at first light, in a bold frontal approach. 'It was clear in everyone's mind that speed and surprise were essential', he said.

'Moore was a great believer, as all sensible military commanders are, in decent intelligence', said Walden. 'Jumping off into the dark is asking for trouble. We did not know what number of people there were nor what had happened to the hostages. It was really quite scary, but we had the kit and this was the Royal Marines so we weren't going to lose.'[23]

At midday, Bridges and Patterson met again. Patterson impressed on Bridges that the main aim of the operation was to release the hostages unharmed as soon as possible. The available intelligence estimated that Limbang was probably held by 30 rebels.[24]

'As a cautious approach on sound military lines would have endangered the hostages' lives, the plan adopted was a simple one', said Bridges. 'It was appreciated the enemy would hold the police station, which was the pattern adopted in other areas; so it was decided to make a direct assault from the leading craft onto the police jetty.' The remaining troops would land as and where possible. The rescue attempt was set for dawn the following morning.

Navigating the river would be extremely difficult. It was tidal, with many twists and turns and mud banks as it wound its way through mangrove. Fortunately, help came from the Royal Navy.

Just after midday, two coastal minesweepers, HMS *Fiskerton* and HMS *Chawton*, captained by Lieutenant Harry Mucklow and Lieutenant Jeremy Black, sailed into Brunei's harbour. They had been hunting pirates on the east coast of Borneo under 30-year-old Black's command. Pirates had been killing and looting along the Borneo coast, fighting a running battle with the North Borneo police, the Royal Navy and Royal Air Force. Black's orders were to speed across to Brunei, to lend aid to the civil power by helping clear rioters off the street. The small crews of both boats were surprised by their summons, and generally unaware of the situation in Brunei.[25] 'Neither ship's company were told the real purpose of the trip', said one crew-member. 'We were informed that we were to accompany the Marines up river for a banyan! Consequently we stocked up with loads of cans of Tiger beer.'[26] They took on board some of the men of 42 Commando whom the RAF had flown into Labuan.

Reaching Brunei, they went up the winding river to Brunei Town.

'It was a hot tropical morning, a cloudless day', said Peter

Down RN, 1st Lieutenant to Jeremy Black on HMS *Fiskerton*.

> Playing on the boat was a record of the Royal Marine band
> *Hearts of Oak, Cheer up me lad* as we were steaming up river,
> half expecting to be attacked. The Royal Marines were
> lined up along the bulwark ready to fire, and no one took
> any notice! It was all something of an anticlimax. We went
> alongside the customs jetty at Brunei Harbour and strolled
> ashore. There were not many people around. We eventually
> tracked down the harbourmaster. He was a retired British
> Royal Marine officer who said, 'You chaps should have been
> here yesterday, there was some activity then!'[27]

In fact, the situation in Brunei was tense. The Gurkhas had generally routed the rebels from the town, but it was under curfew,
with sporadic shooting. Moore had been shot at twice during the
morning as he went about the town.

For Moore, Black and his men were a godsend. They helped
with the rescue mission. Lieutenant Down and Lieutenant David
Willis, first lieutenant on HMS *Chawton*, joined the Marines,
with Lieutenant JP 'Paddy' Davis and Captain Derek Oakley
among them, to find river craft with which to mount the operation. They inspected the assorted collection of craft along the
town's waterfront.

In Oakley's estimation, 'There were hundreds of small boats
but none particularly suitable for transporting 100 men up river
for 12 miles [19 kilometres], and then carrying out a frontal
assault'. Standing on the dockside with him was Marine Tony
Daker. After his short stint filming on the Île de Ré, he spent
a year in the desolate Radfan as a Vickers gunner, before being
flown to Borneo at short notice. He was struck by the variety
of craft before him, perhaps not realising how the rivers were

Brunei's highways. 'I was just looking in amazement at the different types of speedboats there. Bloody hell! There's some money here!' he thought. 'Never seen anything like it!'[28]

As they reached the north end of the extensive waterfront, they came upon two unarmoured river lighters, similar to Z-lighters. Marine John Genge described them: 'They were great big things with flat bottoms; used for carrying Public Works Department stuff about the rivers; 120 foot long and 30 feet wide; they looked like landing craft, but with no sides.'[29] They resembled a big long, flat box, and had diesel engines, a wheelhouse aft, and a loading ramp up the front end. 'It was not a military style ramp that could drop down and let people rush out', explained Laurie Russell, 'you had to wind the thing down; and it was a long, laborious task'.[30] In fact, the mechanism to lower the ramp on both boats appeared to be out of order. They never got it to work. 'Not what you think a military unit would be moving in', said Genge. But they were capable of carrying their company.

One of the lighters was loaded with two large, bright yellow caterpillar tracked earthmovers, used to push the craft off the mud when they got stuck. These could not be moved, so they remained there. 'Having no one who could drive them away', said Moore, 'these monsters came with us'.

Though the vessels were far from ideal, they appeared to be in working order, and Moore decided that they were the most suitable craft available. He commandeered both. No one knew then that these lighters belonging to the Brunei Government had been ordered in 1958 by Dick Morris, when Commissioner of Development in Brunei, and now one of the hostages in Limbang.

Moore thought that the two tractors were there if needed, and might be useful as a little bit of protection because the gunnels, the sides of the boats, were no more than 1½-inch planking, varying in height from 6 to 18 inches. 'Hardly good camouflage, but in the event useful armour', thought Lieutenant Down. "'JCB Sangars" the Marine gunners called them but they had to explain the military jargon to us matelots.'[31]

'It was ironic for me who had spent some time becoming a landing craft expert to find myself on the wrong end', said Laurie Russell finding himself on one of the civilian flat-topped barges with their non-functioning ramps.[32]

Each minesweeper's crew helped with preparing the improvised landing craft. Each provided its first lieutenant who brought a midshipman with him, a leading seaman who would be the coxswain to drive each lighter, and stoker petty officer to work the engines. They got the lighters running. Engine room staff ensured that both were in working order. Engineers from the minesweepers welded protective sheets of metal to parts of the sides and the wheelhouse. A heavy torrential downpour interrupted their efforts, with rain so thick, said one Marine, that you could not see the back of your hands.

By the evening, both craft were ready. The medium machine guns were mounted forward where they would be most effective. Ammunition and equipment were checked. The Commando's large packs acting as sandbags, and a few earth-filled oil drums, were the only further protection. If the preparations for the mission were somewhat improvised, they were the best that could be managed in the circumstances.

Moore was satisfied with the day's effort. 'By the time we needed them, both were in working order and the First Lieutenants, with small crews, were ready to take us through the leads in the mangrove swamps to the Limbang River and up to the town.'

L Company was still not at full strength. Moore believed in careful preparation. He calculated:

To complete my task I have two and a half Rifle Troops,

my Company Headquarters and a section of MMGs. I assessed that the enemy had the firepower, at a range of over 100 yards, of a little more than a section, whereas at close quarters it was probably nearly as good as mine if well handled. It seemed reasonable to expect, though, that it would be poorly handled. Certainly I felt that once I had closed with them I would have the measure of the rebels.

His foremost concern was the hostages.

> The important thing to try to assess was what they would do to the hostages. I anticipated that we might be able, by a show of force, to bluff them into surrender; but if this failed, or if operations were prolonged, they would probably either shoot the hostages out of hand or threaten to do so to make us withdraw. If however we could get to the hostages before the enemy had time to react we should succeed, as Skorzeny found when he rescued Mussolini from Gran Sasso in 1943.[33]

In one of the most remarkable escape raids of the Second World War, the German field commander Otto Skorzeny at least knew where Il Duce was being held, after he was deposed and arrested on King Victor Emmanuel's orders. Mussolini was imprisoned at Campo Imperatore Hotel, a ski resort high in the Apennine Mountains.

For Moore, 'The problem was that we did not know where the hostages were, and several possibilities presented themselves: the police station, the hospital, the administrative offices and the Residency'.[34]

His men would have to head to the police station, with its cells and surrounding barbed wire, if not to the administrative offices

Top The new Brunei Town in 1954, showing the wharf area and Chinese shophouses. The marble mosque has yet to be built. Across the river is the attap hut settlement of Kampong Ayer. *British Malayan Petroleum Company Ltd.*

Above left Dick and Dorothy Morris with Sarawak Constabulary, Kanowit 1954. As an administrator in Sarawak, Dick Morris worked with the police force, which was in the process of being developed. *Photographer unknown.*

Above right Most travel in Sarawak's interior was by boat. With few roads, only the rivers offered some means of communication with the communities living near them. This often meant traversing dangerous rapids. *Photographer: RH Morris.*

Top left Sultan Omar Ali Saifuddien III (centre) and Dick Morris (left) during Queen's Birthday Celebrations in Brunei, June 1955. Dignified parades always marked the Queen's birthday to demonstrate the loyalty of the Sultan and his colonial officers to the British sovereign. As the Commissioner of Development for Brunei, Dick Morris worked closely with the Sultan. *Continent Studio, Brunei.*

Left Iban women dressed in traditional ceremonial silver present gifts to the Duke of Edinburgh during his visit to Sarawak in February 1959. His visit saw the largest crowds ever to assemble in Kuching. They expressed the generally held desire for Britain to preserve the status quo in Sarawak. Sir Anthony Abell (left) was a popular governor after the shock assassination of his predecessor. *Photographer unknown.*

Top The Sarawak United People's Party (SUPP) was Sarawak's first political party. Comprising mostly Chinese, it was formed ahead of Sarawak's first General Election in 1959. SUPP's hostility to colonial government is represented by the chained figures shown in the banners at this rally in Simanggang, 1961. *Photographer: RH Morris.*

Above Sarawak State Council member James Wong and Dick Morris (left), District Officer Abang Zainuddin (centre) and Ismail bin Yusof (third from right), who headed the visiting delegation from Malaya in November 1962. Less than six months earlier, demonstrators at Limbang demanded its return to the state of Brunei. *Photographer: Bolhassan B. Seruji.*

Above Captain Jeremy Moore, photographed in Australia in 1963 at the Australian Staff College, Geelong. *Photographer unknown.*

Top left A trading ship delivering supplies moors at the riverfront customs wharf at Limbang, Sarawak's sixth largest town. The newly built Chinese shophouses face the wharf. Rising immediately behind the new bazaar is the thickly wooded hill and jungle interior. *Photographer: Hedda Morrison, ARPS.*

Left Improvised metal sheeting was installed by L Company to shield the Z lighter's wheelhouse and sides. It provided little cover against firing from the elevated river bank. *Royal Marines Museum.*

Below This George Molnar cartoon appeared in the *Sydney Morning Herald* on 27 December 1962: 'All our neighbours claim us as brothers. The Philippines, Malaya, Indonesia. Oh, it's true Christmas spirit.'

"All our neighbours claim us as brothers. The Philippines, Malaya, Indonesia. Oh, it's true Christmas spirit."

Above left The new police station, erected in 1958, shows damage from the Marines' MMGs. The Marines, firing from the supporting Z lighter, generally aimed high to give cover to their own men and avoid harming the hostages. *Photographer: RH Morris.*

Above A 'model' police constable turned freedom fighter, Salleh bin Sambas led the rebels in Limbang. British-trained, his command of the Bren gun meant that he was key to the rebel forces. *Photographer unknown.*

Left TNKU prisoners in the cell where Dick and Dorothy Morris and Constable Max Bisop Kunjan had been held hostage. *Photographer: RH Morris.*

Above Abang Omar (centre) with his Red Cross 'workers', who defied the rebels in their improvised uniforms. *Photographer unknown.*

Left Ever equipped with his camera, Dick Morris knew that he was living through eventful times. He remained responsible for maintaining the civil administration while Limbang was a militarized zone. His wrists bear the scars from being tied by his captors. *Photographer: Lieutenant-Colonel Gordon Shakespear MC.*

In challenging terrain, the Royal Marines conducted widespread foot patrols of the Limbang–Temburong area. By February 1963 they were closing in on the rebels, who were hiding in a ten square mile of mangrove and nipah swamp. *Photographer unknown.*

Only four officers in the Brunei Police Force were trained for intelligence work so after the revolt Special Branch officers were sent to Limbang to cull information from prisoners. All data collected was classified 'Top Secret' and given only to the British Army to help them track down rebel divisional command leaders. Dick Morris (right, second row) listens to the intelligence Iban trackers offer about the jungle trails that the fugitive rebels might use and which the Iban knew well. *Photographer unknown.*

Above On 3 August 1963 leaders of the Combined Services stand at attention while the Governor of Sarawak, Sir Alexander Waddell, unveils the memorial in Limbang to those who lost their lives in the insurrection. It was paid for by subscription raised by the Limbang community, who crowd to watch the ceremony. Dick Morris (seated, right) is giving his attention to a young boy scout. Wearing black behind him is a widow of one of the policemen who died resisting the rebels. *Photographer unknown.*

Right The memorial to those who lost their lives and the men of 42 Commando Royal Marines, some of whom rescued the hostages: Lieutenant Waters (third from left), Sick Berth Attendant Clark (fourth from left), Corporal Bill Lester (fifth from left, front row), Marine Underwood (fourth from right, front row), Marine Downey (immediately behind). *Photographer unknown.*

and Residency area. 'I assessed that the police station seemed the most likely place for the rebel headquarters, and I hoped that if we could knock this out, before the enemy commander had time to give orders for the disposal of the hostages, our chances of rescuing them might be increased.' Moore pondered on how this could be achieved without bloodshed. Clearly it would be desirable to do so.

> I therefore planned to go straight for the enemy with the intention of overwhelming his headquarters very fast, but decided to hold my fire until he opened up on me, and to call upon him to surrender, in the hopes by a brave show, of bluffing him. I chose, as my prime objective the police station, and gave this as the objective of my leading troop. From there I intended to move to the Residency area, clearing the hospital on the way.[35]

These locations were separated from each other by about 300 yards (275 metres). Moore's plan was simple: to overwhelm the rebels' likely positions as fast as possible, holding fire until the rebels opened up. 'We had to get to the hostages before the enemy had time to react.'

The plan of attack was for one of the craft to go ahead and land, with the other following. In the first landing craft would be 5 Troop: they were to be the snatch squad. They would make straight for the police station, the expected location of the hostages, storm into it and capture it. The second lighter, carrying 4 and 6 Troops with two Vickers medium machine guns, would give covering fire. That boat would also carry a reserve section of Royal Marines to deal with any strong points in the town. The MMGs would give covering fire to 4 Troop, which would go ashore on a jetty in front of the police station, where 4 Section would act on a shop behind the police station, thereby assisting 5 Troop (from the lead boat) in capturing it. 6 Section would give additional close covering support. The remainder of the company, from 4 and 6 Troops, would land further down the river and sweep towards the other sections, in a pincer type movement.

Moore would be in the first lighter, with his signaller, the commando intelligence sergeant, and the rifle troop led by Lieutenant Davis, who had trained his troop himself at Kota Belud. Moore's second-in-command, Lieutenant Waters, would be in the second lighter with the company sergeant major (CSM), Cyril Scoins.

The primary objective was to liberate the hostages and transfer them to the safety of the lighters. Secondary objectives were to clear the town of rebels and, if possible, to obtain prisoners and further intelligence.

Given the risk to the hostages, it was judged inappropriate to put heavy gunfire directly into the buildings. The tactic was to rely on surprise and fast, aggressive action.

By 8 pm, Moore counted that he had 89 men, including seamen from the minesweepers and one section of MMGs, under command.[36] The remainder of his company were still somewhere in the pipeline, making their way to Brunei.

Later that evening, Moore gathered his officers in a room in the Brunei Hotel, which they had requisitioned, and in which the troops encamped through the day. 'I gave my orders', Moore said. He was heading into an operation as a Company Commander for the first time.

> Big moment in life. In many ways. I was giving orders for real. For an operation. Serious stuff. Tomorrow people were going to get killed, unless we were very lucky... It was pretty serious with me. No levity about this. The responsibility, and getting it right. Have I got it right? There is so little

information: am I making the right choice?

Few of the men had seen live action before. 'I had been in action in Malaya as subaltern and I had been shot at in Cyprus', Moore reflected. 'I had been on operations before. Peter Waters and the CSM had, but none of the marines had been in operations before.'

The atmosphere in the room was tense. 'Very close tension', Moore said.

> Because, for everybody else, no-one had been in this situation before. Now it was for real. With live ammunition. This was serious stuff. I was hoping they were trusting their company commander. I gave them their orders. I got some one or two questions, as you will, and then they went off to give their orders to their marines.

'At that, some pictures were produced', said Daker, who was Number One on one of the Vickers MMGs. 'No maps. They gave a rough idea of what the terrain was like, and the river reminded me very much of being at Stourport.' Having anticipated that he would by now have seen more action than he had met with in Brunei, Daker was under the impression that moving into Limbang would be easy; he imagined that going into Limbang was 'going to be like going into Stourport, on the river Severn'.[37] He was thinking of the inland port that grew in the eighteenth century, a relatively tranquil West Midlands market town, served by canal basins and locks between the canals and the river.

At that Marine Matty Cooper came up to him. Daker explained they were very good friends. 'He was a Welshman. Always singing. Nice chap.'

'Cheerio, Tony.'

'What do you mean? You're coming with us, aren't you?'

'But who is the first one you think they are going to shoot?'

'Aw, nothing is going to happen anyway', said Daker. 'Then I thought about this, and thought he's right! I am the main target! Then I thought, Aw nothing will happen.'

Daker recalls, 'Nobody said anything. The Sergeant did say to me, "just relax a bit, Tony. Your knuckles are turning white"'.

'We joked on', said Daker, 'joked on, for a bit of time'.[38]

Later that night, around 9 pm, as the company assembled, Moore realised there were still only 89 men. 6 Troop was one section short, but this had been made up by ranks from Company HQ.

'When, bang! goes a rifle! Into the night', Moore tells. 'Someone had a negligent discharge. Tension. That was what it was. It gave me the opportunity to go around to say to them "come on, calm down, I know it is tense, but you have got to calm down. We are going to get it right."'[39]

Moving among the men, Moore continued to reassure them: 'Don't worry about it. I know you're frightened but don't worry about it, we are going to get this right'.

In Limbang, something had to be done about the hostages. Police Constable Essa, who was hiding in the roof of the police station, overheard the TNKU leaders planning to hang them. Their executions were to take place the next day.

As yet unaware of this, Omar was encouraged by his success so far. The growing support that he received, and the noticeable turn in the rebellion that was apparent from the increasing number of older rebel guards at the jail, emboldened him. He set up a 'Red Cross delegation'. Ten of his 'Red Cross' group, each dressed in their 'Red Cross' uniform, accompanied him to the police station. He demanded that the hostages be removed to the hospital, and impressed on the rebel leaders that the hostages be treated as patients. Commander De-Erah, a deputy of Salleh bin Sambas, agreed, giving him written orders from the Revolutionary Government of United North Borneo that no English could be spoken with the hostages.[40] 'If they found I speak English, they will take action upon me', Omar said. He also feared what they might do to anyone who spoke with him.

It was exactly a month since the Morrises had arrived in Limbang. In their cell, they reflected on the calamitous position in which they now found themselves.

'I counselled myself to be patient', Dorothy records, 'thinking how wonderful it would be to be free and safe, instead of the situation we were in'.

The Morrises stand-off with their guards continued. 'The behaviour of individuals varied between the rigidly correct and beastly', recalls Dick. 'Certain facts do stand out. The general attitude had become anti-European, anti-Police and anti-Government.'[41]

Yet, the attitude of many of the guards was clearly changing. Dorothy recalls:

> They took every opportunity to whisper to us that their hearts were not in the enterprise and that they hoped the Tuan Resident would deal gently with them when *Perentah* British was in charge again. Our suspicions that something was going to happen very soon were further strengthened by the increasing number of visitors who were permitted to bring us food, cigarettes (even cigars). These same friendly visitors were also trying to convey news of successes in Brunei Town, Kuala Belait, Seria and Miri, and for these many kind and brave acts we shall never forget them. [42]

Now a regular visitor to the jail, Omar came again to tend to the hostages that morning. He handed them some rice and a bottle of water and in Malay he said to Dorothy that he had been unable to find the medicine which she required but would try and find something in the dispensary which would do. As Dorothy had not asked for any medicine, it was obvious that a message was intended, Dick thought. Just what?

In the early afternoon, Omar returned to the jail, again accompanied by grim-looking armed guards. This time he made sure that the Morrises understood the news he could give them.

Ordered to speak only in Malay, so the guards could follow his conversation, Omar had devised a method of getting his news across to the Morrises. He brought with him a bottle of medicine which was labelled in English. He impressed upon the guards that he could not read the English instructions on the label and would need help to do so from the Resident before he could issue the correct dosage. He impressed upon the guards that this was vital to avoid possible severe medical consequences.

Through the bars of Cell No. 1 he spoke in Malay to the Morrises. He began his conversation with an apology to the Resident's wife. He said that he had found some tablets in the dispensary but all the instructions were in English which he did not understand. If he were able to spell out the instructions maybe the Resident's wife would be able to tell him which, if any, of the medicines would meet her needs. Very slowly he began to 'spell out' indications and doses of the label of one bottle.

'B – T – N – R – HENS – – 2 – H – M – S – N – B – T – – R – M – 2 – N – B – T – – B – T – A – PT – N – R – HENS.'

'Then the same on another', said Dick, 'and in the same slow voice he went on'.

Holding the bottle out so that the Morrises could follow him, Omar pretended to read out the label's instructions, slowly spelling out each letter. Making sure to keep up a dialogue in Malay as he did this, so as to not raise suspicions among the guards, he interspersed his 'reading' of the label with 'letters' by stringing them into abbreviated 'English' phrases 'read' from the label that the Morrises might follow. This way Omar managed to convey his 'coded' news.[43]

The Morrises quickly appreciated Omar's ruse. They played along by pretending to slowly follow each letter of the label, as if to work out with Omar the correct dosage. They pretended that this was a matter of severe concern. Omar continued 'reading' his 'information' for as long as he could manage without raising suspicions, and all the while making certain that Dick understood his news.

In Malay, Omar asked, 'Can Mem understand what that means? Because I cannot understand English.'

'B – T – N – R – HENS – – 2 – H – M – S – N – B – T – – R – M – 2 – N – B – T – – B – T – A – PT – N – R – HENS.'

'Yes', Dorothy replied, 'I think that is the right medicine'. The Morrises understood.

'Brunei Town is in our hands. There are two of Her Majesty's ships in Brunei Town. There are Royal Marines too in Brunei Town. Brunei Town Airport in our hands.'

For the Morrises, this was wonderful medicine.

Abang Omar conveyed to us with real thespian talent the
state of the emergency in Brunei Town, Brunei Airport,
Kuala Belait, etc., from which we were able to assume – or
hope – that matters had turned our way and that it appeared
to be only a matter of days (or hours) before Limbang would
also be 'N. R. HENS' (in our hands).

'But had Omar's "Minder" understood that message', writes Dick, 'then Omar would almost certainly be for the "chop". However, the guard was obviously as puzzled as Omar appeared to be by the detailed instructions on the bottles of tablets.[44] From then on, we realised that a critical stage had been successfully achieved in planning our recapture.'

The afternoon saw more activity in the jail. Dorothy described how they were ordered to march out of their cell. 'There was quite a flurry when one of the TNKU top brass visited us all and "invited" us to proceed to the hospital, where the other expatriate hostages were being taken.'

She described Dick's response when they were singled out. 'When we received our orders to leave the jail and proceed to the hospital Dick demurred, saying "Thank you very much" (Lady Troubridge could have found no fault) "but what of our fellow prisoners in the jail, namely the police?"'

Dick was concerned about the fate of the Malay policemen. In his view, they had been loyal in their duty and he would not abandon them.

Dorothy recalls:

He requested that the police hostages be moved with us also. Further to-ings and fro-ings between TNKU headquarters, and then we were told that the police would be also brought to the hospital, but that we were ordered to proceed first. We feared for their safety and suspected the rebels had other plans in mind for them.

Later that evening, the Police Inspectors were taken to the cells of the police station.

The Morrises were marched onto the road. They gulped in the late afternoon air. 'One of the happiest events of that day', said Dorothy, 'was the all too short walk down the road to the hospital (emptied of patients) at about 5.30 in the afternoon. We had grown very stiff and sluggish from the long hours spent just sitting or lying on the floor of the cell.' Changes they had noticed before among their guards also buoyed their spirits. 'Very heartening too was the evidence of lowered morale in the whispered assurances of our escorting guards (armed, fore and aft) that they were not really bad chaps and would be very glad to see the old set-up in force again.' The move to the small general hospital gave Dick and Dorothy renewed hope.

> More 'highs'! Dick and I were put into the doctor's
> consulting room, which the 'Red Cross' had equipped with
> two beds and two mattresses. Utter bliss! Shortly afterwards
> we were taken into the ward where to our great joy we met
> the six fellow-hostages, who had been held in the police
> station. They were all in good heart and we were told we
> could '*sheken*' with them, which we gladly did.

The other Limbang captives included the three Mill Hill missionaries; Peace Corps volunteer Fritz Klattenhoff; and a Public Works Department employee, Mr Withers, whom Dorothy singled out. She was curious to meet him because he had seemingly shunned all social occasions, refusing all invitations to the Residency. Doubtless he had his good reasons for his solitary existence, she thought. Still, she enjoyed, in view of the well-armed guards, thrusting out her hand and greeting him. 'How nice to meet you at last. I'm Dorothy Morris', while thinking to herself, Lady T would have cheered from the side-lines.

The Morrises were not to keep their company for long. More guards arrived. The Morrises were returned to their room and locked in. As Dick later discovered:

the hospital and the police station (the latter was rebel HQ) together formed the centre and pivot of the rebel defences and were manned by approximately a company of rebels. The other two companies of rebels were deployed along the river bank and in the jungle fringe which at Limbang lies about a hundred yards or so from the river bank. This was the situation on the evening of 11 December.[45]

Dick overheard the guards, from their conversation nearby, say that they planned to hang him and Dorothy the following morning.

It was difficult to settle. 'There was not much sleep for us that night, in spite of those wonderful beds', recalls Dorothy. 'The guards were too many and too noisy, we'd had nothing to eat or drink since midday, and we both sensed that something was going to happen, and soon. And of course it did – early the next morning.'

The rescue force set out in the dark, at 11 pm. 'The idea being that we motor up to within about a mile of Limbang, put into shore, just keep quiet, lay up during the night, then get into position for the dawn attack', says Marine David Greenhough.[46] 'We were fully loaded up with front-line ammunition, with grenades of all types, bandoliers hanging from us, all the automatic weapons.' There was also the attachment of MMGs. 'The old Vickers guns: these particular weapons at close range are quite frightening with their sound of fire. And so we left.'

Their route up the rivers lay along a series of complicated winding channels between 50 and 100 yards wide, flanked by thick Nipa swamp. They took this indirect route as the direct route up the river, while shorter, passed a number of kampongs, which might harbour rebel sympathisers. Being uncertain of the routes through the Nipa, they set off with time allowed for wrong turnings. They estimated that Limbang was perhaps six hours' steaming away up the rivers.

Finding their way was no easy task. At best, during daylight, the thick belt of Nipa palm, crowding the river banks with long feathery foliage up to 30 feet (9 metres) high, narrowed vision to the river alone for much of the journey. Despite a full moon which assisted with navigation, visibility was very poor. The flat barges were difficult to manoeuvre and it was hard going. Their progress was slow, at 3 or 4 knots. They had no charts, and were navigating with an ordinary compass. The leading craft had an engine breakdown. They took a wrong turning and had to back down the narrow waterways to the right route. 'We did have some alarming moments', recalls Corporal Jones. 'Three or four times we found ourselves ploughing through the *ulu*, and of course the mosquitoes gave us a busy time.'[47]

Earlier that day, Moore had found Brunei's harbourmaster, Captain Muton.

'He knew the Brunei River but didn't really know the Limbang River well and he certainly had not been through the Nipa palm swamps which were the recommended route by anybody who knew anything about it. He had heard of the route, but never travelled it.'

'That's the way they all go', he told Moore.

'You're coming with us', said Moore. 'Help us find the way.'

Apart from Muton as pilot, Moore also had the naval personnel who joined the mission. 'Our parent service came to our rescue', said Moore. 'The Royal Navy got us to our objective.'

'It was not quite like the preparations for D-day', said Lieutenant Down.

We had no Ordnance Survey maps and the Hydrographic charts did not extend that far upriver. Navigators will be familiar with the outline sketches that adorn the edges of some coastal charts with shading for high ground and the general shape of rivers, but no depths or detail indicated. Local information was not much help. The local boat traffic did not move after dark, so there were no buoys or navigation lights. There had been no recent survey, so no depths could be confirmed. Captain Muton had marked his preferred channel by placing spars on the main mud-banks – which were prone to shift after the monsoon rains. The vessels we commandeered had no log to judge speed and the (uncorrected) compass was of dubious value in the confined waters of the river. It was back to the techniques of Nelson's navy when approaching an unknown shore.[48]

The two craft, keeping just within sight distance, slowly edged their way through the narrow channels as silently as they could. The atmosphere on each lighter was tense.

'There were some speculations among the lads as to what we were going to expect and I know we were all a little scared', recalled one Marine.[49]

'Older sergeants had seen action, but 90 per cent of us had never had anything fired at us in anger before', said Marine Genge. 'We weren't sure what to expect.'

Some were thinking, 'This is for real!' Some, like Marine Daker, were in a state of disbelief. 'Nothing is going to happen', he reassured himself.

'You are so full of yourself that you think that nothing is ever going to happen to you', Genge said. 'I was apprehensive. You think, "I might be dead in a few hours". I didn't think that apprehension was about doing my job! But, I was confident. Whatever lay ahead', he thought, 'I know I could do it'.[50]

Others took comfort in their training. They had all done their basic training together; they knew that they were all equally capable, selected members of an elite, and respected each other for that. 'The training is so rigorous, it brings out in you a belonging and trusting in each other', says Corporal Rawlinson, 'and builds that great camaraderie'.[51]

Sitting alongside Mike Bell, a young Marine wondered whether he would remember his training when faced with fire. He decided that not doing as you had been trained would be more frightening.[52]

Another, Richard Jennings, muttered, 'I am a coward: if we are going to fight, I'd change sides and fight for the other side'.[53]

By 2 am, both craft reached the main Limbang River some 5 miles (8 kilometres) from the town. The muffled grinding of their engines and the wake from their vessels was all that could announce their presence. They kept out of sight of the town, several miles downstream. They pulled into a side channel where they laid up, hidden in the shadows of the jungle edges, until 4.30 am. From there they could reach Limbang town just after first light.

'I remember vividly laying up with mosquitoes all around us all that night', says Marine Greenhough. 'Light in the Far East arrives generally speaking at a certain time so we synchronised quite easily as to what time we were going to arrive.'

Marine Tony Daker was relieved when they pulled in to the riverside, to lay up. He thought, 'Oh, nothing is going to happen here!' He moved from under the gun, having been in that position for the past couple of hours. No light or noise came from the men, who were alert to their surroundings. 'Nobody was talking', says Daker.

I sat with my back to the ramp. Going though my mind

was my folks. I could imagine them being at home. I could see the fire; my mum and dad at the table, talking … If my mother knew where I was and what I was up to, she'd be going mad! … The sweat was running off you.

'I heard "we're going to get a move on now." It was just breaking light … and we sailed in.'[54]

Signallers in Brunei made the best of the confusion of the past two days. Batteries and charging engines for the type 62 radio sets were mislaid somewhere between Singapore and Brunei. The weight of their responsibility dawned on them as they prepared for the Limbang operation.

'Unlike on exercises, no excuses could now be tolerated', said the signaller. 'This time, there would be no wash-up for me to blame out-of-date equipment if communications failed, no detailed investigations in two days time into the failure of essential equipment to arrive by air, no calm official or unofficial criticism of the exercise planning. The 62 just had to work.'

'I crossed my fingers. They were to stay crossed for a long time.'

If the sets failed, 'we would fail to get anywhere in this roadless, trackless country, or at the best, grind slowly on from point to point, never taking bold leaps, never getting the rebels off balance'.

'It was only as I was giving the Company signallers their final instructions that I suddenly realised that this was no exercise but the real thing. How tough it was going to be, no-one knew.'[55]

7

WEDNESDAY, 12 DECEMBER: RESCUE THE HOSTAGES

The build-up continued. Seventy-four airlift sorties had flown out of Singapore so far.[1]

A spokesman for the British armed forces said in Singapore that Brunei Town was quiet and clear of rebels, but the jail was still in rebel hands. It was reported that 300 British troops from the 1st Battalion Green Jackets landed at Miri from the Royal Navy Cruiser HMS *Tiger*. It was also reported that about 400 Kenyah and Kayan Tribesmen were fanning out from the Sarawak town of Marudi, close to the Brunei border, to prevent insurgents withdrawing to the jungle.[2] Aerial reconnaissance in the Sibuti area of Sarawak, southwest of Miri, revealed that the Indonesian flag was flying over the government office there. The small Sarawak fishing town of Bekenu, south of Miri, appeared to be in the hands of the rebels: armed men were seen, and one saluted the aircraft. A spokesman for the Commissioner-General in South-East Asia reiterated that the Sultan, was safe in Brunei Town.

The Press had to make sense of such seemingly contradictory reports, from briefings given by military spokesmen. Correspondents were not allowed in Brunei for their own safety (although some ignored this).[3]

In Manila, Sheikh Azahari challenged Britain to prove that

the Sultan was supporting the British forces as a free agent. He challenged the British to produce proof of their claim that the Sultan still controlled Brunei and opposed the revolt.[4] He told a press conference that the Sultan was with the rebels. He said that Britain had committed an act of aggression by sending troops to Brunei because the 1959 treaty between Britain and the Sultan had provided for troops to be sent only at the Sultan's request. He ignored the fact that this request had been made.

The British Government withdrew Azahari's British passport. With Azahari in Manila was Zaini bin Ahmad, executive secretary of the PRB, who also had his passport cancelled. Seemingly unperturbed, Azahari retorted that he was continuing to petition U Thant, UN Secretary-General, and intended to visit the United States, but American officials replied that because their passports had been withdrawn, the United States could not entertain their applications. A spate of diplomatic cables were exchanged between London, British Borneo, Manila, Djakarta, Washington and New York.

Reuters reported that 42 Commando was given the task of operations on Limbang, and a company of 1/2 Gurkha Rifles was to rescue the European hostages at Limbang.[5]

42 Commando Royal Marines was formed from the 1st Battalion Royal Marines in October 1943. At the war's end, it took part in Britain's end-of-empire activities. Between 1950 and 1952, 42 Commando was operational in Malaya, where 22 months of active service saw the unit engaged in a number of highly gallant engagements. It was deployed for Suez in 1956 and the Lebanon Crisis in 1958; and it came to the aid of Kuwait, which expected an invasion by Iraq in mid-1961.

A recruit who was undergoing training in 1962 wrote how an essential part of a Marine's training was to learn the Corps' history. 'The Corps revolves around its history and is very proud of what it has achieved over the years, something that was drummed into us at every conceivable opportunity ... items like our battle honours and "Victoria Cross" winners, there being about ten of them so far.'[6]

Commando units were ready to deploy at short notice anywhere in the world. Marines could be assigned as they were needed, within and even across Royal Marine units. Therefore it was essential that their training be the same, as was their organisation within units. Troop sections each consisted of 'a two-man Bren gun team, plus a Bren gun commander, a three-man rifle team, a front scout, a rear end Charlie and a corporal in charge of the whole section'.[7]

Commandos specialised in amphibious and land assault. In approaching Limbang, Moore and his men of 42 Commando were doing what they were trained to do.

Marine Mike Bell was among the youngest of the men in L Company. 'Dinger' Bell was from Shedfield, a village in Hampshire surrounded by good pasture for grazing livestock. He was on his first posting, having barely passed out of the commando's training school when sent to Borneo in September. At 18, the husky, blond-haired Bell stood six-feet-three-inches tall. When asked why he had enlisted, Bell replies casually.

Why did I join up with the Marines? I think that the first time I heard about the Marines was from a story in my comics about the Marines that I read when I was a boy. When I left school I worked on a farm, crawling through mud there. The year before I joined up was really wet, and I was up to my knees crawling through mud. I joined the force the following year thinking, that if I was going to be crawling through mud, I might as well be doing it with the Marines.[8]

Selection and training for the Royal Marines was rigorous. In 1962, it was more customary to walk and cycle to get around, and many recruits came from occupations which involved physical labour, such as miners, builder's mates, or farm workers like Bell. 'Half the squad had earned their living working with their hands', explains Julian Thompson, military historian, and former Royal Marine.[9] Physical fitness was a feature of recruits to the Royal Marines, who prided themselves on being the fittest service personnel in the world.[10]

Trainees were tested to the limits of their endurance. Bell appreciated the training that he received to qualify as a member of a small fighting force, a battalion-sized unit, able to survive in alien conditions and used for making quick destructive raids. The intensely physical training tested their mental fortitude, the ability to keep going until the job is done. Demonstrating the fortitude to withstand pressure of every kind earns a trainee the much-coveted green beret.

Giving their best and respecting that commitment was inherent in being a Royal Marine. Recruits started their training in squads that could be about 40 strong to begin with. Progressing through their training, the men shared more than 'memories of agonising moments on the death-slide, of blistered hands on the ropes, of bleeding blisters on the marches, of aching shoulders on the load-carry, of freezing water and clinging mud on the obstacle course, and the moment of hopelessness on the fifth attempt at a regain'.[11] Individual character was tested, as was group cohesion. 'You did everything in syndicates', said Bell, and those who succeeded in completing the course and finished their training together, remained close and worked as one.[12] 'The spirit was the thing! Pulling together – every move calling for the maximum effort … to make one worthy to carry the mark of a Royal Marine – the Green Beret.'[13]

Recruits were instructed in their handbook that Marines are part of a highly organised machine. The trickle draft recalled a Marine from overseas service after 18 months. Marines returning to England were replaced in the unit, with three, four or six Marines at a time arriving in a section. Marines underwent continuous training with this rotation; officers trained with their men, and were expected to outdo them. Marines were at once self-reliant, and loyal to each other.

Other factors besides their training fostered a mental attitude that set the Marines apart as elite troops. In the days of National Service, conscripts made up only 30 per cent of Royal Marines; the corps enjoyed the highest number of regulars among personnel in the forces.[14] Commitment built firm bonds. Service overseas established further ties among the men. 'In a commando unit, when you are a long way from home', one Marine explains, 'people seem to find a closeness uncommon to civilian life, and lasting friendships develop'.[15] Good fellowship or 'mess spirit' followed. Royal Marine units worked as an integrated, single body, making them a most effective and elite fighting force.

This cohesion was evident in training they did at Burma Camp, 16 miles (26 kilometres) to the north of Singapore Island. They learned that:

> One cannot afford to have 'the thin red line' in the
> assault. Section and troops must work forward by fire and
> movement. Control must be retained without shouting and
> arm waving … movement forward to an assault position
> will often have to be on a narrow front … The LMG [light

machine gun] groups of the assaulting sections should be used on the flanks of their sections [where] they can either act as a 45 degree fire unit or as flank protection and cut off.[16]

Marines had an outstanding record for showing initiative and unswerving devotion to duty.

Among the men heading for Limbang, Bell looked across at Gerald 'Scouse' Kierans and David Formoy. Kierans was not much older than Bell. Aged 22, Kierans came from Widnes, Lancashire. Qualified in naval gunnery, he had been with 42 Commando since July. At 24, 'Dave' Formoy was a married man from Deal in Kent; his wife was at Sembawang in Singapore with their three-month-old son. He had joined the Commando in January. Bell observed that they were probably on their second posting, whereas it had been just three months since he had joined 42 Commando.

Just before dawn, the two boats slid away from their lay-up position just off the Limbang River. They moved slowly up the river so as to arrive off from the police jetty a few minutes after first light.

As they set out, Paddy Davis passed the order round his troop to fix bayonets. The midshipman who was on the craft looked over from the top and exclaimed, 'Good lord! Do they *really* do that?'[17]

They chugged towards the town in the breaking dawn. All was still and quiet. Mist rose from the trees and the surface of the river. Limbang came into view, a couple of miles away, at 5.45 am.

'We could see the street lights: the electric lights were on; it was still dark. Suddenly they went out.' Corporal Jones describes the mood that took hold of the men on the two boats. 'Whether this was due to the coming dawn, or the sound of the Landing

Craft, I don't know but it made the atmosphere pretty tense.' They did not know then that the town lights were routinely switched off at dawn.

They came to a bend in the river, nearing the town. Little sign of life appeared in the kampong north of the town. The leading craft rounded the bend leading to the customs wharf and the boats picked up speed, owing to the current in the river.

They headed towards the small jetty in front of the police station. Lieutenant Peter Down was expecting that 'we would go alongside this jetty like any sensible boat; intelligence was that Limbang was deserted, so if the rebs were still up there, if we turn up looking fearsome and warlike, we might frighten them off'.

'We got within about 300 yards before there was any movement in the town', Captain Moore says, 'but then it erupted like a disturbed ants nest as the rebels stood to'. Men rushed out of buildings, and ran into positions with their guns.

The first boat made for the river bank at a point 30 yards upstream of the police station as the Marines recognised it and slowed when about 200 yards away from it. The Commando Intelligence Sergeant, David Smith, using a loudhailer, informed the rebels in Malay that the rebellion was over and that they should lay down their arms and surrender.

The answer was a hail of fire directed at the boats. Muzzle flash, from weapons aimed at them – an LMG, sub-machine guns and about 100 shotguns – stunned the men.

'We were expecting a minor incursion, or perhaps, a putting down of people shouting at us – not actually firing at us!' Greenhough says.[18]

At the time, the men on the two boats did not know that they faced a force more than double the size of their own. Rebels held positions along the length of the town. They faced the river from the police station; from elevated positions such as the upper floors of the bazaar, the hospital and District Office; and in monsoon drains beside the road running along the river.

Heard among firing against them was the unmistakeable sound of the magazine-fed Bren gun. 'This was the first that we knew that they had a Bren gun!' says Peter Down. 'And, as fire increased, we heard the noise of the American Armalite! In my job, I wore a rubber suit and worked under water. Using a rifle alongside a marine was something I had never, ever considered!' Down and his sailors were equipped with the normal ships' weapons of a few old wartime .303 rifles, three to four submachine guns, 1942 pattern weapon, a few pistols. '*We* had the wrong kit all round!'[19]

'Christ almighty! I wonder if they knew we were coming after them!' thought Tony Daker, in position with the MMGs.

'We were not quite expecting the surprise we got!' says Greenhough, who led 3 Section from 4 Troop. 'We hadn't opened up at this stage – but the full weight of fire from the bank, coming toward us – sort of threw our plans into disarray … The whole thing changed from a minor furore or confrontation to a major frontal assault.'

Some of the men, like Greenhough, Daker and Russell, who were on the second boat (Z-craft/*Fiskerton*) slightly behind the advance boat, were in a position to follow what happened.

The lead boat (Z-craft/*Chawton*) headed in to ram the bank, so as to enable the men to jump onshore. The Marines on that boat took cover on the open decks, but had little protection. 'They were firing down on us', says Corporal Bob Rawlinson. 'Then again we were lucky.' He praised the efforts of the naval welders from the previous afternoon.

The bulwark saved us. That piece of metal from the ship's side was about 3 feet high. It was well built, made of metal from WW2. It gave us shelter from that fire, gave us cover from that angle, that arc. Very quickly GPMGs [general-purpose machine guns] opened up after we'd taken the initial bursts.[20]

'It was decided by the commanders', says Greenhough, 'that the rear boat would give as acute a cover from the Vickers machine guns as was possible, by strafing at overhead height, with the hope of frightening the rebels to lay down their arms and offer no resistance'.

'We were given instruction to open on rifle fire that we could see coming', says Marine Laurie Russell.

'We started firing', says Daker.[21] He began counting. 'One banana, two banana, three ...', thinking, 'This is ridiculous! It is stopping nobody! This is serious! They are shooting at us! Couldn't get my breath! I wasn't frightened, but thought I wouldn't like to be at the end of this!'

With the Vickers firing, Moore's boat beached some 30 seconds later. It went straight into the bank, near where it had been planned they should go in, by a small jetty.

4 Section of 5 Troop leapt over the bow of the craft. They stormed ashore, heading for the police station. They faced a 30-yard dash across open ground through a hail of heavy machine-gun fire.

Sergeant Johnny Bickford, a Corps footballer and PT Instructor and the senior Section Commander, with Corporal Bob Rawlinson, who was second off the boat, and Corporal Bill Lester, pressed home the attack. Lester urged his section to charge the rebels and over-run their position.

'It was a marvel how we got through', says Rawlinson. 'The firepower was so tremendous. I never heard noise like that firing. I couldn't hear myself shout, it was so intense.'

From the gunboat, Russell saw them go ashore. 'They went so fast, and carried out drills they'd been taught.'

Moore watched the Marines from 5 Troop surge ashore.

> Some firing, some moving. They were doing their job. It was a beautiful sight. What was going through my mind was, 'That training period worked! They're doing it right!' Bullets were falling in all directions. Yet I knew every time the corporal gave an order. I knew he had given it, because I could see blokes doing right things. It was lovely to watch.[22]

According to plan, Corporal Lester led his section to the rear of the police station while Sergeant Bickford with Corporal Rawlinson and his section pressed the attack from the front. Supporting cover came from both boats. Marines fired at a rapid rate into windows, doorways and any likely cover to stop the rebels from shooting at the men from 5 Troop who were racing ashore.

'On each boat were 30 to 40 rifles and two machine guns', Peter Down recalls.

> That much lead being shot into the air knocks holes into brick buildings and would conceivably wound, injure, or kill people inside. Killing hostages defeats the exercise. So it was decided not to fire onto the police station, where it was thought the hostages were, but to fire enough rifle fire at the rebels to enable a Marine snatch party to jump ashore and collect the hostages, without too much fear of being shot themselves.

The rebels returned intense fire. 5 Section were pinned down on the bank under heavy fire from rebels using a monsoon drain as a slit trench. The Bren gun at the police station returned the fire from the Marines' MMGs.

The leading troops, and those on Moore's boat, took the brunt of the resistance coming from the rebels. Two Marines were killed before they got to the bank. The Troop Commander, Lieutenant Davis, was hit in the leg while jumping ashore. Corporal Rawlinson was wounded in the back. Ignoring pain, he led his men, attacked the rebels from the flank, put them to flight, and pursued them into the jungle. Only when certain that the fight was over, did he seek treatment for his wounds.

Moore's boat drifted off the river bank when the helmsman, Petty Officer PJ Kirwan RN, was hit.

The second craft, the gunboat, remained standing off. 'We were giving covering fire to 5 Troop', says John Genge. 'The sergeant in charge of the machine gun, Sergeant Wakeling, said: "Watch where you're shooting as our lads are on shore."'[23] They concentrated their fire on targets in the town to prevent the Marines ashore from being shot at. It was not yet wholly apparent to them that they had the superior firepower.

They had experienced the Vickers firing in training. As Corporal Rawlinson describes it, the guns were fired then 'above us, all on a safety arc, to just give you an appreciation of what it might be like; with dummy mortars going off'. That simulation amounted to little preparation for what now faced them. 'Nothing prepares you', says Rawlinson.

> You could never ever get to the position that we were in …
> The Vickers saved us. The fire blast went for quite a few
> minutes; it seemed like a long time of course. If the Vickers
> hadn't opened, if we hadn't had them, we'd have been more
> or less annihilated.

'The rebels in the police station could see us and the firing coming at us had intensified', says Daker.

> I could only fire through some fuel pumps and a Land Rover which was on the jetty. The jetty was a lot higher than us with a number of oil barrels on it, and amongst them was a rebel shooting a double-barrel shotgun at point blank range, giving off two big blue smoke rings.

'We knocked a petrol pump over', recalls Peter Down. 'A large flare 20 feet in the air illuminated the scene and those nearby.'

'I was directly behind the left-hand gun and saw the damage we were doing', recalls Daker. 'Quite impressive!'

Lieutenant Peter Waters was wounded in the wheelhouse of the gunboat.

'The front of the craft started to turn out into the river, and at this point I could see the front of the police station properly for the first time', says Daker. 'I gave it all I could, and this had the right effect, silencing the Bren gun, which was on top of the police station.'

Salleh bin Sambas, who was manning the Bren gun, was wounded and withdrew, followed by most of his force. Three rebels remained in the police station, including Salleh's second-in-command.

At this stage, Moore's boat, which had drifted away from the bank, was moving upstream in the fast-flowing river.

Moore gave orders to get back to the bank. 'I could see the firing at us had stopped at the police station. We clearly had the fire initiative thanks largely, I am sure, to the MMGs.'

The Marines on his drifting craft were frustrated: 'We were riflemen too far away to engage!'

Lieutenant David Willis, who was serving as captain of that

lighter, grabbed its wheel. He took control of the awkward craft and drove it back towards the bank.

'We went forward', recalls Moore, 'but not in the same place, because we had drifted off'. The current was vigorous. 'And, the boat was unwieldy.'

It broached some 150 yards upstream from the initial landing, past the jail, at a spot between the hospital and the Residency.

Moore was concerned about the section at the back of the police station. He called down to the troop sergeant who was still on board, Wally Macfarlane. 'Take the remaining section and clear the shoreline down to the police station and join up with the rest of the troop.'

As the men scrambled over the upended ramp, they found themselves waist-deep in thick mud and slime. Seeing the boat stuck fast in the mud, Moore decided, 'Right. I'm going ashore.' He would take his MOA and his signaller with him, catch up with Macfarlane's section just ahead of him, and head to the police station.

'I went down the vertical ladder at the back of the bridge structure to get on to the deck', recalls Moore, 'and there is a marine lying facing aft'. He turned him over; Marine Powell, aged 18, lay dead. Only with the Corps for one year, he joined the Commando in November, and was known for his 'all or nothing' approach to life. He was manning a Bren gun when he was killed.

The petty officer mechanical engineer popped his head up through the hatch where he was working the engines. He shouted, 'Jesus Christ! Some fucking exercise!'[24]

Troop Sergeant Macfarlane, by now ashore with the reserve section, pressed on northward, to the hospital. He brushed past the jungle edges, that came from just behind the hospital to some 40 or 50 yards from the river in some parts, and gave the enemy cover. As they reached the hospital, a group of rebels opened fire. Sergeant Macfarlane and two Marines were killed by a shotgun fired at close range.[25] They were 24-year-old David Formoy and 19-year-old Richard Jennings.

All the while, the gunboat manoeuvred in the fast-flowing river to give the best supporting fire possible. It took up a position in mid-stream, covering any eventuality with its MMGs. The tractors on board gave the men some protective cover. Greenhough recalls:

> I hunched low as possible under the 18 inch gunnels, blessing the fact that we had the agricultural implements [as he called the tractors] behind me, sort of shielding me from the back. I saw the front boat going hell for leather into the bank to offload the marines. We were then told by our troop commander, a guy called Soapy Waters – so-called because he had short-cut blond hair – that we were going to follow them, as soon as that boat had cleared. We would assist them and give them as much cover as possible.

The volume of fire coming at them seemed to be coming from a light machine gun, from the side of the town near the police station. 'It appeared that the fire was coming directly at me', says Greenhough. 'Which, I might add, was quite frightening! I had never had one fired at me before!'

> And then one or two people on our boat started getting hit. One was a friend of mine. 'Scouse' Kierans got hit in the neck. Beside me. Also our commander, Soapy Waters, got hit. He was up in the driving seat of the landing craft,

and he was shouting a bit. And the midshipman who was in charge of the boat was calling for the next marine commander.

The CSM Cyril Scoins took command of the situation. Scoins asked the lieutenant controlling the lighter if he could pull the craft out of line to give the machine guns a better fire position. 'Can you get us a little closer, Sir!'

Pulling the boat into a more exposed position, to give the best supporting fire, the naval officer responded, 'Sergeant Major, Nelson would have fucking loved you!'

Scoins landed the two troops from the gunboat, 200 yards to the right of the police station. He then took the boat back into mid-stream to give further fire support with the MMGs. They neutralised a number of rebels in an attap house about 30 yards up the hill behind the hospital. The boat returned downstream opposite the bazaar area.

At this point, an elderly Chinese man walked to the flagpole of the District Office. He removed from it the tri-colour Red, White and Green rebel flag with the PRB symbol of the Head of the Buffalo. He ran the Union Jack up the flagpole. This was Law Ah Kaw, whose courage and generosity deeply impressed Dick Morris. He had kept up his and Dorothy's spirits, bringing food and cheerfulness to them in their cell. Dick would later write to thank him 'for all that you did for my wife and me and for the others held prisoner by the rebels'. Dick never forgot how Ah Kaw pulled down the rebel flag 'even before the firing had ceased ... Your action can well make you proud and I for my part am proud to be able to say that "I know Ah Kaw".[26]

At the same time, 6 Troop cleared the police station, and 4 Troop moved behind and north of it, past the mosque to the back of the town. Most of the rebel resistance collapsed from this time on.

The Vickers section came ashore. Daker, the Number 1, carried the 54-pound tripod, 10-pound sight and his Sterling; Marine Shoubridge, the Number 2, took the gun, which weighed 52 pounds, and his Sterling; and the Number 3 carried the 5-gallon jerry can of water, which was strapped to a carrying frame, and his self-loading rifle (SLR). Each man also carried their personal equipment and two belts of 250 rounds. Daker and his crew settled their machine guns by the river bank. They were to hold the southern end of the perimeter which the Marines held, being the only area which afforded a field of fire of more than about 50 yards.

Daker looked towards the hospital. 'Just down the road, Marines were lying about, wounded. Some crying ... I was shocked.'

The road was narrow, eight feet wide, and fringed by bushes and scrub. Daker and his co-gunners were alarmed when one of them decided to relieve himself into the bush. At this, 'Three rebels stood up. Just like that!' They had taken cover in the bushes, but it became clear that they were more startled. 'We saw that they had no weapons, and we pulled them out and took them down to the police station.'

Marine Taff Coombs was told that his section, led by Corporal Parrish, was to secure the area around the police station. Coombs kept to the monsoon drain, firing at potential cover the TNKU might hide behind, until he and his section arrived at the police compound. He entered this, believing the police station had been cleared, checked the rear building and then went into the police station itself. He saw movement behind a door left open. He fired two warning shots into the ground, and shouted orders to come out. 'Two TNKU emerged, both very frightened, and one turned out to be second-in-command to Sallah bin Sambas', says Coombs.[27]

Appearing in the compound behind him was Sergeant Bickford, running from the jungle fringe, carrying a wounded Marine on his back.

Bickford's 5 Troop had suffered the heaviest casualties. They regrouped at the police station. They were reorganised and ordered to hold the perimeter from the area from the police station to the attap house behind the hospital. This involved clearing a number of houses. Doing so, an old woman was killed by a 36 grenade in her house.

Marine Greenhough was among the Marines who regrouped at the police station. 'That was where we stopped – to try and take account of what was going on and who was where and what had happened', Greenhough recalls. 'Really it was a case then, of picking ourselves up, finding out who was where, and re-planning a new course of action.'

In Brunei, the signallers waited nervously. L Company were expected to land at dawn. The control signaller tapped at his morse key. An expectant group surrounded him, willing him to get through to Limbang. His head turned, as the first faint messages from L Company came through. 'There they are', he muttered. Faces peered over him to read what he was writing – 'Heavy fighting on landing. Some casualties …'

At the hospital, Dick kept alert:

By my watch it was 0602 when I heard the sound of
powerful marine engines and shouted commands from
the direction of the police station. By standing on the bed
I could just see over the translucent glass in the windows
and, in the very pale light which precedes the tropical
sunrise, make out the form of two "Z" craft. 'This' was very
obviously 'it'.

The Morrises were in a room by themselves. The night before,
they made plans as to the action they should take when shooting
started. 'The aim of these plans was to avoid being shot', said
Dick, 'apart from keeping our heads down to protect ourselves
from glass, which would start flying when the bullets started to
come through the windows'.

They had to be quick. 'Before I had jumped down from the
bed', said Dick, 'a voice, speaking in Malay, called on the rebels
to surrender'. The answer to this was a prolonged burst from the
rebels' Bren gun. Then the fire-fight was on. The guards held
positions around the hospital, which came under heavy fire.

The Morrises moved the beds to a location protected from
any fire which might come through the door and got under them.
The firing surrounded them. 'Quite a lot of stuff came through
the windows and the windows came with it', Dick recalls. 'Most
of the stuff that came in was "ours". The rebels either by accident
or design put a couple of charges of buckshot in as well.'

The Morrises swung into action with the next part of their
plan. Dick and Dorothy began singing their two-verse ditty about
'dark green bonnets' to the tune of the folk song 'She'll be Coming
'Round the Mountain.

Fittingly, given his Welsh extraction, Dick Morris had a rich
baritone voice of considerable strength. He sang at the top of his
voice, in an effort to ensure that the Marines realised where the

hostages were, and did not shoot them.[28]

> We kept on singing. I'm afraid it wasn't very tuneful. But
> then, you see, our mouths were rather dry – from all the
> brick and plaster dust – well, that's my story! It's just as well
> we did sing because Sergeant Dennis Smith of Commando
> HQ was just about to toss a '36' into the concert hall when
> he heard the soft dulcet strains of our duet.[29]

The sound of their singing could be heard through the firing.

Things moved fairly quickly then. 'A short crisp dialogue of
challenge, response and identification, and a window on the sheltered side of the room disintegrated under the impact of an SLR
barrel, vigorously wielded by the same Sergeant Smith. He was
the first member of 42 Cdo RM we met.'

Dorothy said:

> We didn't enjoy the bangs and the flying glass one bit, but
> I do well remember the glorious sound of Sgt Smith's voice
> calling on the rebels to surrender. This was followed by a
> great many more bangs and noise and flying glass during
> which we sang our little ditty about 'Green Bonnets'.
> In between verses I repeated almost hysterically verse 4
> of Psalm 23 (which had figured very much in our quiet
> moments during the previous four days).
>
> *Yea, though I walk through the valley of the shadow of death,*
> *I will fear no evil: for thou art with me;*
> *thy rod and thy staff they comfort me ...*
> *Surely goodness and mercy shall follow me all the days of my life:*
> *and I will dwell in the house of the Lord for ever.*

Their identity established, she heard Sergeant Smith's voice again, this time saying, 'Out you come, old girl'.

'Whereupon "old girl" clambered out in Dick's wake', she continues, 'through the rather jagged aperture of the window obligingly broken by Sergeant Smith'.

Dick later joked, 'If my wife ever gives another man a look similar to the one she gave Sgt Smith and those other Royal Marines outside that window, there's going to be trouble'.

'He looked so large and calm and capable', she recalls, 'crouching down with gun aimed at the thickly wooded slope immediately behind the hospital, into which the guards who had survived had fled'.

The Morrises themselves narrowly escaped being shot at. 'One of the rebels had loosed off with his shotgun', said Moore, 'fortunately inaccurately, at the Resident, before taking to his heels, but no one was hurt'. The Morrises were not aware that three Marines had been killed in the jungle which encroached onto the back of the hospital.

Dick noted:

It was 0620 when we climbed out of the window. The last eighteen minutes were now part of history, minor history maybe, but terribly important to all those who had played a part in its making. The fire-fight was over, but there was still quite a lot of shooting and the occasional crump of a grenade as the beach-head was extended.

Dick recalls, 'It was I suppose three or four minutes after we "got out" that I met Capt. Jeremy Moore. I don't suppose for one moment he was as calm and cool as he appeared to be.'

Moore had heard Dick's warning to the Marines not to kill them from inside. When Dick sang 'they won't be singing sonnets', Moore introduced himself by announcing to Dick, 'You are wrong!'[30] He pulled a copy of Shakespeare's Sonnets from his pocket.

The missionaries, Withers and Fritz Klattenhoff had taken cover in the adjacent room in the hospital. 'As the first shots were fired', Fritz said, 'everybody seemed to go under the beds except the two fathers who were praying in bed for all of us'. His leg was grazed by gunfire.

Moore learned from Dick Morris that there were further hostages elsewhere in the town, and about 300 rebels. He set about organising his company to clear the town.

'We didn't waste time in pleasantries', says Dorothy, '(very sorry, Lady T), but darted into the ward to find our fellow hostages all present and correct and, like us, a trifle dazed. Mercifully the police officers held in the jail were rescued.'[31]

She was relieved that she could busy herself. 'Fortunately there was plenty to do, the first casualties were soon being brought in and we all did our fumbling and inefficient best to help.' She prepared beds and bandages for the wounded whom she nursed. 'The next few hours passed quickly enough.'

'I don't suppose we were really much help', Dick would say, 'but I like to think that, maybe, we civilians did one or two things which may have eased the task of "L" Coy and those who came with them'.

Moore made contact with the signaller at Brunei. The signaller lacked adequate power, his battery supply not yet having been brought in from Singapore. He remarked, 'I must have sounded very agitated because he spent a lot of time assuring me that everything was under control. I did not tell him that we had no spare batteries nor any charging engines yet, and he was probably going to run out of communications very soon.'[32]

Mugs of tea, made with water from a Vickers condenser, were

produced for the hostages. 'Not the cleanest thing', Daker says, 'but they were all pleased'.[33]

The first phase of the engagement was brisk. 'All this had taken twenty minutes', Moore recalls. 'Quite a short time. It is funny how time goes in a battle. You find that time seems long.'[34] Now the remaining hostages and the town had to be secured.

'I cannot say much about the sharp end', Dick notes. 'There were the usual "little" jobs of course; house clearing, the rescue of odd civilians being held in houses far beyond the perimeter; there were many others too.'[35]

Moore left his men to clear the area between the hospital and police station, before they started clearing the town. For the moment, Moore observed that some firing came from the shops in the bazaar. The whole bazaar area, where some rebels remained, would have to be cleared. 'The presence of civilians in these buildings prevented the Marines from taking normal counter-action, and it became a case of house clearing, each shop-house in turn being checked by Marines.' They would also have to cut off the rebels' retreat.

Moore directed two young subalterns, who were new to L Company since the exercises at Kota Belud, to move systematically through the town and clear it. Both seemed disconcerted by the prospect of street fighting.

'You two are looking a little blank. Have you got a problem?'
'A bit, sir.'
'Has your training covered fighting in built up areas?'
'No sir.'

'So, I then conducted a TEWT (Tactical Exercise Without Troops) with them on how to clear buildings. I stepped forward to take them through what to do.'[36]

The bazaar area contained the largest buildings in the town. They faced the Customs House located on the river bank, near the bend in the river where L Company first saw Limbang. They were two-storeyed concrete blocks. Shops occupied the ground floor, with residences above reached by a staircase from a separate entrance on the street.

The Marines were despatched to skirt up and secure these buildings, and cut off anybody who was attempting to escape. The insurgents hid where they could shoot at the Marines, who came under fire as they moved. 'There was shooting going on all over the place all the time; you couldn't tell where it was coming from', recalls Marine Genge.[37] Grenades could not be used, because families sheltered inside.

The Marines got themselves into position to support each other in what was obviously going to be a house-clearing job. Two separate rifle sections began with the first property on the bazaar's three-sided square. 'We adopted the normal Pepperpot movement, which is some protect whilst others move', says Greenhough.[38] 6 Troop held the northern end of the perimeter and gave support, as 4 Troop cleared the first east–west block of shops in the bazaar area, then 6 Troop cleared the first south–north block, supported by 4 Troop.

They progressed, slowly: 'One house, two houses, three houses', Greenhough adds. 'But it does take quite an amount of time. Interspersed with this searching method, my cover group, with their automatic weapons which had been covering us, are also on a high, with adrenalin running.' He gives an example of this.

There was a guy who was obviously killed, not by me
personally but whom my section killed, lying outside of a
door; so we assumed, on arriving at it, that it was empty
or open but in fact it wasn't. I think the complete contents
of one magazine was emptied into the door, to effect an
entrance, where the normal lock would be. Only to find
the door had been bolted top and bottom! In the heat of
the moment, with the adrenalin running, that hadn't even
been considered! So after the contents of one magazine,
and I think, one grenade as well, we eventually effected an
entrance.

One also had to guard against one's own force.

Whilst communications exist, and they are fully in the
picture about what is happening on our progress, there is a
no-man's land area where people shouldn't be. And if people
do appear there, then firing came from the cover group. This
stopped your progress through the houses, because any time
you heard fire, of course you stopped.

Further casualties occurred. Marine 'Smudge' Smith, a section
radio operator in 4 Troop, weighing 15 stone and encumbered
with a radio, insisted on helping. Moore describes what happened
to him.

Big chap, with a light machine gun, had gone into a
building. He worked his way up into the roof. He went
belting along, and the roof gave way. He fell through to the
first floor. And that gave way. He arrived on the ground
floor, with his gun. Shook his head. Got his breath. Beside
him was a concrete bath in which there was a Chinese

family, with their eyes popping out at this chap who came through the roof!³⁹

Smith was not alone in falling through a roof or floor of the buildings they were clearing, which were found to be far from sturdily built.

As soon as the first blocks of shops in the town were cleared, 4 Troop took over the northern end of the perimeter and 6 Troop was transferred to the eastern side while the SP Company elements cleared the southern end of the town and released the remainder of the hostages.

Everyone they found was rounded up and escorted to the police station. 'We didn't know who they were; they were all dressed the same; it was difficult to work out who was who. We took quite a lot of people into the police station, and let the police identify them.' An open-air fenced-off compound belonging to the Public Works Department, adjacent to the police station, and with a high wire fence around it, held people while the police processed them. They were screened by the police along with Sergeant Smith.

They found that the leaders of the rebel body had melted away in the main. 'They withdrew into the jungle area immediately behind Limbang', says Moore, 'and to the kampong area immediately to the north of the bazaar. Although shots were fired at the Marines, and others in the perimeter area, for some time, no attempt was made to counter-attack, but prisoners were taken'. They were held in the fenced-off compound.

'By the afternoon', Moore recalls, 'we had cleared the southern area and released all the fourteen hostages who had been held by the rebels'.

That night, 4 Troop fell asleep in the seats of the town's empty cinema.

Action at Limbang cost Moore's L Company heavily. 'The action had cost us five dead and six wounded – one of the latter a sailor', Moore records. 'Of the 350 odd rebels who we subsequently learned had been in Limbang, we had fifteen bodies to dispose of and took fifty or so prisoners.'[40]

Greenhough adds, 'The task of collecting up the dead bodies [was] an onerous task, but an experience for young marines who perhaps had never seen dead bodies before'. They carried a medical attendant to look after their own dead and wounded.

> If he can achieve anything in the way of first aid, then
> that is carried out. But we don't stop. Unfortunately, or
> fortunately, whichever way you look at it. It is a fact of life.
> The aim of course in all warfare is to injure. If they are dead,
> then you don't worry too much about them. In our instance,
> the fact is, if they drop, it is most unfortunate, but you carry
> on until the task is completed, and *then* you go back and
> look after them.

Much later Dorothy would say, 'I still have most unhappy reflections when I remember those who were killed in getting us all free again. They, or the ones I saw, were so young, and it is still one of the things I find hardest to forget.'

Marines who were killed were no more than teenagers like her own son, Adrian, who was then aged 13. She wrote to Dick: 'Perhaps you could ask Jeremy to let you have the names of their parents, so that I could write one day soon and tell them of our grief for them and our great debt of gratitude'.[41]

The Brigade Commander, Lieutenant Colonel Bridges would report on the success of the operation. 'It was carried out in the face of intense fire at short range from an LMG, rifles, and shotguns with the utmost bravery and determination. I consider it was undertaken in the highest traditions of our Corps.'[42]

During the morning, four RAF jets came sweeping down the river. 'Typhoons!' recalls Marine Laurie Russell. 'Great sight! Must put the fear of God into the Rebs!'[43] They circled the town for 15 minutes. More firing was heard.

However, as they would learn, the rebels would show determined resistance. Apprehending them would be a larger operation than the Marines were aware of at the time, and become guerrilla warfare.

Later that day, more of the Commando as well as members of 40 Commando came to relieve the men at Limbang. Few realised then, that their mopping-up process would mean sending scouting patrols into the hills and the jungle adjacent to the town, and broaden from there. Patrols would eventually reach the Temburong River, which was the river adjacent to the one by which they first reached Limbang. 'We were in jungle warfare at that stage', says one Marine, 'attempting to identify the whereabouts of all the Terrorists'.

The action at Limbang, as at Brunei, was to be the start of action that would keep troops engaged in Sarawak and North Borneo for the next four years.

The casualties and some civilians, including Dorothy, were evacuated on the 'Z' craft/*Fiskerton* at about 10.30 am. The wounded were laid out on the deck.[44] Fritz Klattenhoff rested himself against the side of the craft. Father Cronin was suffering from shock.[45] He was in no state to remain in Limbang, unlike the other two priests who did not leave the town. The craft was peppered with bullet holes, leaving those on board feeling exposed as they made their way to Brunei Town. It was unclear whether they may be shot at.

'I most clearly remember trying to crawl under a bulldozer on the deck of the Z craft on the advice of someone', recalls Dorothy, 'and then being advised not to do that by someone else, and finally being persuaded to go down into the engine room, where the walls were thicker and more likely to withstand possible fire from the shore. I wondered just how long I could keep my claustrophobia in check'. She was apprehensive about joining Peter Waters and the wounded on the bullet-riddled canvas-walled deck.

The men on board were solicitous of Dorothy. Lieutenant Down recalls that she gripped on to everything, as if to reassure herself that, yes, she was indeed on the boat, and alive.[46]

Dorothy told Dick later:

After I went aboard the Landing Craft at Limbang I didn't catch sight of you again, though I hung around at the blunt back end until we were about to take off, and then, on the advice of a Marine officer, Father and I went down to the engine room (imagine it!) and I stood just under the ladder so that I could see some light and air and keep the old claustrophobia in check more easily. We both prayed again – at least I did. Then when we were nearly to the border of Sarawak and Brunei one of the officers suggested we come up to the wheel-house and the fresh air. I wasn't awfully keen, but the Captain who had been wounded in the leg while on the bridge during the landing, and was getting about with a broom for a crutch [she meant Peter Waters] – well he assured me he was the world's biggest natural coward and if he was prepared to sit up there with only canvas around him I need have no fears. So I emerged, and they were all wonderful to us. Some Naval rum in a

Gordon's Gin bottle appeared, and we all took turns at taking a pull at it. I must say I didn't feel at all confident that someone might not be sitting up in a tree along the river banks somewhere waiting to pop off at us, but we did reach Brunei Town without incident.[47]

She appreciated the kindness shown to her by Lieutenant Willis and his men.[48]

'The Purser's rum helped no end', she said, 'and it was at least possible to relax a trifle. In fact the kindness and hospitality I received from the moment I stepped aboard that craft would have left Lady T standing, as would that which followed on board HMS *Fiskerton* at Brunei Town.'

Unexpected loud sounds threw her off guard, in an understandable nervous reaction. Harder to digest was 'the fact that our dear friendly Sarawak, with its neutral rivers, jungles, villages, suddenly became hostile and unfriendly'.[49] She was saddened that the traditional easy-going ways that typified Sarawak for her may never be quite the same again.

She would say at the end of December:

Whenever I remembered all that jungle up behind the
Residency and of what it held and could hold again, I feel
convinced I could never go back – and those long stretches
of river where we always waved to fellow voyagers – I'm sure
I could never travel happily on those again; where any bend
could produce some snipers, hoping to cover themselves in
honour and glory for the cause (what cause?).[50]

Ambulances and military personnel were on the wharf at Brunei, awaiting the arrival of the lighter. They did not know what to expect. Radio contact had been imperfect. Derek Oakley was with them. He had seen the lighters take off for Limbang the night before. It had been a long wait. 'We hadn't any idea of the wounded. Only the sick berth attendant, Terry Clarke, was with them. We had no idea what we were going to see or meet, how badly the wounded were or anything else!'[51]

The first lighter, without the tractors, arrived, with the dead and wounded lying on deck. Oakley found that his close friend Paddy Davis was severely wounded.

> He was very badly hit. He was shot in the back, and he vaguely recognised me. This was though we knew each other very well. He lived next door to me. We played in the same hockey team and saw a lot of each other. But he was badly hit. I didn't think he was going to make it.

> He was hit from the machine gun being fired at the boat, that was doing so much damage, and being fired by Salleh bin Sambas, the leader, who was an ex-policeman, a weapons training officer. It took him a long time to recover, six months. My wife had to tell his wife that he had been wounded. She had no idea how badly. Before she went to her – she told me after, that it was the only time of day when – she had a whiskey in the morning.[52]

Dorothy approached Oakley when she alighted. She wanted to get news to her children. She had written to them on the boat and needed to get the letters to them. Her presence of mind impressed Oakley.

> I had never met her before. When the boat came in from Limbang, I was standing there, watching it pull in. I suppose I must have looked official, as they came off the boat. And

Dorothy came up to me and said 'could you post these two letters to Geraldine and Adrian who both live in Australia?' The point is that she had already written the letters![53]

Dick remained in Limbang. The difficulty of communicating with Brunei was overcome by requisitioning the stock of car batteries in a Brunei garage and getting them by boat to Limbang.

Later that afternoon, Oakley accompanied Brigadier Patterson up the river to Limbang. They spent the afternoon on a debriefing, which Oakley describes. 'We spent a longish afternoon walking around and talking to the Marines, learning about what had happened and what was happening next.' Oakley then first met Dick, who confessed that, although 'the day passed comparatively quietly', he was feeling 'slightly frightened and rather shattered'.

Limbang was now a military zone, with sporadic firing as fugitive rebels tried to escape. Sergeant Wakeling's MMGs knocked out a rebel speed boat and its driver who tried to make a break for it from a riverside hide-out, some 300 yards up river. Men of 1/2 Gurkha Rifles were flown in. They patrolled the Limbang River in their assault boat, weapons at the ready.

Salleh bin Sambas, though wounded twice – in the arm and in the chest – escaped on a bicycle with his brother, Rosali bin Sambas, accompanying him. They rode to the ferry at Ujong Jalan, where they crossed the river by boat, and then made their way to Bangar, the small capital of the Temburong district.

It would take a few days more to clear the Limbang area of insurgents and settle it down. The offensive against remnants of the rebels would continue in the district for some time.

Restoring order in the town was essential. Fear and alarm among the townspeople created an immediate problem. Many sought refuge in the police station and hospital, and in shop-houses closest to the police station.[54] Most would shelter near these buildings for the next few days, needing food and water.

Dick found that his District Officer, kept captive in the District Office, was too badly shaken by his ordeal to return to work. Dick was thankful that two of the hostages remained with him. The Catholic priests, Irishman Father John Jackson and Dutch-born Father Joop Vaneman, refused to be evacuated, so as to help with the refugees. Dick describes how they organised themselves: 'Cpl Horn RM took over as Director of Hygiene and Sanitation and Father Jackson who had also been "let out" became Curator of Refugees – over three hundred of them – at the police station'. Dick had little time for reflection. 'There were other tasks too and one way and another the day passed with unbelievable rapidity.'[55]

Help came from Iban tribesmen. They appeared on the river, Union Jack flying proudly from their longboat. They brought in rebels whom they had captured 40 miles (64 kilometres) up river from Limbang. They handed the unharmed prisoners over to the Marines who had delivered Limbang a few hours before. They would be part of a Home Guard that voluntarily sprang up to assist the British. Their action was symbolically important and empowering for both the terrorised local population and for the Marines. 'I think', says Greenhough, 'some of us still had unvoiced fears of counter-attacks from some source or other before reinforcement for "L" Coy 42 Commando could arrive ... We had very little idea of what strength we had over here at that time.'[56]

'It was still difficult to believe that the worst was over, personally speaking', Greenhough reflected. 'Any sense of joy was tempered for us all, to one of quiet thankfulness, mixed with great sadness, and the consciousness of a debt we could never repay, by the presence of the dead and wounded around us.'

Though he did not know it at the time, Marine Mike Bell would find 'This was my only time in action. I was proud to take part in this raid but five men gave their lives.'[57]

8

THURSDAY, 13 DECEMBER: ENEMIES WITHIN

The evening before, with L Company secure in Limbang, Moore halted operations for the night. The Marines had known little sleep since the morning of 11 December. It was pointless to enter the bazaar during the night. The jungle reached right down to the backs of some of the buildings. It was clear that some rebels were hiding in its fringes. Some had been flushed out, within 15 or 20 yards of the hospital. So, with Limbang only partially cleared at that stage, Moore established a perimeter from the first east–west cross street of the bazaar, along a track through the edge of the jungle to the attap house, and then south past the jail, then west down to the river bank. It was manned by sections. 4 Troop held the forward perimeter. The river was covered by Company HQ and Sergeant Wakeling's Vickers machine guns. Marine Downey's LMG covered the road heading southeast. A sentry was posted on the LMG behind the hospital, which became headquarters for the Royal Marines and the civil administration.

Meanwhile, Police Constable Essa hoped that he could be freed from his hiding place in the roof of the police station. When the police were told to surrender on the previous Saturday morning, he had climbed up through a hatchway into the roof. He hid there for five days, able to drink from rainwater leaking from the roof, but without food. During that time, he observed through chinks in the hatch the rebel leaders beneath him. He emerged, on Wednesday evening, fearing that he might be mistaken for a rebel and be shot. Intelligence that he gave to Moore was invaluable, because he identified the rebels and their leaders whom he had watched. Moore applauded his courage: 'A tremendous effort! I take my hat off to that chap. He was a Malay. So he was a bit of a hero.'[1] He revealed a lot of information about what happened in the town, as did the interrogation of released hostages.

From his hiding place in the roof, he had heard the leaders on the evening of 11 December decide that the Morrises would be hanged the following morning. Had L Company arrived later than they did, it would have been too late.

The Marines also learned that the rebels had a fair amount of weaponry. Most were armed with shotguns, but they also had a Bren gun, Sterling machine guns and 15 rifles captured from the police, besides a variety of .22 rifles, muzzle-loading muskets and other weapons like parangs and daggers. The Bren gun and eight rifles were recaptured, and their main ammunition magazine was found in the police station. The Marines learned that the rebels were inexperienced. Two LMG magazines had been badly filled and one Sterling magazine was recovered with 30 rounds in it, all of them the wrong way round. 'Had they been correctly filled, in other words had the rounds or the bullets been put into the magazine in the correct way and used effectively, I doubt very much that we would have got onto shore', said Marine Greenhough.[2]

They bunkered down for the night in the hospital. 'Captain Jeremy Moore and a great many others, including myself, shared our prison of the night before', Dick recalls.

It was not a restful night and none of us I think got much

sleep. The rebels, who the morning before had taken refuge in the jungle, were pretty active. Some no doubt were anxious to get away, but many, very obviously, were still inclined to be aggressive. The night was interrupted at irregular but quite frequent intervals by shots and two '36s' went off less than a cricket pitch away from our cabin. Jeremy and I must have smoked a good hundred cigarettes between us that night and we didn't get much, maybe any, sleep. It had been a long long day.[3]

Moore reported that they spent 'an interesting night during which a number of enemy, who had clearly been lying low awaiting darkness, attempted to escape from within our perimeter'. Most succeeded in slipping away. Rebels fired on the L Company positions from the north. The sentries posted on the LMG behind the hospital shot at any movement. Two rebels were killed.

Much of this scuffling took place within fifty yards of the hospital and at the third grenade going off so close I was unkind enough to accuse the troop concerned of shooting at shadows. However, the following morning they produced a body ten yards from one of their LMGs to prove their point.[4]

The corpse was found at daybreak by 22-year-old Marine Ken Fyffe, of the Commando Intelligence Section. He found in the dead man's pockets

a tiny red plastic box about the size of a small eraser – in it was a miniature copy of the Koran – I felt remorse at that point; I suppose his need of spiritual reassurance paralleled my own needs … I kept that little Koran as a sad little reminder of friends I had lost and the futility of it all.[5]

That morning L Company continued the work of clearing the town. Their task became one of house clearing, with each shop-house checked in turn. Grenades could not be used as civilians, fearing for their lives, had barricaded themselves inside the locked shop-houses. It took them the full day to clear the western and eastern halves of the town.

K Company of 42 Commando arrived in Brunei in the early hours of Thursday morning in the *Woodbridge Haven*. They were given news of L Company's successful attack on Limbang. Later that morning, they embarked for Limbang with ammunition (303s and Carlsberg/Becks, noted one company member).[6] Haste and primitive conditions at Brunei called for improvisation, such as loading kit and supplies onto smaller boats from upended domestic tables.

Once in Limbang, K Company set to clearing the road from Limbang to Bangar (which M Company would occupy), thus linking the Commando's sub-units as they continued the offensive against remnants of the North Borneo rebels.[7] That night 42 Commando, with 621 Signals Troop (Air Support Signals Unit) attached, were complete in Limbang and K Company took over the perimeter for the night.

Upon arriving in Brunei, Dorothy had been taken to the home of the High Commissioner, Sir Dennis White, 'and just about cried on D's shoulder'. She received much sympathy from him. Most of White's working life had been in Sarawak, where he joined the service of the Rajah in 1932. He was one of the few experienced Brooke officers to have survived the Japanese Occupation, having been a civilian prisoner of war in Kuching between 1941 and 1945. White's good knowledge of the Dayak and Malay languages endeared him, like the Morrises, to local people.

Dorothy was given rest. 'I'm still finding it hard to believe that I can walk past a window without crouching. I still tend to "twitch" at the least sudden sound.'[8] She was put in the care of White's private secretary, Kay Petrie. 'We are surrounded by gurkhas!!' But it comforted her to see them, 'squatting, helmeted, still and wary, with machine guns at the ready'. She had seen firing from Kampong Ayer when on the *Fiskerton* and sporadic firing continued through the night.

White and Sir Alexander Waddell, the Governor, took her in hand. Nick Waddell (as he was known to family and friends), to Dorothy looking very weary and worried, also gave her support. He too knew about having to draw on inner strength. A Scottish-born son of the manse, he spent his war years with the Royal Australian Naval Volunteer Reserve. As a 'coastwatcher' on Choiseul Island in the Solomon Islands, he established a radio station overlooking Bougainville Strait to report on Japanese naval and air traffic. When the Japanese retook Guadalcanal in 1943, he was vulnerable on the island for 15 months, totally dependent on Solomon Islanders, both for food and his safety.

It was decided, she wrote to Dick, that she return to Kuching with Waddell and 'with my consent, which they feel sure you would prefer, I will then be sent down to Australia to be with the children. It has been generally agreed that the children not be brought up to Sarawak at all for their holidays.'

Up to then, the only news about Limbang was 'garbled and horrifying reports that the Brakes and others were to share the fate of the police'. She was anxious for news. She was pleased to receive 'the most wonderful news ... that Mrs Brake had arrived and was safe and well'.

She heard more about the uprising. On the following day, White sat next to the Sultan, who gave his first press conference after the collapse of the rebellion. White was a member of a 14-man emergency council which the Sultan established to run the protectorate.[9]

Dorothy learned that other hostages were taken elsewhere. She heard about the ordeals they had faced. The hostages and casualties with whom she returned to Brunei were evacuated, she told Dick. 'Nearly all Europeans here were taken to Labuan. So that, my dearest one, seems to be that.'

She worried about Dick. They had been together in Sarawak and Brunei for 16 years. 'You can imagine how I hate to be leaving you.' Unable to rejoin him in Limbang, returning to their children and family in Australia was her only course.

> There's so much to tell, and be told, but a long time till we
> can tell it. Already the edges are getting a wee bit blurred
> and I hope that the wonderful work you are doing up there
> is helping to blur it a little for you too. Longing to get more
> news of you, and of our friends, and 'friends'.

She asked him to thank all who had helped them. Dick sent her down some clothes; others lent her what she needed.

5 Troop received the brunt of fire in the battle at Limbang. It sustained five dead and four wounded, all the L Company casualties of the action save two.

The loss shocked the men. 'In terms of our own casualties we had five dead and quite a number of injuries', says Corporal David Greenhough. 'That is high. In later attacks or major battles my whole unit never encountered five fatalities, so this was heavy casualties for us.'[10]

It was the largest number of casualties suffered in a single day by the Corps between Korea in 1951 and the Falklands in 1982.

It took the men by surprise. As Greenhough puts it, 'I think it was primarily that we were not expecting it'. Having set out with scant intelligence, Greenhough thought that this left them unprepared for what followed. 'Had we been ready for an all-out, we would perhaps have been better off.'

He took stock of his reactions.

> There are many changes in mood. There is a standard fear
> which subsides. I remember well being frightened initially,
> but then as the adrenalin flowed and one is given an order
> to do something, i.e. land, elation starts and you are on
> a particular high. But then that goes, and it becomes a
> job; your training takes over, and you react. Not like an
> automaton, but certainly as a second nature of doing things.
> It suddenly comes flooding back into you: if somebody is
> firing at you and you are down, crawling and observing,
> you are doing it to perfection. I felt no feeling of elation on
> passing a dead enemy or an injured enemy. Rather, I thought
> of the utter waste of it. Obviously, I felt great sympathy for
> personal colleagues who I knew had been injured or killed.[11]

'The one person I felt particularly sorry for', says Greenhough, 'was "Scouse" Kierans'. Greenhough's friend, Marine Gerald Kierans, was 22 when he died. He had joined the Corps four years earlier, was qualified in Naval Gunnery, and joined the Commando in July 1962. He was killed as his craft approached the shore. 'A marine I knew very well', reflects Greenhough.

He was the unluckiest person I ever met. You get this in all walks of life. He arrived in Singapore in May; his kit arrived in August. When he got off the aircraft at Singapore, he fell and broke his arm. In fact he had only just got out of plaster. Misfortune troubled him from whenever. I felt very badly about 'Scouse'.

Greenhough thought of Kierans's mother in Widnes, a Merseyside centre for the manufacture of chemicals.

On reflection, it is very difficult to say one gets hardened to death or injury. I suppose you get hardened or you harden yourself; it is not a conditioning process, it is a case of hardening yourself.

We have a very old saying in the services that exercises are made to be boring so that the real thing comes as blessed relief. In active service, while there is the remote possibility of attracting some reaction or response to your being there, a lot of the time is spent in routine after routine. And it is only by continuing in this particular task that the opposition sees there is no point in going on. So therefore a lot of *that* wins battles rather than the actual direct attack.

Anger to me is an emotion which is a luxury. I get more angry at what I see as waste: people revolting at something they can do something about. In the Service, with somebody firing at you, anger will not help you. If you are in a particular task of aggression, you cannot afford anger.

In Singapore, David Formoy's young widow was in shock. She and their baby were flown home to relatives in Deal, Kent.

Lieutenant Colonel Robin Bridges reported that the successful action at Limbang undoubtedly broke the back of enemy resistance throughout the Limbang and Temburong districts, and saved casualties which would have occurred if the enemy had continued to hold Bangar.[12] He quickly appreciated that, together with the Gurkha actions in Brunei Town and the landing by the Queen's Own Highlanders at Miri, the victory at Limbang broke the rebellion completely in the first few days.

At Limbang, the insurgents were subjected, for the first time, to devastating MMG fire, and heavy fire from all company weapons. They met head-on the speed, mobility, surprise and firepower that characterised Commando operations. The news of the defeat of the strong rebel garrison at Limbang by an under-strength company group spread quickly. Rebel garrisons everywhere left their posts and withdrew rapidly into the jungle. L Company's action at Limbang changed the course of operations decisively.[13]

Fifteen insurgents were killed during the battle. Initially, 11 prisoners were taken, of whom three were wounded. However, many more were taken or surrendered subsequently. Yet most of their leaders remained at large.

The Commander-in-Chief Far East Land Forces, General Sir Nigel Poett, announced at a press conference that the first phase of the Brunei rebellion had collapsed.[14]

However, as British and Gurkha troops recaptured rebel-held towns like Limbang, Lawas, Seria and adjacent Kuala Belait, insurgents withdrew into the interior. British troops now needed to fan out to prevent this.

For the men of L Company in Limbang, it was operations as usual. Their efforts went to hunting down the Limbang insurgents and TNKU leaders. 'After the Limbang assault itself things came back to a form of Royal Marine norm', David Greenhough recalls. 'It would appear that the uprising had served its purpose or died a natural death.'[15] L Company fanned out through the district in jungle patrols, and engaged with the local population, gaining intelligence and enlisting support. 'You satisfy some people that all is well, that the terrorists had left that area and were no longer a nuisance.'

There was still no accurate estimate of the strength of the total rebel force. At the time, this was roughly guessed at around 2000. Of these, 250 were taken prisoner. Mainly equipped with rifles and shotguns, they were clearly surprised by the swift arrival and bold tactics of the British troops.

'The terrorists were caught by members of the company', says Greenhough. The Temburong District Commander, Salleh bin Kerdin, was arrested.[16] Salleh bin Sambas was running. Unknown to British command, he was lying low, living on sweet potatoes and rice with a party of 60 rebels, not far from Temburong's Batang Duri, between Limbang and Bangar, where the local people were thought to be more friendly towards them.

The efforts of the British military forces also went to restoring normal conditions, working jointly with the civil administration. Asked whether there was the possibility of the rebellion dragging out into guerrilla warfare, General Poett replied, 'It is difficult to tell at this stage. Our counter action and build-up have been swift and if our operations continue at this speed we may very well avoid this danger.'[17]

On 13 December 1962, none could predict the difficulties that lay ahead.

9

DECEMBER AND BEYOND

The rebellion was contained and broken in Brunei by 17 December. Some 40 rebels were dead and some 3000 captured. The remainder had fled or melted away. Azahari was in the Philippines and Yassin Affandy among the fugitives. Many spread into Sarawak, some perhaps trying to reach Indonesia to escape. Speaking over Radio Brunei, Sultan Sir Omar Ali Saifuddin said he would show clemency 'to all of you who have been misled'.[1] The Sultan called for a return to the forces of law and order. 'There must be no more resistance, no more bloodshed', he urged.

Brigadier Glennie handed over command to Major General Walter Walker, who assumed the newly created post of Director of Operations and Commander of British Forces, Borneo Territories. Newspapers reported that in Walker the rebels could expect a formidable foe. He masterminded the organisation and training of Malaya's jungle fighters, who had spearheaded the destruction of the Malayan Communist Party's military arm. Now 50, he was an experienced counter-terrorist commander.

The Sarawak Government faced the problem of insurgents and rebels who were driven out of Brunei State taking refuge in Sarawak and going underground. A massive operation was under way to flush fugitive rebels from their jungle hide-outs. Military spokesmen reported that the main rebel strength was now concentrated in the jungles around Limbang (as well as Lawas and Bangar, straddling the border between Brunei and Sarawak). The mopping-up operations by the Marine Commandos, Gurkha troops and Sarawak Rangers went into full swing in the Limbang–Lawas–Bangar area where about 1000 rebels were believed to have gone to ground or were making their way to the Indonesian border.

Crossings into Sarawak were easily made from Indonesian Borneo across the porous border. Insurgents could destabilise Sarawak's internal security, and threaten the safety of its people. They had to be rooted out.

'It was a matter of searching for them', says Marine Laurie Russell. 'We had pictures of who we were looking for and kept searching through areas where they were suspected to be hiding to see if we could find them.'[2] The Marines were soldiering in rugged terrain. Local Ibans, masters at visual tracking, helped the Marines. 'They knew the way. They knew the tracks. I had an Iban attached to my Troop. Fabulous fellow.'[3]

Helicopters from the aircraft carrier HMS *Albion* transported 450 Commandos to strengthen local forces on the Sarawak–Indonesian border and keep a close watch on insurgent activities there. Sarawak welcomed troops like these. As the *Sarawak Tribune* put it, 'Their presence is not to start a war but to give us confidence and strength and to ensure that we are able to proceed without interference on our own way of choosing our own government'.[4]

Moving into the jungle to flush out rebels, Commandos were backed by the Sarawak Government's efforts to undermine rebel support by the use of radio. Isolated outlying communities were kept informed of the emergency as it developed, and of progress made in talks about Malaysia. Radio Sarawak at Kuching broadcast in English, Chinese and Malay, and occasionally in Dusun and Iban. Hearts and minds would be reached in the remote jungle areas, and rebels would be captured.

The front page of *The Straits Times* for 15 December, continuing full coverage of the crisis, featured Indonesian official denial of involvement in the revolt. Dr Subandrio, Indonesia's Deputy Prime Minister, Foreign Minister and intelligence chief, said that if Indonesia was accused too much over the Brunei Revolt, 'she will get very angry'. Subandrio, a skilled political manipulator, refused to comment on Azahari's threat to use Indonesian volunteers. Azahari was reported to have asked three Indonesian political groups offering him volunteers 'to stand by but not to take action for the present'.

Radio Sarawak broadcast that Azahari appealed to 'peace-loving nations' for assistance – when his rebellion had collapsed. It declared that what Azahari achieved was to make it glaringly obvious there could be no possible satisfactory alternative to Malaysia.

It seems now to be perfectly understood why Azahari
and his political associates in Sarawak were demanding
independence before Malaysia, which, of course, meant out
of Malaysia. It is difficult to find any remaining doubts on
this score and for this reason alone the rebel leader, Azahari,
has defeated the very cause he claimed to promote.[5]

On 17 December, during the visit to Indonesia of the Vice President of Yugoslavia, Edvard Kardelj, President Sukarno took the opportunity to praise the Brunei Revolution. Sukarno called the Brunei Revolution a manifestation of the New Emerging Forces in the struggle against colonialism and imperialism.

Talks went ahead in Kuala Lumpur despite the emergency. The final details for the formation of Malaysia were expected to be mapped out during the Inter-Governmental Committee's plenary session. As Sir John Martin put it, 'All the delegations are determined to press on and not allow events in Brunei to mar the talks'.[6] He was central to the three-day meeting.

He wrote to Dick:

You and Dorothy have seldom been out of my thoughts in these last few days and I have been miserable with anxiety for you. There are no details yet, but you must have had a frightful ordeal and I do hope you are both none the worse for it and that the same goes for all the members of the little European community and James Wong and his friends.[7]

Over the radio all the time, recalls Marine Bell from 42 Commando, could be heard the jingle 'Merger and Malaysia as sure as the sun rises, Merger and Malaysia as sure as time goes by'.[8]

News of the ordeal endured by 'white hostages' was spread over the front pages of newspapers worldwide.[9] The press sensationalised rebel intentions and incorrectly portrayed Dick as being found with the noose around his neck. According to RAF sources, the rebels were 'at the stage of looking for a tree to hang Mr Morris from' when four RAF jet fighters hurtling low over Limbang caused the rebels to take off and gave Dick, 'left with the rope still around his neck', a chance to escape.[10] Closer to the truth was the report from Labuan on the front page of *The Straits Times*. This read that the Hawker Hunter pilots were cock-a-hoop to know their flying had been effective as they had been feeling more than a little out of things because they had not been allowed to fire on any targets and had been restricted to low-level buzzing of targets. Indeed, *The Straits Times* carried a small column rebutting the report of the RAF saving Dick. The battle of Limbang, read the column, was over in 45 minutes and well before the RAF arrived. This column carried the by-line 'RM

Wives'.[11] Dorothy confirmed that the RAF story was completely untrue.[12]

With Limbang still cut off by phone, letters flowed into the Residency. Close friends caring for Dorothy in Kuching told Dick:

> Dorothy, bless her, has told us the story of your ordeal and I realize just what hell you have gone through. Lack of news at this end was terrible and we can only say Thank God that the final news of you two was good news. We do hope your area will be cleared very soon as we don't like to hear news that the rebels are still around.[13]

In Kuching, Dorothy was overwhelmed by the kindness shown to her.

> I can't remember all the local people who have greeted me and said they couldn't sleep but just cried for us, and then prayed to *Tuhan* for us. Pangkalan Batu police station was always a long stop. Dear old Manoor – Jaker's *sais* rushed across the Secretariat parking lot, and took my hands, with tears running and no words coming.[14]

Dorothy's five-day ordeal was detailed in the newsletter issued by the Sarawak Information Service, *Sarawak by the Week*. Her thoughts were for others. 'I should like to stress the courage and devotion of the small police detachment', she said, 'which helped out against greatly superior forces for as long as possible'. To Dick, she wrote: 'My love and thanks to those Chinese who sent us food. I would so love to know how some of our guards fared, who appeared to be sympathetic to us. I'd hate to think that was an act.'[15]

She was incorrectly reported in the local press as being in Brunei Hospital recovering. 'Recovering from SHOCK', she exclaimed. 'What rubbish!' She spent two days in Brunei with Sir Dennis White 'while plans were being hatched for my removal to Kuching by the flight which was conveying Sir Alexander Waddell back after a brief visit to Brunei'. She returned to Kuching with him on 14 December, 'sniping going on around the air field' and 'the airport stiff with troops and arms'.[16]

There she stayed with very old and dear friends, John and Kay Williams, while flights were being checked which might convey her to Sydney and to the children. Williams worked in the Secretariat, assisting Jakeway. On her arrival, Mahomet Yen, their Malay cook, welcomed Dorothy warmly. 'He was keen to hear all the details which I could supply', she said.[17] 'He was an excellent boy of rather solemn countenance, and normally dead-pan expression, but devoted and loyal and hardworking.' The Williamses decided the occasion called for celebration. When John asked Yen where he put the champagne, the reply came: 'I took the bottle outside, to the back garden so that when I drew the cork the pop wouldn't startle the Mem'.

For some time after the events of Limbang, Dorothy said, 'I did tend to jump a trifle at the sound of back-firing cars'.

She flew to Sydney on 18 December, the events still sharply in her mind. A letter to her captured the emotions she felt.

> Phew, thank goodness that's over! I could never imagine that
> a week could last so long … I expect the reaction afterwards
> was probably worse than at the time. It was very sad that so
> many of our chaps should have lost their lives – coming in
> from the jetty, they were sitting ducks.[18]

Dorothy wrote to Dick en route from Darwin, 'I still can't believe that these horrors are really a thing of the past'.[19]

As one letter writer expressed it, 'It is dreadful to think that undesirable elements can spoil things in such a delightful country with wonderful people'.[20] Another read:

> I can only hope that the holiday at home with the children
> will help to remove the memory of the nightmare you have
> been through. I am so sorry that poor Dick has to stay in
> Limbang instead of coming with you to spend Christmas
> with the children. It will be extremely bleak for him. One of
> the many occasions on which one wishes that one had gone
> in for a different career.[21]

Kindness helped her come to terms with their experiences. She wrote to Dick, 'Our friends of all races have been so wonderful to me and send so many messages to you. We can never repay them for what they've done to get me back to a relaxed and even keel'.[22]

The shock and strain of those past days on family and friends is evident in their letters. Friends wrote from Moss Vale, 77 miles (124 kilometres) southwest of Sydney: 'Thank God Britain arrived in the nick of time'.[23] Dick and Dorothy's deliverance overjoyed Dorothy's elderly mother and Dorothy's sister, Carol Helm.

> We do hope and pray you are not suffering a relapse after
> the great strain of it all. Mother is alright so you must not
> worry about her. The reaction after learning you were safe
> had her feeling sick but she really is better today. There is so
> little to say when all you feel is relief.[24]

Many letters told the Morrises 'how much we admire your bravery and respect you for the truly magnificent way you came through that ordeal'.[25] Many congratulated them on their remarkable escape. They described how Kuching responded to news of their release. 'The cries of joy when the news of the relief of Limbang came through (sounds rather like Mafeking Night and we all felt much the same) could almost have been heard in Limbang itself.'[26] Others dwelt on the toll that the ordeal could take. They acknowledged 'it will take quite a time to recover from the strain'.

Many still tried to make sense of the events. 'We've had very little news of what really happened – whether you were ill-treated or not – don't even know who was imprisoned with you, but I expect James Wong would have been grabbed with you', wrote Phyllis Jacks, who had lived in Limbang when her husband was the Resident there in the 1950s.

> I was astonished to learn that you were in Limbang at all, and it's my guess that Dick was sent there in anticipation of trouble from the bloody Bruneians. I keep wondering how many local people were involved – they were more Brunei types than Sarawakian in the Kampongs – Sheikh Salleh was in it up to his neck. I never trusted that bastard.[27]

Others looked beyond the euphoria. 'You will feel for a bit, Dorothy, that you never want to see the place again. I do hope you will be able to get well away from Borneo for a couple of weeks until the nightmare seems less acute.'[28] One wrote to Dorothy from Kuching, 'I purposely didn't bother you while you were in Kuching – I know you must have needed to be quiet'. She learned of Dorothy's departure for Sydney on Monday.

I took it for granted it was going to be the Viscount at 6 pm, and took myself off to the airport, armed with the most beautiful bunch of orchids for you. I looked a real Charlie when they told me you had gone in the afternoon – there I was with me flowers and no one to give them to ... forget this place for a while ... and keep smiling.[29]

A more sober note reached Dick. This came from one of his colonial service colleagues who had been detained as a Japanese prisoner of war and had been unable wholly to put his ordeal behind him. He warned, 'I doubt whether the thought of the past experience will ever be forgotten by you two'. He advised Dick, 'I do hope that your wife has since got over the effect and if not, I would advise her to consult a doctor and don't delay as so many of us did in the old days. May the new year bring us some peace.'[30]

In Limbang, the aim was to restore normality as quickly as possible, but armed rebels in the immediate vicinity made this difficult. As Dick put it, 'The civil population, including the majority of Government servants, are still very much afraid of the rebels, even though they have not made any attempt to carry out acts of terrorism'. Curfew was imposed. All-night patrols and watches were in force – 'that make our eyes disappear into the back of our heads', said the troops.

Dick added:

Rumours have been rife and a considerable amount of time has had to be devoted to dealing with these. These rumours usually take the form of a report that an enemy group proposed to attack the houses of Government servants or people living on the outskirts of Limbang, or alternatively that they will ambush the roads, or that they will attempt to steal food from houses. These rumours gained some strength from the fact that in Lawas a man was murdered in his house by rebels seeking food.[31]

Dick received letters commiserating on his detention. One said: 'It has brought it home to all of us what an extremely cut off place is Limbang, quite hopeless to defend unless you have a strong resident force'.[32] Security issues were not the only ones that Dick faced. With river access under military patrols, food was in short supply. The Royal Marines took charge of distributing limited supplies.

Commandos moving into the jungle to flush out rebels were now assisted by helicopters brought in by HMS *Albion*. Wessex helicopters increased the mobility of the commandos, ferrying men and ordnance. However, travelling lightly proved best when on the ground, on the few and inadequate roads and through the heavy jungle terrain. 'Our time went to foot patrols, all over the place, into the jungle, following reports where people were', said Marine Genge. 'We had to try to find them. We were after the main leader of the rebels, in patrols of seven marines and a corporal, with special orders where to go and what to look for.'[33] Commandos were also helped by the Sarawak Rangers with their dogs.

Security forces patrolled upriver to intercept rebels fleeing from Brunei. Surrenders occurred over 17 and 18 December, including one man surrendering to a helicopter.[34] He was among 41 more prisoners brought into Limbang, where over 100 prisoners were now held. Some were believed to be TNKU leaders.

Commando helicopter activities caused Salleh bin Sambas to move furtively at night from his hiding place to the Sarawak side of the Pandaruan River, returning to his father's house. He hid in a nearby hillside, accompanied by his brother and fed by his father for about a month, until troops searching the area made his hide-out insecure. He moved to Yassin Affandy's hide-out on the Pulau Kibi. Parties from this group who were sent out for food were captured.

Prisoners were vital to gaining information that could assist in the mopping-up operations. One Marine described the task of questioning prisoners. 'Sgt Smith, the "I" Sgt, he lately consumed a daily diet of an average of 20 prisoners a day, a monstrous interrogation machine, which could be heard around the clock.'[35] Many of the captured were dazed and appeared completely bewildered with little idea of what they had been trying to do or what they took up arms for. It became known that large numbers of rebels had been misled and threw away their arms.[36]

David Greenhough was among Marines who were assigned to guard over prisoners. He was struck by how demoralised they seemed.

> To actually see the people that evoked all this action, one looks at them, and says, well, was it really worth it for all the loss and everything else? All Malays are quite small of stature and they were just dejected, very dejected, having been captured. Now, detained themselves, they were awaiting whatever the end result was.[37]

Information from the prisoners, besides from voluntary informers or from evidence found on troop patrols, provided a clearer picture of the overall size and fighting power of the insurgents. The police learned the names of rebel divisional commanders. Leaflets with their photographs and information about them were dropped by air into remote communities. Loudhailers on vehicles, boats and voice aircraft were used to try to persuade the rebels to hand themselves in.

Most of the prisoners found in the Limbang District were Kedayans, one of the smaller ethnic groups in Borneo, with smaller numbers of Brunei Malays.[38] Of lower social rank than the Malays, Kedayans are said to be of Javanese origin and are mainly found in the southwestern parts of North Borneo. They were believed to form the majority in the insurrection. When evaluating the revolt a year later, Tom Harrisson, Sarawak's leading ethnologist, pointed out that the Kedayans numbered only about 10 000 in Sarawak. He said that if the revolt had taught anything from an ethnological point of view, it was 'that you cannot afford to ignore small racial groups'. He pointed to how the Kedayans 'have not been taken into account. There are practically no responsible Kedayans in any positions. They are not adequately represented in government.'[39] He warned that this observation also applied to larger groups, like the cohesive Chinese in Sarawak.

Dick learned how many in Limbang were complicit in the revolt. 'It now seems fairly certain that virtually all Malays and Kedayans in Limbang district had a foreknowledge of the intended rebellion. This knowledge in some cases appears to have been quite detailed. Despite this no information was passed either to the Police or to myself.'[40]

More worryingly, as he wrote:

There are some grounds for believing that some civil servants knew of the proposed rebellion, but despite investigations it is unlikely that we shall ever ascertain how much they really knew. The Chairman of the Limbang District Council made a comment which may be an indication of local feeling. When questioned, he said: '*Orang sudah bali dua ticket* (Bet a bob each way)'.

Help came to Dick with Terry Weekes, formerly stationed in the Fifth Division, and until recently District Officer in Simanggang, 340 miles (550 kilometres) south. His wife, Mickie Weekes, wrote to Dorothy from there. She gave Dorothy a picture of how the country was overrun. Fear of insurgency had spread beyond the Fifth Division. 'We have plenty of Army buzzing around, especially in the ulu where the majority of the hardcore rebels are fleeing', wrote Mickie.[41] 'We have 100 Home Guard parading Simanggang for 24 hours, and yesterday several trucks of Army personnel moved in. I suppose they will be relief for jungle work.' She added, 'Personally I don't think the Brunei Government are capable of putting their house in order – especially with such a pusillanimous Sultan'.

Clearing the wreckage of battle in Limbang and elsewhere, the heroism of the local police force became better appreciated. It was learned that, had the police at Kuala Belait surrendered, the rebels would have seized 'an arsenal of modern arms and at least 100 000 rounds of ammunition as well as gas grenades, armoured vehicles, and other key weapons'.

Pride was also taken in the Limbang Group of the Red Cross for the tireless and determined way in which it responded to the turn of events. Abang Omar and Kathleen Brake, together with Mohammed Edin and Inche Kasim, were especially praised. Omar, who was entirely loyal to the Sarawak Government, returned to his postmaster duties, and assisted as an interpreter with the respective British services during the following months of their operations around Limbang.

Lima Company of 42 Commando remained in Limbang until mid-January, when it moved east to Bangar, from which the Commando continued the mopping up and search for terrorists in the surrounding district. A Marine described the daily activity there: 'The helicopters land, as always, on the *padang*, driving locals into shelter and covering the town in dust. Craft of all types, from large unwieldy Z-craft to tippy dugouts with outboard engines tie up at the jetty to the muddy river.'[42]

The usually quiet district was a hive of activity. 'All over this county, day patrols are setting out and night ambushes are returning.' No. 5 Troop, commanded by Lieutenant Davis who was wounded at Limbang, was now under the command of Sergeant L Poole.

> They have returned to the company from the wilds of
> Batang Duri with the addition of a dog. 'K' Company, is also
> based here, widely spread out along the banks of the rivers
> Pandaruan and Temburong.

> If you look at the battle maps in the Ops Room here, and
> draw lines out to all locations, 42 Commando would represent
> a huge octopus, squatting firmly on the central rivers, its
> suckers thrust out to the northern coast of Lawas, the western
> river port of Limbang, the deep jungle to the south bordering
> to Indonesia. Up and down these tendrils pass the supplies
> and reinforcements, communications and patrols helicopter
> borne, river borne, in landrovers, and on foot.[43]

Locals and troops worked side by side. Royal Marines and the jungle-trained Gurkha Brigade garrisoned at Limbang built friendships with the local people throughout the Fifth Division. Sergeants mended sewing machines, others repaired outboard motors for longboats. Their mechanical ability was sought after for all sorts of repair jobs, which won over the local community. They taught village folk how to go about draining the areas around the longhouses and how to attend to minor medical requirements. Major General Walker summarised the result in March 1963, saying, '… the people are regarding the soldier as the chap to see when they need help'.[44] The confidence of the local people was severely shaken by the revolt, but it was gradually restored by the servicemen's spirit of friendliness and practical helpfulness.

This was vital when Indonesia began guerrilla raids into Borneo from April 1963. British Borneo territories became a target for Indonesian ambitions. Inspecting the Serian district, 40 miles (64 kilometres) from Kuching where a company from 40 Commando was stationed, General Walker found 'the people are very scared', anticipating trouble from armed raiders. Despite Walker's assurances, 'the towkays still dare not sleep in their respective shop-houses during night time'.[45]

Help with the challenging operational logistics came from the locals, such as with man-packing stores and equipment. Particular help to the patrols came from Iban trackers with local knowledge. They had shown their value in Malaya, where Ibans from Sarawak were attached to every fighting patrol and demonstrated their phenomenal ability to track where people had been. 'They could tell how long ago a particular track had been used, by how many people, which direction', said a Marine with 42 Commando in Malaya. 'They seem to have a sixth sense and could feel the presence of the terrorists and they were extremely useful.'[46]

The Marines were engaged in a silent and deadly game of cat-and-mouse. To set ambushes, they had to blend into the environment (as did their enemy), to move about quietly and to develop their sense of sight, hearing and smell. They could leave no trace of their presence (burying all their rubbish) as they combed through the jungle for tracks or signs of the enemy's presence. They drew on jungle warfare skills, and in developing these they learned additional fighting skills.

The men were in a state of constant preparedness. Tension was part of the everyday. One Marine wit pictured the strain of always being on the ready:

Twas the night before Christmas, and all thru the bash
Was the odour of 'Tommy Cooker's, but none of a rasha
The weary Marines were sacked out in their beds
And visions of home danced in their heads.
When out in the ulu, there arose such a clatter,
Sgt Shail's machine-gun had started to chatter.
I rushed to my rifle and threw back the bolt;
The rest of the lads awoke with a jolt.
We tumbled outside in a swirl of confusion,
So scared that each man could have used a transfusion.
'Get out in the ulu and silence that Reb,
And don't come back till you're sure that he's dead.'
Putting his hand in front of his nose,
Cpl King took leave of us shivering Joes;
But we all heard him say, in a voice soft and light,
'Merry Christmas all, may you live thru the night.[47]

Yet it became clear to the Marines they were achieving results, restoring the land to its own. 'It would be hard to complete a day's march in any part of this area without being constantly aware of the green beret.'[48]

They adjusted to local customs that were adapted to the equatorial rainforest environment, such as going about scantily clothed. They acclimatised to the enervating steamy conditions. A Situation Report for a troop on longhouse patrol noted that 'way out in the wilds their sitrep might have read "the constant presence of near naked females is distracting to military efficiency", and we thought they were chasing rebels!'[49] One Marine observed:

To quote the old saying, 'when in Rome do as the Romans do', could be aptly applied to the Borneo Bootneck who could be seen often, clad in jungle green shirt, sarong and wielding an evil looking parang, which as you could imagine, was not the general rig of the day.[50]

Indeed they were under strict dress orders. Marine William Ewing, from K Company, described the encounter. 'Living amongst a people who lead a life completely different to your own, you will find strange at first, but with a little understanding either way, you settle down to life sharing each other's way of living as a matter of course.'[51] Children swarmed around them, 'uncontrollable after their long confinement', once curfews were lifted. Men on various patrols, who disappeared into the *ulu*, gained in the process. 'So far they have all returned far fitter than they went out and with tales of the wonderful longhouses and their even more wonderful inhabitants.'[52]

Villagers were grateful they could go about their lives without fear of being terrorised. The troops dispensed medical treatment that would otherwise not have been available, conducting medical evacuations that saved lives. They received a few unusual requests. 'One of these was a request from the Sarawak Agricultural Department to move a swineherd and 12 pigs from Kuching to Limbang, a distance of 450 miles [725 kilometres].'[53] It was hoped the pigs would be airlifted by helicopter. 'Regrettably we were not able to comply, but this was about the only request that we haven't been able to fulfil.'

As they restored calm, most Marines found their experience in Borneo made deep impressions on them. They encountered a grace of living in the people they met.

Squatting in longhouses after wet patrols, sipping coffee and surrounded by countless children, and suddenly being made 'to feel at home', though as a complete stranger you had just walked in uninvited. This is one important thing you learn, amongst the Iban, Malay and Murut peoples, community life is shared, to walk into a strange household, sit and eat, is the done thing, for a people who live together and work together, this life of complete unselfishness is a lesson for people all over the world.[54]

From Sydney, Dorothy wrote to Dick:

I would give almost anything to see you again but realise I must be patient and I never cease to recall how God did come to our aid, as well as those wonderful troops. Still don't feel one little bit drawn to Limbang except for your presence there and of course to be able to say thank you to the Commandos and the Red Cross and those others who kept our morale up and our tummies full. Give them all my thanks and my love.[55]

His letter to her on 19 December informs her of developments in Limbang. 'Where does one begin? We have had our alarums and excursions but all is now more or less quiet. A burst of m.g. fire last night at – you guessed it – a pig or *bruang*. Over 200 prisoners taken in Limbang and the place nearly back to normal.'[56]

On the morning of their release, there had been little opportunity to speak to each other. Dick wrote now:

I didn't have time to tell you very much before you left but all I do have to say can't be said here. I can however say a little. I've always loved you and it would not be possible to love you more than I do but if ever there was a time when my love is greater than it is possible, it was during these days. Your guts and your faith and your strength were the things that kept me going. And darling, your guts when the metal started to fly was magnificent. When you started on the dressings with the wounded and the dead around you, I could have burst and sung with pride.

His thoughts were also for others. 'There is one task more that I must ask of you and that is letters to the next of kin. I also will write but it may be some time before I can get round to it.' He enclosed a list of addresses.

Dick juggled civil administration with military requirements. On 15 December, Dick, Jeremy Moore and several other Royal Marines returned up the hill to the Residency. They repaired the damage left by the rebels.

> The Residency is now the officers mess of 'Limbang Coy' 42 Commando RM and as you can imagine we get on very well together and it is wonderful to have them here. Light is on so they get a hot bath which they regard as the very height of luxury. Jeremy Moore is in Geraldine's room with 2nd Lieut Derek Lamb (just 19 years) and the others in Adrian's room. They refused point blank to share ours and said that I at least was entitled to some privacy.[57]

> We have had our visits from various Brass. Brigadier Barton, Commander of the Third Commando Brigade, Royal Marines and Lieutenant Colonel Bridges, Commanding Officer of 42 Commando, visited Limbang in the morning. Admiral Sir David Luce, British Commander-in-Chief,

together with Brigadier Glennie visited in the afternoon.[58]

Border patrols were deployed along the Sarawak–Indonesian border. Reuters reported that a company of Gurkhas was airlifted into Tawau, the North Borneo port close to the Indonesian border.

Security remained sensitive as through late December a nervous cat-and-mouse game was played between Indonesia and Britain and its supporters. Already anxious about how the emergency in Borneo might affect moves towards independence for Malaysia, they waited to see how Indonesia might act upon the threats it made.

On 21 December, Sultan Sir Omar Ali Saifuddin suspended the September 1959 written Constitution under powers granted him under the Constitution. He dissolved the state's 33-member Legislative Council and appointed a new Emergency Council, over which he would preside.

Over Radio Sarawak, Sir Alexander Waddell assessed the events of the last ten days 'not as a record of police, military, Home Guard and volunteer operations ... but in terms of human endeavour and of the outstanding courage, initiative and loyalty with which the people reacted to the threats to our country'. He summed up, 'this has not only been an emergency: it has been a test of loyalties and integrity'.[59]

He singled out the courageous deeds at Limbang. He noted the bravery of the police who defended the station to the last.

Then there is the Postmaster who gathered his group of Red Cross in makeshift uniforms, tended the wounded and brought food and comfort to those captured and defied the rebels to interfere with their brave and humane work. And there are the people from the bazaar who stood firm and brought aid and comfort. And upriver longhouses defiantly flying home made Union Jacks in the path of retreating rebels.

The steadfast and loyal conduct of many at Limbang was notable. Government staff stayed at their posts and kept essential services running and members of the public enlisted in large numbers in the newly raised Home Guard.

In London the House of Commons was told that the rebels' coup had been frustrated, organised resistance had ceased and order was largely re-established. Life was returning to normal in the towns and villages. Rebel activity was confined to certain rural areas. Seven British servicemen were killed and 28 wounded.[60]

In Limbang, river transport was re-established, with supplies coming in regularly. Dick paid tribute to the efforts of the Public Works Department, who promptly saw that all transport needs were met. Divisional Engineer Joseph King Shih Fan, who had been held hostage with the Morrises, had with his men in Limbang 'virtually erased all signs of damage done during the fighting'.

'Nevertheless', Dick said, 'the situation is far from normal in the hardcore rebel areas along the Pandaruan Road where some of the Kedayan villages remain virtually deserted. Steps are being taken to call these people back to their homes from their hiding places.'[61]

There were by then over 100 prisoners still held in Limbang. They were believed to include some TNKU leaders. 'A large number of suspects are still held in Limbang and more have been taken to Brunei. Hai Bakar, of Kampong Epai, and his people have brought in approximately 80 suspects, including a leading Kedayan who is alleged to have played an important role in the attack on Limbang.' Kampong Epai was just over 12 miles (19 kilometres) from Limbang.

Further afield, in the Fourth Division, interrogation of prisoners revealed that most of the rebels had been recruited within the past two months.[62] As was discovered in Limbang, they were demoralised. When interviewed, a captured rebel leader, 'General' Momin bin Ahmad, told his interrogators that he was fed up. He blamed Azahari. He said, 'Azahari tricked us all into this rebellion. Azahari has played us out.'[63]

The massive operation under way to flush fugitive rebels from their jungle hide-outs was achieving results. By the end of the week, civil administration was functioning normally in Limbang town, but the curfew remained in force. Firing broke out overnight on 19 December in Limbang when security forces guarding the radio tower on the hill behind the Residency detected people moving there. Intensive patrolling continued in the District. Dick announced that, 'A number of rebels however, still remain at liberty'.[64]

For the Marines who were on patrol, it was clear that it would be a strictly operational Christmas and New Year. For most Marines, North Borneo was an unforgettable experience. Looking back, as the *Globe & Laurel* recounted, 'We know our presence has raised the morale of remote and forgotten areas of Borneo, and that practically all the people we met there are enthusiastically on our side'.

Close friendships had developed between Dick and the Royal Marines. A memento of this remained when L Company left Limbang. The number one estaminet, most favoured by the company, was re-christened the 'Bonnet and Sonnet', with a swinging sign that Dick produced. While the sign was hung in their honour, most Marines thought it referred to Dick's announcing to the Marines his whereabouts and that of his co-hostages in the hospital, to the tune of 'She'll be Coming 'Round the Mountain' and the words 'they'll be wearing light green bonnets, but they won't be singing sonnets'. To Dick, it referred also to their Company Commander, Captain Jeremy Moore, producing for him an edition of William Shakespeare's Sonnets.

Writing to Dorothy he said, 'During the last couple of days I have had two good night's sleep and now feel as fit as a fiddle – my only sorrow is that Christmas will be a little lonely. Jeremy too may have gone and that will make it worse – *Apa boleh buat* (too bad).'[65]

The Indonesians would step up operations by the use of parachutists, attempted landings on the mainland of Malaya, and incursions into Singapore.[66] In early January 1963, President Sukarno whipped up popular support for the crushed rebels.

That month, Captain Kenneth Toft, a Singapore-based Anglo-Thai pilot with Malaysian Airways, and two British co-pilots were threatened before a firing squad upon landing at Djakarta airport. They had flown to Djakarta on a Garuda commercial flight to collect and return to Singapore a MAS (Malaysian Airways System) Comet aeroplane that had needed undercarriage repairs in Djakarta. The Comet was freshly painted with anti-Malaysian slogans, in a protest against the merger of Singapore and Malaysia. The Indonesian military ordered them to fly. 'After we got airborne the radios went dead and navigation aids were switched off', said Toft. 'We were flying with no radio aids on the ground ... just dead reckoning.' One of the British pilots, Scotsman Tommy Duncan, was an ex-Second World War bomber pilot who, in the war, had flown in many similar instances. 'Tommy Duncan had done this all over before in World War 2. He knew what to do. We switched off the navigation lights; didn't fly at constant altitude; deviated all over the sky; we flew all over the place.' They returned to Singapore, by flying 'like we were flying in a real World War 2 environment'. The pilots thought that the Indonesians intended to 'send up fighter jets and shoot us down and make propaganda of it and start a war that way'.[67]

The following day, Indonesian Foreign Minister Subandrio announced that Indonesia would pursue a confrontational policy (*konfrontasi*) with the Federation of Malaysia, Sabah and Sarawak. Toft said:

> That was when we realised they were looking for an excuse to start a war. That was why we were lined up against the wall, but they let us go! They were going to shoot us down! They had MIG fighters in the Indonesian Air Force. The next day, when we opened the newspapers, we realised the political intent; that was when the chill set in.[68]

Fears of an Indonesian invasion of Brunei were real, noted Captain Daniels, working for the Brunei Shell Petroleum Company.

> Panaga School long continued to serve as an emergency headquarters; a store room was made over for security equipment and cooking utensils; the Headmaster's office housed a powerful radio-transmitter that was regularly tuned into the military base in Singapore. There were also secret evacuation plans for Shell staff should the invasion take place.[69]

British Command would face many difficulties in Borneo. They were conducting an operation that would require a firm approach. In fact, they would be engaged in an undeclared, secret war. Indonesia's military potential concerned Britain and her defence staff. In 1965 Indonesian armed forces would number 412 000 men, with 350 000 in the Army.[70] The paratroop arm of 30 000 men on its own would outnumber the whole of Malaysia's armed forces.

Indonesian forces were equipped with an impressive armoury of Russian and American arms and equipment. Its Navy and Air Force were equipped with guided missiles.

10

AFTERMATH

Mopping-up operations absorbed the troops into 1963. Festive celebration was the only distraction the men enjoyed from their active engagement.

> There were no holidays – we were busy right through till the second week in January, what with the collection of weapons and suspects, patrolling of kampongs, ladangs, sungeis, ulu and so on. Troop Sergeants became honorary Ibans, Section Sergeants developed into trackers, and CQs [Company Quartermasters] learnt to cope with buffalo haunch and wild boar for lunch.[1]

For the Morrises, it was their first Christmas apart. Christmas, as Dick described it to Dorothy, was 'two working days rolled into one for we decided on maximum activity as a counter to any reb. ideas that we might decide to take things easy'.[2]

Sobering for the men was the death on Christmas Eve of a young soldier, aged 20, from Warwickshire. With the unit for just three months, he died in a tragic shooting accident at Limbang, and was buried in the Military Cemetery at Labuan.[3]

In keeping with the Marines' experience of the district, their Christmas was spent in ways that had been as varied as December had been for them. As one Marine described it: 'one company was lucky enough to be embarked that day, but some had their turkey and plum duff flown in, and others shared the local feasts in up river longhouses'.[4] One Marine wrote home, 'We caught our turkey in the trees, well frozen, in sacks weighing 200 lbs, supplied by courtesy of the RAF'.[5] One patrol is reported to have had braised monkey for their Christmas dinner.[6]

After Christmas, 42 Commando concentrated on the largely undeveloped Temburong District and were replaced in Limbang by the Gurkhas. By 5 January, the sparsely populated Temburong District was believed to be clear of enemy, with 421 insurgents captured.

A new enemy faced British troops and rebels alike in mid-January. The worst floods in Sarawak history turned everyone's efforts to survival, then to meeting humanitarian need. A large-scale operation took place to bring relief to flood victims, some 25000 of whom were left destitute. Tons of food were taken to marooned villages by helicopter or dropped by parachute, and security forces assisted refugees and distributed supplies. The very real help that British servicemen gave to the victims saved many lives and mitigated much suffering. Their effort was seen to be given without thought for their own safety or comfort, so was seen as unselfish.

By 6 February the British troops returned to their counter-insurgency purpose. 42 Commando were withdrawn from the Temburong area to Brunei's coastal regions, from Tutong in the south to Muara at the tip of Brunei Bay. Operation COLDSHOWER, intent on mopping up and capturing TNKU leaders, went into full swing.[7] One arrested insurgent, Bujang bin Tali, described how one of the rebels, Moksin bin Atai, was miserable in hiding and 'tired of the whole affair'. He evidently wept frequently but was terrified of giving himself up as he feared that British troops, not being able to speak Malay, would shoot him on sight. Voice aircraft were flown over where he was hiding north of Lawas in an attempt to persuade him that this was not true.[8] Messages broadcast from loudspeakers attached to RAF voice aircraft (such as Austers) had influenced insurgents to surrender in Malaya. Following the Americans who had experimented with loudspeaker aircraft in Korea, the British adopted air propaganda with loudspeaker planes in Malaya as a way to reach underground forces. The same tactic was used in Sarawak with flights broadcasting loudspeaker messages. A reward of $15 000 was issued for information that would lead to the arrest of Yassin Affandy. Instructor Lieutenant Colin George RN and Intelligence Sergeant Smith RM formed an interrogation team focused on tracking him down, but Affandy eluded the net until he was captured by Gurkhas when ambushed at the mouth of the Brunei River in May 1963.[9]

By then it was noticeable that:

> things are slowing down here, the stream of willing prisoners
> has abated, the press have pushed their inaccuracies back
> from the headlines to small columns on the middle page,
> and have erased us altogether. True the offensive prosecution
> continues to the end, but information which at first poured
> in loud and clear has become more flimsy and hearsay,
> uncomfortable operations in the deep mangrove swamps on
> the coast and river banks draw less results and rebel leaders
> have become fewer and more crafty – one feels that the
> movement inside Brunei has died.[10]

42 Commando embarked in HMS *Albion* for Singapore on 29 March 1963. However, just days after, a raid on a police post at Tebedu, a small border town 39 miles (63 kilometres) south of Kuching in the First Division, signalled the start of attacks by Indonesian volunteer forces. Men claiming to belong to the TNKU made another armed intrusion into Sarawak nearby,

northwest of Tebedu, a few days later. The Brigade Headquarters and 40 Commando, with L Coy, 42 Commando, moved quickly back to an area most had just left. From July to October 1963, 42 Commando was responsible for the First Division, whose frontier with Indonesia was more than 180 miles (290 kilometres) long. It was a critical position because the Federation of Malaysia, consisting of Malaya, Singapore, North Borneo and Sarawak, was proclaimed on 16 September 1963. Malayan Premier Tunku Abdul Rahman was inaugurated as premier of the new federation. At 8 am on that morning a large crowd gathered around Kuching's Padang. Across the river, the guns of Fort Margherita fired a 21-gun salute to celebrate Malaysia Day. A week later, on 23 September, President Sukarno announced that Indonesia would *ganyang* (literally, 'gobble raw') Malaysia. Following Sukarno's launch of *Konfrontasi*, Indonesian troops made armed incursions into Malaysia and particularly into Sarawak. Armed incursions of increasing strength culminated in a major assault on a remote post at Long Jawi in Sarawak's Third Division on 28 September. The post was held by locally recruited Border Scouts led by Gurkha soldiers, a number of whom were killed.

Threats on the border from Indonesian-based terrorists, and contact and skirmishes with them, continued through to May 1966 and saw 42 Commando undertake five tours in Sarawak.

At the news that they were to stay through the year, the Marines submerged themselves into the jungle. As the conflict dragged on, they penetrated deeper into the *ulu*. They patrolled extensively over what at the time seemed a vast area. From January to May 1964, the Commando was responsible for the West of the First Division in a tour that was mainly concerned with building up friendly relations with the local population. In 1965 they were in Tawau, in southeast Sabah on the Indonesian border. They were back in 1966, at the other end of the Indonesian border, on the southwest of Sarawak, engaged under heavy mortar fire in a major clash with Indonesian regular troops near the border south of Biawak.

President Sukarno continued to urge the people of Borneo to rise up and 'crush Malaysia'. Foreign Minister Subandrio said that 'Indonesian support for the TNKU is likely to take any and every form of open military assistance'.[11] In August and September 1964, small-scale landings by Indonesian troops took place on the Malay Peninsula. On 2 September, about 100 Indonesian guerrilla paratroopers were dropped into Malaya south of Kuala Lumpur, and infiltrators planning bomb attacks would be arrested in Singapore. On 3 December, Prime Minister Rahman told Parliament that the Indonesia–Malaysia dispute had changed from a state of confrontation to a state of war.

In the former British colonies of northern Borneo, Indonesian policy achieved the very opposite of the effect Sukarno intended. Resistance to Indonesian aggression strengthened local solidarity, and welded northern Borneo to the Malaysian Federation – with the exception of Brunei.

British troops adopted the 'Hearts and Minds' policies that had been so successful in Malaya.[12] Patrols assisted local communities, treated minor medical cases, and saved lives by flying out more serious cases. Their interaction with the locals overcame resistance to Federation.

The end of Confrontation was unexpected. 'There didn't seem to be any end to Confrontation', said a staff officer with Headquarters, Far East Land Forces in Singapore. 'It seemed that it was going to go on forever, but it stopped quickly and events in Indonesia took a lot of people by surprise.'[13] When Sukarno was ousted in a coup in March 1966, peace finally came to the region. The Bangkok agreement of 11 August 1966 marked the end of Confrontation.

The London *Times* noted that 42 Commando's raid at Limbang 'was carried out with great dash and courage'.[14] Captain Jeremy Moore was awarded a bar to his MC. Corporal Lester and Corporal Rawlinson were awarded the Military Medal (MM). Lieutenant David Willis was awarded the Distinguished Service Cross (DSC), and Petty Officer Kirwan the Distinguished Service Medal (DSM).

It was the heyday of the junior leaders, the Troop Commanders and their Section Commanders. Unconventional but inspirational leaders like Lieutenant Commander Jeremy Black RN enjoyed the action, which saw different military organisations combining forces. However, Black was summoned to be court-martialled for irregularities that had occurred in his minesweeper at the time and had escaped his attention.[15] In a nice twist, halfway through the court martial, Black was awarded the MBE.[16]

This was at a time when Lord Louis Mountbatten's principal objective as Chief of Defence Staff from mid-1959 to mid-1964 was the integration of the three services and a unified Ministry of Defence. Inter-service rivalries were anathema to him. His ultimate aim was a functional, closely knit, smoothly working military machine.[17]

General Walter Walker held similar views. In Borneo he led British, Gurkha, Malay, and eventually Commonwealth land, air and sea forces, knitted together by tight inter-service command. However, he earned the ire of the Army Board, which overruled the recommendation that he be knighted, and threatened him with court martial. It recalled him in 1965 from the successful covert counter-insurgency operations, codenamed CLARET, that he was leading. Subsequently, Denis Healey, the Secretary of State for Defence, called Walker's Borneo campaign a brilliant example of the use of minimum force, and described Walker as 'the best fighting general in the British Army'.[18] The PRB acknowledged that Walker was a 'military genius' who 'neutralised the military threat of the TNKU and extinguished the fire of revolution before it spread to Sarawak and North Borneo'.[19] Walker was knighted in 1968, and in 1969 he was appointed Commander-in-Chief Allied Forces northern Europe under NATO.

The Marines found the same cooperative approach from Dick Morris in Limbang. He ensured a smooth collaboration between the civil administration and military command and operations. He had the benefit of experience as an officer in the AIF and military administration at the end of the Second World War, as well as intimate knowledge of the circumstances of the region. He represented Sarawak on the Brunei Eastern Sarawak Executive Committee (BESEC), which met weekly in Brunei Town to deal with operational security and administration matters.

Jeremy Moore wrote to Dick:

> Whilst it can never, of course, be a pleasant business to lose
> any of one's men; it nevertheless gives me personally, and
> I think all of us, the greater sense of satisfaction to have
> been instrumental in your release now that we have been in
> Limbang long enough to get to know you better.[20]

The Marines appreciated Dick's understanding and help, which made their task easier when mopping up around Limbang. They thanked him for his kind hospitality and hoped to meet again 'in the Bonnet and Sonnet in more peaceable times'.[21] The Gurkhas did too. Letters at the time reflect the bonds made. A soldier, preparing to return to Britain from Singapore, wrote to Dick, 'It seems strange to be among the bright lights once more and trying to come to terms with packing up, selling cars and the hundred & one mundane things, that have to be done before we fly home in about 10 days time'.[22]

Salleh bin Sambas was captured by the Gurkhas, who acted on information given by a food carrier. His capture was the culmination for the patrol of the 2/7 Gurkha Rifles of seven weeks of gruelling and often hazardous operations, wading through streams, mud and mangrove. Sambas was badly wounded when ambushed near Serdang, and was in desperate need of a blood transfusion. The first to volunteer was Captain David Cutfield, who commanded the patrol. 'I shouldn't do this you know', he said, while giving Sambas his blood. 'The poor blighter will probably be tried, sentenced and hanged. I should let the poor blighter die quietly.'[23] Sambas was sentenced to 15 years' imprisonment when he pleaded guilty to three separate charges connected with the rebellion in Sarawak.[24] His father, Sambas bin Murah, was sentenced to one year's imprisonment for consorting with him. The same day, the Malaysian Prime Minister, Tunku Abdul Rahman, met President Sukarno in Tokyo, as a messenger of peace, hoping to smooth the way for hoped-for summit talks in Manila.[25]

Improvements came to Limbang. Damaged property was repaired. The bullet-battered facade of the police station was replastered. An airfield was constructed at the northern end of the town.

The prisoner who asked to be allowed to remain in the jail to help the Morrises returned to the jail to complete his sentence. Dick saw to it that he was not readmitted, but completed his sentence as an orderly for the Field Forces. 'I have had him decked out in khaki, armed him with a shotgun, and all of us are happy.'[26]

The strain of the emergency on Dick was telling in his face and in how thin he became, evident in a photograph of him taken by Gurkha commander Lieutenant Colonel Gordon Shakespear.

In late April, Dick received a new appointment to Kuching as Resident of the First Division. He wrote to Walter Walker, telling him how much he enjoyed working with Walker and those under his command.

The inherent differences in approach and attitudes between civil and military authorities only too frequently lead to disagreements and to strained personal relationships. In this Division there have been no strained relationships and the rare initial disagreements have in all cases been merely a prelude to agreement. The credit for this harmony must, in the main, go to you as Commander.[27]

Dick applauded the pains taken by Walker's senior officers to help him and his District Officers. 'It was clear that they were personally interested in the human problems of the local population', he told Walker. 'At no time did the urgency of operations produce disregard of the basic civilian needs.'

He credited their assistance as being very largely responsible for the rapid return to near normality in the Fifth Division. In his judgment, there were many occasions when members of Walker's command did more than their orders demanded. 'There have been numerous cases of personal kindness to the civil population and I can assure you that all ranks of all units both in Limbang and Lawas Districts have made many friends, nor will they be forgotten after their departure.'

He told Brigadier Patterson that he was leaving regretfully. 'I would have wished to have stayed here until the last rebel had been eliminated and I should have liked to have seen at least some convicted rebels released in accordance with a policy of clemency and rehabilitation.'[28]

While the last few months under emergency had been difficult, working with Patterson, his staff and those under his command to restore community life in Limbang had been rewarding. He told Patterson, 'The understanding of the civil problem which you, and all those under your command, have constantly shown has made my task much easier'. He remarked on how there had been no frictions between the military and civil authorities in his Division, and on how much the troops in Patterson's brigade had done for the local population. 'Even in those Kedayan areas, which were disaffected and which are now denuded of fit men, there is a remarkably friendly attitude to the forces.'

In a final note he thanked Patterson for 'the decision which you made on the 10th and 11th December. My wife and I and the other hostages are so grateful to you for your decision as we are in somewhat more intimate way to the wonderful fellows of 42 Cdo RM'.

'It is most encouraging for all of us to know that our feelings of friendliness, admiration and respect which we all entertain for you and the Civil Administration of the Fifth Division of Sarawak are so fully reciprocated', replied Patterson. 'It has indeed been a most pleasant experience to cooperate with a senior Government Official who so fully understands the way soldiers think and work as yourself.'[29]

Walker wrote to Dick. 'All of us with experience of internal security operations, especially in Malaya, are very alive to the necessity for cooperation between the civil, the military and the police', he said.

> I have noticed with pleasure how close this cooperation has
> been in the Fifth Division, and I put much of the credit
> for this to the friendly and easy relationship you have
> maintained with my officers. They, on their part, have told
> me how pleasant it was to work with a man of your ability
> and good sense.[30]

Patterson conveyed to Dick an honour which gave him great joy. He was made a life honorary member of the 99th Gurkhas' Officers Mess for his contribution to counter-insurgency, and

Patterson told Dick that he should freely avail himself of all the amenities of the Mess whenever the opportunity arose.

In April, Dick inspected a Police guard of honour before Limbang's old fort before departing for Kuching. There, he subsequently met up with some of the men from L Company in Kuching.

Others were reunited again, when on 3 August 1963, a memorial to those who lost their lives in the insurrection was unveiled on the spot where they landed at Limbang. A bronze plaque, mounted on a plinth of plain local stone, was inscribed with the names of those who died. The memorial was raised at the express wish of the residents of Limbang and paid for by public subscriptions.[31]

Early that morning, a Gurkha band led the Royal Marines down the road which Dick had trod as a human shield. The Governor, Sir Alexander Waddell, officiated at what would be among the last of his official duties before he departed from Sarawak, as the country's last British Governor. Representatives of all the British forces stood at attention and saluted before the stone memorial.

Three guards, provided by 42 Commando Royal Marines, the Police, and the Police Field Force, paraded with the band of the Sarawak Constabulary. The guard of one Officer, one SNCO and 22 Marines from 42 Commando, was provided from 5 Troop, L Company, and included men who had taken part in the assault. Lieutenant Peter Waters was the Guard Commander. Wreaths were laid by three of the men who had been decorated for their part in the action.

Misfortune dogged Marine Gerald Kierans, even in death. His name was misspelled on the plaque, as 'Kiernans'.

On the same day as the unveiling of the Limbang Memorial, Inspector Abdul Latif Ben Besah and Constable Bisop Anak Kunjan were awarded the Colonial Police Medal for Gallantry.

Abang Omar bin Abang Samaudin and Joseph King Shih Fan were awarded the Queen's Commendation for Brave Conduct. The Limbang Division of the Sarawak Red Cross received the Governor's Commendation. Their awards were presented while the Band of the Sarawak Constabulary played Elgar's Morceau 'Salut d'Amour'.

Dick, dressed in a civilian suit, not a colonial service uniform, said:

> Limbang has not forgotten, nor will it forget the debt it
> owes to 42 Cdo RM. My wife and I have a rather personal
> debt to and affection for 'Morris' Own Light of Foot'. Our
> association with 42 has continued in Kuching; so far as we
> are concerned it will always continue and so will our debt.
> Oh, one more thing, if ever I get into trouble again, I'll send
> for the Royal Marines – '42' for choice.[32]

A year later, a smaller group stood before the memorial. The error made with Marine Kierans's name was corrected, with his name reinscribed.

Dick retired from service in Sarawak in 1964, aged 49. Major General Walker told Dick that his departure saddened 'all those of the Armed Forces, particularly the Army, for whom you have done so much'. He thanked Dick for his unfailing support and 'abundant kindness'. 'Your wide experience of local problems and your advice have been invaluable to those of us who have had the benefit of working with you.'[33] In a personal cable, Walker said, 'You have been a staunch ally to all and a personal friend to so many'.

The new Governor of Sarawak, Dato Abang Haji Openg, expressed his appreciation of Dick's long and loyal service to Sarawak and its people. 'Your ease of manner, fluent command of language and great energy have made you a most valuable administrator.' He also thanked Dorothy for her support, and said that her 'kindness, and untiring sympathy and work for the social services of the country' had earned his deep gratitude.[34]

For David Greenhough, 'Limbang was the only frontal attack which the Royal Marines put in for some considerable time, or indeed thereafter in my service career. That attack was remembered and celebrated every year up until the Falklands incident twenty years later in 1982.'[35]

L Company commemorates Limbang Day every ten years. On 12 December 1972, some of those who were in Limbang reunited at HQ 42 Commando in their barracks at Bickleigh near Plymouth. Jeremy Moore and Dick Morris were among them. Photographs taken at the time show the respect the two men had for each other.

The Tercentenary of the Royal Marines was celebrated in August 1964. The Tercentenary Parade held on 23 July was reviewed by the Queen, in a parade which was claimed to be unparalleled since the time Queen Victoria presented colours to the Royal Marine Light Infantry at Osborne in 1894.[36] When the Queen addressed the troops, she stressed the loyalty of the Marines through the centuries.

Dick Morris became an Officer of the Order of the British Empire (OBE) in June 1963. Congratulations were cabled to him from around the world, including from 42 Commando, 40 Commando, and 1/2nd Gurkhas. In 1970 the Sultan of Brunei conferred on him the Most Honourable Order of the Crown of Brunei Class III (Sri Mahkota Brunei).[37]

The rebellion played a role in the Sultan of Brunei's decision for Brunei to not join the Federation of Malaysia. On 4 October 1967, Sultan Omar Ali Saifuddin, then aged only 53, abdicated in favour of his 21-year-old eldest son, Hassanal Bolkiah. The Sultan calculated that he could thus buy time for British protection, and a company of Gurkhas remained detached to Brunei. Lee Kuan Yew, Prime Minister of Singapore, who became a close friend, remarked: 'The history of Brunei has been a most unlikely story of a Sultanate that has survived into the 21st century as an independent oil-rich state in a turbulent part of the world'. Brunei and Singapore both kept their independence from the Malaysian Federation; Singapore, originally part of the Federation, ceased to be a member in 1965. In Lee's estimation, 'Sultan Omar Ali took calculated risks with courage. He had a keen sense of what was politically possible.'[38] The State of Emergency which was imposed in 1962 remains in force.

Azahari's absence from Brunei on 8 December was seen as reason for the rebellion's failure. The military might of the British aside, his colleague Zaini, who was with Azahari in Manila, believed that 'Azahari should have personally led the revolution himself'.[39] Zaini later blamed Azahari's absence for causing a turnaround among his followers. 'In the midst of confusion, [they] saw the Sultan as the new symbol of group leadership and, of course, the centre of loyalty.'

Azahari went to Indonesia, where he received protection, encouragement and aid, but not recognition from the government. He remained dedicated 'lastingly' to democracy.[40] He died in Indonesia in 2002.

The last of the 2342 PRB and TNKU detainees, who were detained without trial in December 1962, were released on 7 January 1990.

Diplomatic ties between Indonesia and Malaysia were resumed in 1967. In August that year was formed the Association of Southeast Nations (ASEAN), comprising at that time Indonesia, Malaysia, the Philippines, Singapore and Thailand. Members saw their principal security threats as internal and aimed to avert these by promoting economic development through regional cooperation. Malaysia has been an ardent supporter of regional cooperation, although relations with Indonesia have not always been cordial. British Far East Command ended in October 1971. Brunei joined ASEAN in 1984, soon after achieving independence from Britain. It achieved independence without a fully elected legislature or a government responsible to the people.

In September 2002, former members of Lima Company at Limbang stood in parade before Sir Jeremy Moore, by then a retired major general, in front of the not-long-opened Imperial War Museum North, in Manchester.[41] Their reunion occurred to mark the deaths of their fellow Marines at Limbang 40 years earlier. It coincided with the filming of the Limbang story.[42] This film was part of a series made by American-based Brushfire Films on the wars that are known as the Brushfire Wars (also known as the Forgotten Wars). Since the end of the Second World War, Britain has fought over 50 military campaigns, including that which followed Limbang. The making of this film took Sir Jeremy Moore back to Limbang with retired Royal Marines Brian Downey and Tony Daker, who appears in this film as himself. In Limbang they met with Salleh bin Sambas who, after serving his time in prison, had become a *penghulu* and village hero.

The Morrises maintained their close ties with Sarawak. They returned often. Through the Australian Malaysian Singapore Association, established in 1970, and its fellowship program, which Dick led for many years, the Morrises assisted many Malaysian students to study in Australia. Their home was always open to visitors from Malaysia and to Australian students of Malaysian affairs. They kept in regular touch with Abang Omar until his death in 1992.

On Thursday, 12 December 1963, a notice appeared in *The Times* of London. It read: 'In Memoriam 42 Cdo R.M. In grateful memory of those who fell at Limbang, Sarawak on 12th Dec.

1962 – Dick and Dorothy Morris.'[43] Since then, the same notice has appeared on 12 December every year. It is a simple thank you from the family of Richard and Dorothy Morris. Dick died in 2000 aged 85, and Dorothy in 2002 aged 86. The debt that they and their descendants owe to the Royal Marines will never be forgotten.

NOTES

1   1962: Countdown to emergency

1. For the central position of the South China Sea, see 'South China Sea: Full unclosure?', *The Economist*, 24 March 2012, 62; Rowan Callick, 'Awash on a Sea of Trouble', *The Australian*, 30 July 2012, 11; On the South China Sea involving the peace and security of Asia as a whole, see Marwyn S Samuels, *Contest for the South China Seas*, London and New York: Routledge, 2005.

2. 'East Asia', in Arthur Cotterell, *A Dictionary of World Mythology*, Oxford University Press, 1997, online at <www.oxfordreference.com/views/ENTRY.html?subview=Main&entry=t 73.e118>, accessed 25 June 2012; 'Borneo', in John Everett-Heath, *Concise Dictionary of World Place-Names*, 2005, 2nd edn, Oxford University Press, 2010, online at <www.oxfordreference.com/views/ENTRY.html?subview=Main&entry=t209.e941>, accessed 25 June 2012.

3. The word comes from the Sanskrit *bhmi*: John Everett-Heath, 'Brunei', in John Everett-Heath, *Concise Dictionary*, 2010, online at <www.oxfordreference.com/views/ENTRY.html?subview=Main&entry=t209.e1050>, accessed 14 August 2012.

4. Per Letters of Exchange signed in March 2009, Malaysia ceded two hydrocarbon concession blocks to Brunei in exchange for Brunei's sultan dropping claims to the Limbang corridor which divides Brunei. However, new disputes have arisen since then: 'Malaysia and Brunei carry out border demarcation, new disputes arise over Limbang', Singapore Institute of International Affairs, 23 March 2009, online at <www.siiaonline.org/?q=programmes/insights/malaysia-and-brunei-carry-out-border-demarcation-new-disputes-arise-over-limbang>, accessed 12 August 2012.

5. *The British Commonwealth Year Book*, 10th edn, London: MacGibbon & Kee, 1963, 581–82; George Lawrence Harris, *North Borneo, Brunei, Sarawak (British Borneo)*, New Haven, Conn.: Human Relations Area Files, 1956, 57. Literacy rates were highest in Brunei, reflecting its relative prosperity and largely urban character; 14 per cent were literate in Sarawak in 1956, and 12 per cent in North Borneo.

6. Roger Kershaw, 'Challenges of historiography: Interpreting the decolonization of Brunei', *Asian Affairs*, vol. 31, no. 3, 2000, 314–23 especially 316–17; 320.

7. AVM Horton, 'Omar Ali Saifuddin III (1914–1986)', *Oxford Dictionary of National Biography*, Oxford University Press, 2004, online edition, January 2008, <www.oxforddnb.com/view/article/66336>, accessed 27 Feb 2012.

8. Gregory Poulgrain, *The Genesis of 'Konfrontasi': Malyasia, Borneo and Indonesia 1945–1965*, London: C Hurst & Co., 1998, 226.

9. Anthony Burgess, *Little Wilson and Big God*, London: Heinemann, 1987, 437.

10   It was generally agreed that Azahari was a charismatic personality. For Azahari as an orator, see AVM Horton, *The British Residency in Brunei, 1906–1959*, Hull, Yorkshire: Centre for South-East Asian Studies, 1984, 54; For a description of Azahari as a messianic figure, see Bob Reece, 'An interview with Dr. Hj. Zaini Ahmad, Kuala Lumpur, 1985', online at <www.thefreelibrary.com/An+interview+with+D.+Hj.+Zaini+Ah,ad,+Kuala+Lumpur>, accessed 27 May 2012.

11   Burgess, *Little Wilson*, 426.

12   Burgess, *Little Wilson*, 429; 426.

13   Particularly in a country with no machinery for, nor lawful right of, public criticism. Captain GF Daniels, *The Brunei Rebellion*, unpublished memoir, 1995, 3. Private Papers of Captain GF Daniels, IWM09/53A.

14   Horton, *The British Residency in Brunei*, 54.

15   Khoon Choy Lee, 'Political History in Singapore 1945–1965', Oral History Interview, 000022, Transcript, 525, National Archives Singapore.

16   HQ British Forces Joint PERINTREP No. 1, Part III Army Intelligence, No. 4 (7/20/11), Royal Marines Museum Archives.

17   Policy in regard to Malaya and Borneo Cabinet Memoranda, 29 August 1945, cab-129-1-cp-133.pdf, online at <commons.wikimedia.org/w/index.php?title=File:Cabinet_Memoranda_29_August_1945_(cab-129-1-cp-133).pdf&page=1>, accessed 12 August 2011.

18   State of Brunei, *Annual Report*, London: HMSO, 1959, 261.

19   Burgess, *Little Wilson*, 429.

20   Ah Chon Ho (comp.), *Kuching 1950–1959, Sir Anthony Foster Abell's Era, Vol. 1*, Kuching: Ah Chon Ho, 1960, 37.

21   'Sarawak head asks three-colony union', *New York Times*, 8 February 1954, 4.

22   'Briton suggests Asian Federation', *New York Times*, 20 August 1955, 6.

23   Sarawak Information Service, *Sarawak by the Week*, Week no. 21, 1959, 3, cited in Michael Leigh, 'Party Formation in Sarawak', *Indonesia*, no. 9, April 1970, 197.

24   David Walder Esq. ERD, MP, 'Malaysia', *Royal United Services Institution Journal*, vol. 110, no. 638 (1965), 106.

25   Robert Trumbull, 'Poverty plagues oil-rich Brunei', *New York Times*, 24 September 1961, 26.

26   John L Esposito (ed), *The Oxford Encyclopedia of the Modern Islamic World, Vol. 1*, New York: Oxford University Press, 1995, 233.

27   'Imposing Mosque with elevator is opened in oil-wealth Brunei', *New York Times*, 27 September 1958, 8.

28   Only 4 per cent of Brunei's land was in use in 1955. RH Morris, 'Rural Settlement and Resettlement', 1951; 'Rural Development in Brunei'; Morris Papers.

29   Jeremy Moore, Interview (1999), IWM31692, Reel 37; Reel 52.

30   Laurie Russell, Interview (2012), IWM33214.

31   'Major General Sir Jeremy Moore', *The Times* (London), 17 September 2007, online at <www.timesonline.co.uk/tol/comment/obituaries/article2469102.ece>, accessed 2 February 2012. The Royal Marine Commando Brigade

fought in Malaya from 1950 to 1952.

32 John Shirley, 'Obituary: Major General Sir Jeremy Moore', *The Guardian*, 18 September 2007, online at <www.guardian.co.uk/news/2007/sep/18/guardianobituaries.military>, accessed 6 February 2012.

33 *The Times* (London), 17 September 2007.

34 Shirley, *The Guardian*, 18 September 2007.

35 Shirley, *The Guardian*, 18 September 2007.

36 'Major general Sir Jeremy Moore', *Telegraph* (London), 19 September 2007; Moore, IWM31692, Reel 10.

37 *The Times* (London), 17 September 2007.

38 Moore, IWM31692, Reel 13.

39 Moore, IWM31692, Reel 60.

40 Moore, IWM31692, Reel 60; Reel 61.

2   Friday, 7 December: Counting the days

1 Richard Morris, *Sarawak Memoirs*, 23–24, unpublished manuscript, Morris Papers.

2 Morris, *Sarawak Memoirs*, 23–24.

3 'The Arrangements for the visit to Sarawak', 12 December 1960; Programme: Visit of Senator The Honourable JG Gorton and Mrs Gorton to Sarawak (9–17 December, 1960), Morris Papers.

4 Bob Reece, Review: Alastair Morrison, 'Fair land Sarawak: Some recollections of an expatriate official', *Crossroads*, vol. 9, no. 1 (1995), 153.

5 V Porritt to RH Morris, 15 August 1994, Morris Papers.

6 B Meikle to RH Morris, 12 August 1962, Morris Papers.

7 GG Briggs to RH Morris, 10 December 1962, Morris Papers.

8 B Meikle to RH Morris, 12 August 1962, Morris Papers.

9 RH Morris to A Morris, 31 October 1962, Morris Papers.

10 Dorothy Morris, 'V.A.D.: Concerning certain activities of the Sarawak Branch of the British Red Cross and Limbang', unpublished manuscript, 2, Morris Papers.

11 Morris, 'V.A.D.: Concerning … Red Cross', Morris Papers.

12 Sir John Martin to D Morris, 4 December 1962, Morris Papers; For an introduction to Martin see: Donald Norbrook, 'Remembering Winston Churchill, Someone in Particular, Sir John Martin', 11 November 1973 BBC Archive, online at <www.bbc.co.uk/archive/churchill/11020.shtml>, accessed 1 June 2012.

13 Sir John Martin to D Morris, 7 December 1962, Morris Papers.

14 William R Roff, 'Islam obscured? Some Reflections on Studies of Islam and Society in Southeast Asia', in *Studies on Islam and Society in Southeast Asia*, Singapore: NUS Press, 2009, 3–32.

15 Essential reading that he would recommend to appreciate the change that continued in the area after the war included Gavin Long's *The Final Campaigns* (1963) and writings of Sukarno; RH Morris to RHW Reece, 17 February 1999, Morris Papers.

16 RH Morris to RHW Reece, 17 February 1999, Morris Papers. See Bob

Reece, *Masa Jepun: Sarawak under the Japanese 1941–1945*, Kuching, Sarawak: Sarawak Literary Society, 1998.

17 In March 2009, Malaysia and Brunei exchanged agreement to declare that the Limbang Question was deemed solved; however, this awaits demarcation of the boundary between the two countries. Nurbaiti Hamdan, 'Limbang border to be set', *The Star*, 20 March 2009 online at <thestar.com.my/news/story.asp?file=/2009/3/20/nation/3518846&sec=nation>, accessed 10 February 2012.

18 Morris, *Sarawak Memoirs*, 23–24.

19 'Sarawak wants Borneo to join Malaysia', *The Straits Times*, 3 October 1962, 5, online at <newspapers.nl.sg/Digitised/Article/straitstimes19621003.2.30.aspx>, accessed 1 June 2012.

20 RH Morris, OBE, 'Limbang – An Inside Story', in Inst Lt Ll Evans, RN (ed), *42 1962–1963, The Magazine of the 42 Commando Royal Marines*, Singapore, 1963, 8.

21 Outram had served in the Sarawak Constabulary from 1952, and as Senior Superintendent from 1955. RH Morris to Chief Secretary, Confidential Report detailing the situation during the period 7/12/62 to end January 1963, 8 March 1963, Morris Papers.

22 Daphne Richards, Interview (1983), IWM8450.

23 '"Return Rule to Brunei" Demand, Limbang Issue', *Sarawak Tribune*, 21 May 1962.

24 RH Morris to Chief Secretary, Confidential Report detailing the situation during the period 7/12/62 to end January 1963, 8 March 1963, Morris Papers.

3 Saturday, 8 December: Black Saturday

1 Azahari's father married Affandy's sister: Bob Reece, 'An interview with Dr. Hj. Zaini Ahmad, Kuala Lumpur', 1985 online at <www.thefreelibrary.com/An+interview+with+D.+Hj.+Zaini+Ah,ad,+Kuala+Lumpur>, accessed 27 May 2012.

2 Zaini Haji Ahmad, *The People's Party of Brunei, Selected Documents*, Petaling Jaya, Selangor: Institute of Social Analysis, 1987, 72 and note 29.

3 'The first eye-witness account of attack on police station', *The Straits Times*, 10 December 1962, 20.

4 Peter Kedit, 'Eyewitness of Brunei Revolt', *The Sarawak Tribune*, 12 December 1962, 3.

5 This is yet to be acknowledged: 'Sarawak seeks out missing link', *Brunei Times*, 1 March 2012, online at <www.bt.com.bn/news-asia/2012/03/01/sarawak-seeks-out-missing-link>, accessed 19 April 2012.

6 Anthony Farrar-Hockley, 'Poett, Sir (Joseph Howard) Nigel (1907–1991)', *Oxford Dictionary of National Biography*, Oxford University Press, 2004 <www.oxforddnb.com/view/article/49929>, accessed 27 February 2012. General Sir Nigel Poett, *Pure Poett: The Autobiography of General Sir Nigel Poett*, London: Leo Cooper, 1991.

7 Poett, *Pure Poett*, 119–22.

8   The British wanted to improve their contacts with Sukarno, so Poett began this by paying a visit to the Indonesian Army during 28 October to 1 November 1962; Poett, *Pure Poett*, 152; Philip Murphy, *Alan Lennox-Boyd: A Biography*, London; New York: IB Tauris, 1999, 139.

9   In early 1962 the Far East was the only important British overseas command still organised on a single-service basis. 'Unifying Far East Command', *The Times* (London), 7 February 1962, 11. It was envisaged that the new command structure could also improve defence coordination in the Southeast Asia Treaty Organization (to which Luce was United Kingdom military adviser). Less than a week after his appointment as the first Commander-in-Chief of the new unified three services command in the Far East, Luce was promoted to the Navy's senior post as First Sea Lord and Chief of Naval Staff. He would turn his attention to the building of the first two British Polaris submarines announced in May 1963. 'Adml. Sir D. Luce is First Sea Lord', *The Times* (London), 4 December 1962, 8; 'Start On Polaris Submarines', *The Times* (London), 18 November 1963, 5.

10   General Sir Walter Walker, Interview (1989), IWM11120, Reel 1.

11   Walker, IWM11120, Reel 1.

12   Tom Pocock, 'Walker, Sir Walter Colyear (1912–2001)', *Oxford Dictionary of National Biography*, Oxford University Press, January 2005; online edition, January 2011 <www.oxforddnb.com/view/article/76147>, accessed 27 February 2012. See also 'General Sir Walter Walker', *The Telegraph*, 13 August 2001, online at <www.telegraph.co.uk/news/obituaries/militaryobituaries/gurkhaobituaries/1337219/General-Sir-Walter-Walker.html>, accessed 27 February 2012.

13   Walker, IWM11120, Reel 3.

14   Walker, IWM11120, Reel 3; 'General Appointed Borneo Commander', *The Times*, 17 December 1962, 7. When Walker took up his appointment, which lasted four years, Glennie served as Walker's second-in-command for the first two years of this period.

15   Walker, IWM11120, Reel 3. Vitriolic anti-Malaysian and anti-British propaganda on Radio Jakarta reinforced his opinion. For a description of the difficulties he would face: Brig. E. D. Smith, 'The Borneo Rebellion & Indonesian Military Confrontation Against Malaysia' in 'Indonesian Confrontation', *The Proceedings of the Royal Air Force Historical Society*, no. 13 (1994), 19.

16   Fred Bridgland, 'Field Marshall Sam Manekshaw', *The Scotsman*, 3 July 2008, online at <www.scotsman.com/news/obituaries/field-marshal-sam-manekshaw-1-1078732>, accessed 29 May 2012.

17   It was later reported that rebels were expecting Indonesian planes to land: Michael B Leigh, *The Rising Moon: Political Change in Sarawak*, Sydney: Sydney University Press, 1974, 46.

18   Pat Foh Chang, *Legends & History of Sarawak*, Kuching: Chang Pat Foh, 1999, 368; Zaini Haji Ahmad, *The People's Party of Brunei, Selected Documents*, Petaling Jaya: Institute of Social Analysis, 1987, 34.

19   Anthony Burgess left Brunei before the Revolt. He wrote his novel *Devil of*

a State in Brunei shortly beforehand. In it he describes the followers of the local nationalist leader holding to a vow to remain unshaven and 'hairy till Independence was achieved'. Anthony Burgess, *Devil of a State*, London: William Heinemann, 1961, 5.

20   Dennis Wong, 'I led a bloody revolt in Limbang', *New Sunday Times*, 1 May 2011, online at <imageshack.us/f/685/TheLimbangRaidfromthere.jpg/>, accessed 12 August 2012.

21   Mrs RH Morris, 'Etiquette and Alka Seltzers', *Globe & Laurel: Journal of the Royal Marines*, vol. LXXII, March/April 1964, 102; Lieutenant George Vardon Helm served with the AIF in British North Borneo, and was made a Member of the British Empire (MBE). His service records state that he 'showed a high standard of resourcefulness, personal courage and devotion to duty'. Second Australian Imperial Force Personnel Dossiers, 1939–1947, Series B883 Item 4628810, National Archives of Australia.

22   Sarawak Information Service, 'Limbang – A Story of Courage and Kindness', *Sarawak by the Week*, no. 51/62 (16–22 December 1962), 5.

23   RH Morris, 'Limbang – An Inside Story' in Inst Lt Ll Evans, RN (ed), *42 1962–1963, The Magazine of the 42 Commando Royal Marines*, Singapore, 1963, 8.

24   'Peace Corpsman escaped hanging', *New York Times*, 7 April 1963, 4.

25   Kennedy first defined the Peace Corps in a short three-minute speech on 12 October 1960: Stanley Meisler, *When the World Calls: The inside story of the Peace Corps and its first fifty years*, Boston: Beacon Press, 2011, 5.

26   Martin Stephen, 'Obituary: Alec Dickson', *The Independent*, 10 October 1994, online at <www.independent.co.uk/news/people/obituary-alec-dickson-1442037.html>, accessed 8 August 2012. On the Dicksons' introduction to Sarawak, see Mora Dickson, *A Season in Sarawak*, London: Dennis Dobson, 1962. See also, Elizabeth Cobbs Hoffman, *All You Need Is Love: The Peace Corps and the Spirit of the 1960s*, Cambridge, Mass.: Harvard University Press, 1998, 79–80.

27   Robert G Carey, with foreword by Joseph H Blatchford, *The Peace Corps*, New York: Praeger, 1970, 101.

28   Abang Omar bin Abang Samaudin, 'I declare …', unpublished manuscript, Morris Family Papers. The hospital was a small and recently built cottage hospital of 15–20 beds, where it was intended that a doctor would be posted to the Fifth Division for the first time. Sarawak, *Annual Report*, Kuching: Sarawak Government Printing Office, 1959, 103.

29   For explanation of the origins and meaning of 'Abang', see Nela Awang, 'Malay words Awang, Abang have similar meaning and origins', *The Brunei Times*, 21 November 2007, online at <www.bt.com.bn/node/25805/print>, accessed 29 May 2012.

30   Spenser St John, *The life of Sir James Brooke, Rajah of Sarawak from his Personal Papers and Correspondence*, Edinburgh; London: William Blackwood & Sons, 1879, 258–59, online at <archive.org/stream/lifesirjamesbro01johngoog - page/n10/mode/2up>, accessed 13 February 2012.

31   Samaudin, 'I declare …', Morris Family Papers.

32   Morris, 'Etiquette & Alka Seltzers', 102–3. Lady Laura Troubridge
       (1866–1946) was an Edwardian author and translator, whose *The Book of
       Etiquette: The complete standard work of reference on social usage* first appeared
       in two volumes in 1926. She wrote her book to help readers steer their way
       through 'unwritten laws' of social behaviour, telling them how to steer a
       course between old-fashioned courtesy and the new spirit of 'informality'.
       Her short stories and opinions were often serialised in Australian
       newspapers: 'Lady Troubridge', *The Daily News* (Perth), 29 May 1911, 4.
       These included monthly letters that appeared in the *Sydney Morning Herald*
       before the First World War. Robert Latta & Alexander Macbeath, *The
       Elements of Logic*, London: Macmillan, 1929. First published in 1929, it
       was reissued through numerous subsequent editions up to 1964. Alexander
       Macbeath (1888–1964) was Professor of Logic and Metaphysics, Queen's
       University, Belfast, until his retirement in 1954. He was also well known
       for the 1948–49 Gifford Lectures, University of St Andrews. These were
       published as *Experiments in Living: A study of the nature and foundation of
       ethics or morals in the light of recent work in Social Anthropology* (1952), in
       which he defended that moral life and the grounds of moral obligation
       are in principle the same everywhere and for all people. He was Visiting
       Professor to the University of Tasmania from 1959 to 1961. Robert Latta
       (1865–1932) held the Chair of Logic and Metaphysics, University of
       Glasgow, until his retirement in 1925 when he co-authored with Macbeath
       their logic textbook.

4   Sunday, 9 December: 'Highs' and 'lows'

1   Lt Col ER Bridges, Report: 42 Commando Operations in Brunei and
       Sarawak 11th December to 3rd January Ref. Map Brunei FARELF MISC
       1069 (Attached) Annex: The Assault on Limbang, Royal Marines Museum
       Archives.
2   'Commando Brigade HQ', *Globe & Laurel: Journal of the Royal Marines*, vol.
       LXXI, no. 1, February/March 1963, 16. In 1960, 42 Commando RM began
       11 years of service based in Singapore.
3   Air Chief Marshall Sir Robert Freer, 'A Station Commander's View', *The
       Proceedings of the Royal Air Force Historical Society*, no. 13, 1994, 50.
4   Lord Lovatt, who led No. 1 Commando Brigade in the D-Day landings in
       June 1944, served as technical adviser to the film in which he is portrayed
       by the actor Peter Lawford. Eighteen thousand Royal Marines took part in
       the Normandy Landings in June 1944. Churchill described their extreme
       gallantry as remarkable: Winston Churchill, *The Second World War*,
       Vol. VI, London: Cassel & Co, 1954, 177, cited in Julian Thompson, *The
       Royal Marines: From Sea Soldiers to a Special Force*, London: Sidgwick &
       Jackson, 2000, 312.
5   Sandpiper, 'The Longest Day', *Globe & Laurel*, vol. LXX, February/March
       1962, 38.
6   Tony Daker, Interview (2012), IWM33246, Reel 5.
7   David Greenhough, Interview (1992), IWM11144.

8   'Commando Brigade HQ', *Globe & Laurel*, vol. LXXI, no. 1, February/March 1963, 16.

9   '40 Sergeant's Mess', *Globe & Laurel*, vol. LXXI, no. 1, February/March 1963, 18.

10 'Commando Brigade HQ', *Globe & Laurel*, vol. LXXI, no. 1, February/March 1963, 16.

11 'Commando Brigade HQ', *Globe & Laurel*, vol. LXXI, no. 1, February/March 1963, 16.

12 'Commando Brigade HQ', *Globe & Laurel*, vol. LXXI, no. 1, February/March 1963, 16.

13 'Sarawak, Brunei and North Borneo: The Duke of Edinburgh's Tour', *Illustrated London News*, Issue 5923, 14 March 1959: 423. The Queen honoured the Corps by appointing Prince Philip in 1953, in succession to the late King George VI.; State of Brunei, *Annual Report*, London: HMSO, 1962, 23.

14 'Peace Corpsman escaped hanging', *New York Times*, 7 April 1963, 4.

15 Sargent Shriver, 'Ambassadors of Good Will: The Peace Corps', *National Geographic Magazine*, vol. 126, no. 3, September 1964, 297.

16 Mrs RH Morris, 'Etiquette and Alka Seltzers', *Globe & Laurel: Journal of the Royal Marines*, vol. LXXII, March/April 1964, 103.

17 Morris, 'Etiquette', 103.

18 With assistance from the World Health Organization, Sarawak was engaged in attempting to eradicate malaria. It was the most important mass health campaign in the country.

19 Sarawak Information Service, 'Limbang – A Story of Courage and Kindness', *Sarawak by the Week*, no. 51/62, 16–22 December 1962, 5.

20 Power was not restored until some days after the recapture of the town by the Royal Marines on 12 December.

21 RH Morris to Law Ah Kaw, 10 May 1963, Morris Papers.

22 RH Morris to Chief Secretary, Confidential Report detailing the situation during the period 7/12/62 to end January 1963, 8 March 1963, 2 (item 5), Morris Papers.

23 Inst Lt WLl Evans, RN, 'Rebel in Captivity', *42 1962–1963, The Magazine of the 42 Commando Royal Marines*, Singapore, 1963, 12.

5   Monday, 10 December: Standing fast

1   GG Briggs to D and R Morris, 10 December 1962, Morris Papers; The Honourable Justice Geoffrey Gould Briggs later became Chief Justice of Hong Kong and Brunei (1973–79), and President of Court of Appeal, Brunei (1979–88).

2   'Revolt in Brunei', Editorial, *The Straits Times*, 10 December 1962, 10.

3   Colonial Office and Commonwealth Office, Brunei Disturbances 1962, C01030/1070, 54, The National Archives, UK.

4   Bruce Jackman, Interview (1990), IWM11125, Reel 1.

5   Derek Oakley, Interview with the author, 3 April 2012.

6   Lt Col ER Bridges, Report: 42 Commando Operations in Brunei and

Sarawak 11th December to 3rd January Ref. map Brunei FARELF MISC
1069 (Attached) Annex: The assault on Limbang, Royal Marines Museum
Archives.

7   Capt DA Oakley, Chronology, 42 Cdo Confrontation 1962–66 Borneo
     Campaign. Prepared for J D Ladd, April 1980, HR7/20/9 Royal Marines
     Museum Archives; Major P. H. Darling, R.M., 'Operations in Brunei
     1962–3', in Inst Lt WLl Evans, RN (ed), *42 1962–1963, The Magazine of the
     42 Commando Royal Marines*, Singapore, 1963, 4.

8   'Limbang', *Globe & Laurel*, vol. LXXI, no. 2, April/May 1963, 83. The
     following units, or significant elements of them, were deployed to Borneo in
     response to the rebellion before May 1963: 40 Commando Royal Marines; 42
     Commando Royal Marines; 1st/2nd Gurkhas; 1st/7th Gurkhas; Queen's Royal
     Irish Hussars; 29th Commando Light Regiment Royal Artillery; Queen's Own
     Highlanders; King's Own Yorkshire Light Infantry; 1st Green Jackets; 22
     Special Air Service.

9   Admiralty and Ministry of Defence, Royal Marines: War Diaries, Unit
     Diaries, Detachment Reports and Orders: Commander's Diaries: Operations
     in Sarawak. 40 Commando, 101129ADM202/475, The National Archives,
     UK.

10   Jeremy Moore, Interview (1999), IWM31692, Reel 2.

11   'Free Borneo or war to death', *The Straits Times*, 10 December 1962, 1.

12   It was also known as the 'Grey Coast off the Borneo Coast': Julian Thompson,
     Correspondence with the author, 21 September 2012.

13   'Governor gives complete picture', *The Sarawak Tribune*, 10 December 1962,
     1.

14   RH Morris to Chief Secretary, Confidential Report detailing the situation
     during the period 7/12/62 to end January 1963, 8 March 1963, 2 (item 7),
     Morris Papers.

15   Mrs RH Morris, 'Etiquette and Alka Seltzers', *Globe & Laurel: Journal of the
     Royal Marines*, vol. LXXII, March/April 1964, 103.

16   Thaine H Allison, Jr Interview with the author, 8 May 2012; 'Reflections
     of Fifty Years of Peace Corps Service North Borneo/Sarawak 1962–64',
     unpublished manuscript, Morris Papers.

17   Robert G Carey, with foreword by Joseph H Blatchford, *The Peace Corps*, New
     York: Praeger, 1970, 18.

18   Vicar Delegate to Father Figl, 21 December, 1962 R28/12/62 St Joseph's
     College (Mill Hill Missionaries) Archives, MHM Central Archive BOR62-
     Miri1962. Their captors, being of smaller stature and more lightly built,
     thought it necessary to guard against the bulky frames of Cronin and
     Klattenhoff.

19   Chris Ashton, 'From the Highlands', *Highlife Magazine*, vol. 7, no. 1 (October
     2002), 184.

20   D Morris to RH Morris, 22 December 1962, Morris Papers.

6 Tuesday, 11 December: Plans in action

1 'SOS goes out to shotgun tribesmen', *The Straits Times*, 11 December 1962, 20.

2 Zaini Haji Ahmad, *The People's Party of Brunei: Selected Documents*, Petaling Jaya: Institute of Social Analysis, 1987, 35.

3 Colonial Office and Commonwealth Office, Brunei Disturbances, 1962, C01030/1069, 21, The National Archives, UK; Colonial Office and Commonwealth Office, Brunei Disturbances, 1962, C01030/1070, 10, The National Archives, UK.

4 'Fisher's Appeal', *The Sarawak Tribune*, 11 December 1962, 3; Peter Smark, 'As I See It', *The Sarawak Tribune*, 11 December 1962, 8; 'SOS goes out to shotgun tribesmen', *The Straits Times*, 11 December 1962, 20.

5 'Public Opinion, Anger and Indignation', *The Sarawak Tribune*, 14 December 1962, 7.

6 Sharon Ling, 'James Wong dies', *The Star* online, 19 July 2011, online at <thestar.com.my/news/story.asp?file=/2011/7/19/sarawak/9126319&sec=sarawak>, accessed 27 July 2012; When Sarawak gained independence through Malaysia in 1963, Wong became the state's first Deputy Chief Minister in the inaugural Cabinet.

7 W Donough, 'I Saw It All', *The Sarawak Tribune*, 19 December 1962, 5; Hostages held at Seria were released on the morning of 12 December: Harold James and Denis Sheil-Small, *The Undeclared War*, Kuala Lumpur: University of Malaya Cooperative Bookshop Ltd, 1979, 26.

8 'Mr Tan: Veil Lifted', *The Straits Times*, 13 December 1962, 22.

9 'A quick look at how the "war" is going', *The Straits Times*, 11 December 1962, 1.

10 'Stephens: Indonesian Reds helped train rebels', *The Straits Times*, 12 December 1962, 24.

11 The three leaders issued a joint communiqué on 9 July 1961: Zaini, *The People's Party*, 72 and note 29.

12 'Azahari Claim is Condemned', *The Straits Times*, 13 December 1962, 8.

13 *Izvestiya*, 1962, in Colonial Office and Commonwealth Office, Brunei Disturbances, 1962, 11 December 1962, C01030/1070, 41, The National Archives, UK.

14 11 December 1962, C01030/1070, 42.

15 11 December 1962, C01030/1070, 44.

16 11 December 1962, C01030/1070, 64.

17 It took this time to transport the commando to Kota Belud for their earlier training there: '42', *Globe & Laurel*, vol. LXX, no. 6, December 1962/January 1963, 390.

18 Alex Hunter, 'Maj Gen AG Patterson CB DSO OBE MC – My Grandfather', online at <www.haebc.com/2011/11/maj-gen-a-g-patterson-my-grandfather/>, accessed 11 November 2011.

19 Jeremy Moore, Interview (1999), IWM31692, Reel 2.

20 Lt Col ER Bridges, Report: 42 Commando Operations in Brunei and

Sarawak 11th December to 3rd January Ref. map Brunei FARELF MISC 1069 (Attached) Annex: The assault on Limbang, Item 10, Royal Marines Museum Archives.

21   John Shirley, 'Obituary, Major General Sir Jeremy Moore', *The Guardian*, 18 September 2007, online at <www.guardian.co.uk/news/2007/sep/18/ guardianobituaries.military>, accessed 6 February 2012.

22   Bridges, Report: 42 Commando Operations, Royal Marines Museum Archives.

23   Col Bengie Walden, Interview with the author, 11 July 2012. Other reports confirmed that they lacked sufficient intelligence: Peter Down, Interview with the author, 9 July 2012; David Greenhough, Interview (1999), IWM11144, Reel 3.

24   Bridges, Report: 42 Commando Operations, Royal Marines Museum Archives.

25   Lt Peter Down, Interview with the author, Morris Papers, 9 July 2012. Ton class minesweepers usually carried a crew of about 33 men.

26   He added that they 'never knew what happened' to the beer. Laurie Johnson, 'HMS Chawton, 1961–1963', online at <britains-smallwars.com/Borneo/ Chawton.htm>, accessed 4 August 2012.

27   Down, Interview, 9 July 2012; 'Heart of Oak' is the official march of the British Royal Navy. It dates from a William Boyce composition (1759), and was played on the quarterdeck of HMS *Victory* as Nelson sailed into battle at Trafalgar. A copy of the 1962 film *H.M.S. Defiant* starring Alec Guinness and Dirk Bogarde was on board Black's ship. This threw the crew into thinking about Nelson's navy. To lighten the rigours and confined quarters of minesweeper life, Black peppered his orders, giving them in the speech of Nelson's time.

28   Tony Daker, Interview (2012), IWM33246, Reel 7.

29   John Genge, Interview (2012), IWM33210, Reel 2.

30   Laurie Russell, Interview (2012), IWM33214, Reel 6.

31   'JCB' refers to the earth diggers. A sangar is a fortified position above ground built with sandbags with overhead cover to protect against shrapnel.

32   Russell, IWM33214, Reel 6.

33   Moore, IWM31692, Reel 3.

34   Moore, IWM31692, Reel 3.

35   Moore, IWM31692, Reel 4.

36   When recalling events 40 years later, Moore described there being 87: Moore, IWM31692, Reel 2; Veterans today consider the number totalled 89, as Lt Col Bridges reported at the time.

37   Daker, IWM33246, Reel 7.

38   Daker, IWM33246, Reel 7.

39   Moore, IWM31692, Reel 3.

40   Pemerintah Revolusioner Negara Kesatuan Kalimantan Utara to Abang Umar, 11 December 1962, Morris Papers.

41   RH Morris to Chief Secretary, Confidential Report detailing the situation during the period 7/12/62 to end January 1963, 8 March 1963, Morris Papers.

42 Mrs RH Morris, 'Etiquette and Alka Seltzers', *Globe & Laurel: Journal of the Royal Marines*, vol. LXXII, March/April 1964, 103.

43 D Morris to RH Morris, 22 December 1962, 6, Morris Papers.

44 RH Morris, 'Abang Omar bin Abang Samaudin', unpublished manuscript, 3, Morris Papers.

45 Morris, Confidential Report, 8 March 1963, Morris Papers.

46 Greenhough, IWM11144, Reel 1.

47 'Limbang', *Globe & Laurel*, vol. LXXI, no. 2, April/May 1963, 83.

48 Peter Down, *Document for 50th reunion*, unpublished manuscript, Morris Papers.

49 'Limbang', *Globe & Laurel*, vol. LXXI, no. 2, April/May 1963, 83.

50 Genge, IWM33210, Reel 2.

51 Cpl Bob Rawlinson MM RM, Interview with the author, 4 July 2012.

52 Mike Bell, Interview with the author, 2 April 2012.

53 Mike Bell, Interview, 2 April 2012.

54 Daker, IWM33246, Reel 7.

55 Pronto, 'Loud and Clear', in Inst Lt Ll Evans, RN (ed), *42 1962–1963, The Magazine of the 42 Commando Royal Marines*, Singapore, 1963, 6.

7 Wednesday, 12 December: Rescue the hostages

1 Reuters report 59, 12 December 1962, Colonial Office and Commonwealth Office: Brunei Disturbances 1962, C01030/1070, The National Archives, UK.

2 Reuters report 53; Brunei Marines 13; Labuan Reuters RG 0854, C01030/1070, The National Archives, UK.

3 *The Straits Times*, 14 December 1962, 13.

4 Reuters report 11, 12 December 1962, C01030/1070.

5 Reuters report 57, 12 December 1962, C01030/1070.

6 Terry Aspinall, 'Royal Marine Commandos April 1962–February 1963', online at <www.terryaspinall.com/autobiography-chapters/chapter04.html>, accessed 27 July 2012. Added to the ten recipients of the Victoria Cross between 1854 and 1945 is Col Eric Harden, who was in the Royal Army Medical Corps, but attached to a Royal Marines commando unit in 1945. See Matthew G Little, 'The Victoria Cross and the Royal Marines', online at <www.royalmarinesmuseum.co.uk/item/researching-family-and-royal-marine-history/the-victoria-cross-the-royal-marin>, accessed 8 October 2012.

7 Terry Aspinall, 'Active Service February 1963–July 1963', online at <www.terryaspinall.com/autobiography-chapters/chapter05.html>, accessed 27 July 2012. Terry Aspinall was assigned to 40 Commando when he Passed Out in January 1963.

8 Mike Bell, Interview with the author, 2 April 2012.

9 Julian Howard Atherden Thompson, Interview (2005), IWM28361, Reel 2.

10 Aspinall, 'Royal Marine Commandos'.

11 'Ubique from the Royal Artillery', in Inst Lt Ll Evans, RN (ed), *42 1962–1963, The Magazine of the 42 Commando Royal Marines*, Singapore, 1963, 24.

12 Bell, Interview, 2 April 2012.

13 *Globe & Laurel*, vol. LXXI, no. 1, February/March 1963, 42. For descriptions

of how American servicemen valued the green beret in 1964, see Terry Aspinall, 'Burma Camp for the 3rd time, February 1964 to July 1964', 1998, online at <www.terryaspinall.com/autobiography-chapters/chapter09.html>, accessed 6 June 2012.

14 National Service ceased in 1959, and all members of the Royal Marines became Commando trained. Julian Thompson, Interview with the author, 10 July 2012.

15 David Lee, 'A Year in 42 Commando, November 1963–1964 Singapore and Borneo', online at <file://localhost/Volumes/42CommandoBorneo/RM_42 Cdo Folder/A Year in 42 Commando.htm>, accessed 7 August 2012. For a list of British and Commonwealth military forces serving in the Borneo front, see: Britain's Small Wars <www.britains-smallwars.com/Borneo/units.html>, accessed 17 May 2012.

16 'Malaya and all that', *Globe & Laurel*, vol. LXX, no. 4, August/September 1962, 245.

17 Jeremy Moore, Interview (1999), IWM31692, Reel 3.

18 David Greenhough, Interview (1992), IWM11144, Reel 3.

19 Peter Down, Interview with the author, 9 July 2012.

20 Cpl Bob Rawlinson, Interview with the author, 4 July 2012.

21 Tony Daker, Interview (2012), IWM33246, Reel 7.

22 Moore, IWM31692, Reel 3.

23 Deliberately, they aimed high, such as above windows in buildings; they wanted to avoid casualties and to rescue the hostages alive. John Genge, Interview (2012), IWM33210, Reel 2.

24 Moore, IWM31692, Reel 3

25 Sgt Macfarlane is incorrectly named as TSM McDonald: James D Ladd, *The Royal Marines 1919–1980: An Authorised History*, London; New York; Sydney: Jane's, 1980, 310.

26 RH Morris to Law Ah Kaw, 10 May 1963, Morris Papers.

27 This was Haji Pilok. Haji Zaini Ahmad, *The People's Party of Brunei: Selected Documents*, Petaling Jaya, Selangor: Institute of Social Analysis, 1987, 34.

28 John Shirley, 'Obituary: Major General Sir Jeremy Moore', *The Guardian*, 18 September 2007, online at <www.guardian.co.uk/news/2007/sep/18/guardianobituaries.military>, accessed 6 February 2012.

29 RH Morris, 'Limbang – An Inside Story', in Inst Lt Ll Evans, RN (ed), *42 1962–1963, The Magazine of the 42 Commando Royal Marines*, Singapore, 1963, 9.

30 Moore took Shakespeare's Sonnets with him to the Falklands War; he said that he always carried them with him ever since Limbang. Moore, IWM31692, Reel 37.

31 Mrs RH Morris, 'Etiquette and Alka Seltzers', *Globe & Laurel: Journal of the Royal Marines*, vol. LXXII, March/April 1964, 104.

32 Pronto, 'Loud and Clear', *42 1962–1963, The Magazine of the 42 Commando Royal Marines*, Singapore, 1963, 7.

33 Daker, IWM33246, Reel 7.

34 Moore, IWM31692, Reel 4.

35   Morris, 'Limbang – An Inside Story', 9.
36   Moore, IWM31692, Reel 4. The Marines had just been shot at where Moore stood.
37   Genge, IWM33210, Reel 2.
38   Greenhough, IWM11144, Reel 2.
39   Moore, IWM31692, Reel 4.
40   Moore, IWM31692, Reel 4.
41   D Morris to RH Morris, 22 December 1962, 6, Morris Papers.
42   Lt Col ER Bridges, Report: 42 Commando Operations in Brunei and Sarawak 11th December to 3rd January FARELF MISC 1069 Annex: The assault on Limbang, Royal Marines Museum Archives.
43   The first RAF fighter aircraft to be involved were Hawker Hunters, which flew up the Limbang River. Laurie Russell, Interview (2012), IWM33214, Reel 6.
44   'Brunei Released from Rebel Hands: And Aspects of the Hunt for the Leaders of the Rebellion', *Illustrated London News*, 29 December, 1962, 1042–43.
45   Vicar Delegate to Father Figl, 21 December 1962, R28/12/62 St Joseph's College (Mill Hill Missionaries) Archives.
46   Down, Interview, 9 July 2012.
47   D Morris to RH Morris, 22 December 1962, 1, Morris Papers.
48   D Morris to RH Morris, 22 December 1962, 1, Morris Papers.
49   D Morris to RH Morris, 22 December 1962, 6. The UK Commissioner-General for Southeast Asia (1948–60) also described Sarawak as a 'peaceful place': Malcolm McDonald, *Borneo People*, London: Jonathan Cape, 1956, 11.
50   D Morris to RH Morris, 22 December 1962, 6, Morris Papers.
51   Capt DA Oakley, Interview with the author, 2 April 2012.
52   Oakley, Interview, 2 April 2012; Moore, IWM31692, Reel 4.
53   These letters have not survived. A cable was also sent to her daughter in Sydney from HMS *Fiskerton*: Morris Papers.
54   RH Morris to Chief Secretary, Secretariat, Kuching Confidential report, detailing the situation during the period 7/12/62 to end January 1963, 8 March 1963, Morris Papers.
55   RH Morris, 'Limbang – An Inside Story', 10.
56   When interviewed in 1992, Greenhough said, 'I recall that my own private mental picture was of thousands of airborne Indonesians floating down upon us!', although it is thought that Indonesian involvement was apparent to few on the ground in early December 1962.Greenhough, IWM11144, Reel 2.
57   Bell, Interview, 2 April 2012.

8   Thursday, 13 December: Enemies within

1   Jeremy Moore, Interview (1999), IWM31692, Reel 4.
2   David Greenhough, Interview (1992), IWM11144, Reel 2. Moore's report confirmed that the magazines of recaptured weapons were badly filled: 'The Assault on Limbang, Sarawak by "L" Company Group 42 Commando Royal Marines on 12th December 1962', HR7/20/11, Royal Marines Museum Archives.

3   RH Morris, 'Limbang – An Inside Story' in Inst Lt Ll Evans, RN (ed), *42 1962–1963, The Magazine of the 42 Commando Royal Marines*, Singapore, 1963, 10.

4   Moore, IWM31692, Reel 4.

5   Sgt KD Fyffe, 'Bullets and Bumboats: Recollections of the Limbang Raid', online at <www.britains-smallwars.com/Borneo/Bullets-Bumboats.htm>, accessed 8 October 2012.

6   As a photograph shows: '"L" Company – Bullets and Beer', *Globe & Laurel*, vol. LXXI, no. 1, February/March 1963, 21.

7   Capt DA Oakley, Chronology, 42 Cdo Confrontation 1962–66 Borneo Campaign, April 1980, HR7/20/9, Royal Marines Museum Archives.

8   D Morris to RH Morris, 13 December 1962, Morris Papers.

9   'A Window on the World', *Illustrated London News*, 5 January 1963, 11.

10   Greenhough, IWM11144, Reel 2.

11   Greenhough, IWM11144, Reel 2.

12   Lt Col ER Bridges, 'The Assault on Limbang Sarawak 11th December to 3rd January', Ref. map Brunei FARELF MISC 1069, Royal Marines Museum Archives.

13   '"L" Company', *Globe & Laurel: Journal of the Royal Marines*, vol. LXXI, no. 2, April/May 1963, 83.

14   '250 Rebels Taken Prisoner', *The Times* (London), 13 December 1962, 10.

15   Greenhough, IWM11144, Reel 2.

16   Army Intelligence, Joint PERINTREP, No. 1, Part III, 9. Royal Marines Museum Archives.

17   'Poett: First phase of rebellion collapsed', *The Straits Times*, 13 December 1962, 22.

9   December and beyond

1   'General Appointed Borneo Commander', *The Times* (London), 17 December 1962, 7.

2   Laurie Russell, Interview (2012), IWM33214, Reel 6. For an example of the circulars distributed in the hunt for rebel leaders see: 'Wanted poster: Yassin Affandy Rahman', Sea Your History online at <www.seayourhistory.org0uk/component/option/com_gallery2/Itemid,811/?g2_itemid=14762>, accessed 27 May 2012.

3   Russell, IWM33214, Reel 6

4   'Comment: Confidence', *The Sarawak Tribune*, 15 December 1961, 4. 42 Commando was complete in Brunei by 17 December.

5   'Who are Azahari's Supporters in Sarawak?', *The Sarawak Tribune*, 15 December 1962, 2.

6   'Malaysia, The Final Details', *The Straits Times*, 18 December 1962, 6.

7   Sir John Martin to RH Morris, 12 December 1962, Morris Papers.

8   Mike Bell, Interview with the author, 2 April 2012.

9   For an example from Sydney see: 'White hostages', *Daily Telegraph* (Sydney), 15 December 1962, 1.

10   'Australian Saved from Noose', *The Age*, 14 December, 1962, 1; 'The man

with his head in a noose, He is saved by swooping jets', *Evening Standard* (London), 13 December 1962, 13. It was much to Dick's distaste that this incorrect report was further sensationalised: Alan Bayne, *Tuan, In the Morning you hang and other stories*, Lewes: Book Guild, 1996, 181–210, particularly 202.

11 'The Battle of Limbang', 15 December 1962, 12.

12 'Mrs Morris Relates Experience', *The Sarawak Tribune*, 17 December 1962, 3.

13 John Williams worked in the Sarawak Secretariat. K & J Williams to RH Morris, 18 December 1962, Morris Papers.

14 D Morris to RH Morris, 22 December 1962, 7. The area at Pangkalan Batu, diagonally opposite the Brooke Monument, was the reference point from which other settlements outside Kuching town were measured, like 7th Mile, 10th Mile, etc. See, Tengku Reza Affendi, 'Vintage Malaya', online at <www.vintagemalaya.com/Kuching.html>, accessed 31 May 2012.

15 D Morris to RH Morris, 22 December 1961, 6, Morris Papers.

16 D Morris to RH Morris, 22 December 1962, 4, Morris Papers.

17 D Morris to RH Morris, 22 December 1962, 5, Morris Papers.

18 M Weekes to D Morris, 18 December 1962, Morris Papers.

19 D Morris to RH Morris, 8 December 1962, 1, Morris Papers.

20 PJ Shannon to RH Morris, 17 December 1962, Morris Papers.

21 ACM Walker to D Morris, 17 December 1962, Morris Papers.

22 D Morris to RH Morris, 18 December 1962, Morris Papers.

23 O King to D Morris, 16 December 1962, Morris Papers.

24 C Helm to D & RH Morris, 17 December 1962, Morris Papers.

25 ACM Walker to D Morris, 17 December 1962, Morris Papers.

26 ACM Walker to D Morris, 17 December 1962, Morris Papers.

27 P Jacks to D Morris, n.d., Morris Papers.

28 Letter to D & RH Morris, 17 December 1962, Morris Papers.

29 L Chater to D Morris, 19 December 1962, Morris Papers.

30 HP Buxton to D & RH Morris, 19 December 1962, Morris Papers.

31 RH Morris to Chief Secretary, Confidential Report detailing the situation during the period 7/12/62 to end January 1963, 8 March 1963, 5, Morris Papers.

32 Letter to RH Morris, 17 December 1962, 1, Morris Papers.

33 John Genge, Interview (2012), IWM33210, Reel 3.

34 'Large Numbers Surrender', *The Sarawak Tribune*, 18 December 1962, 3.

35 '42', *Globe & Laurel*, vol. LXXI, no. 1, February/March 1963, 21.

36 'Large Numbers Surrender', *The Sarawak Tribune*, 18 December 1962, 3.

37 David Greenhough, Interview (1992), IWM11144, Reel 2.

38 'Back to Normal', *The Sarawak Tribune*, 18 December 1962, 1.

39 Tom Harrison, 'The Arc of Resolution', *North Borneo News and Sabah Times*, 12 January 1963, 5.

40 RH Morris to Chief Secretary, Confidential Report, 3, Morris Papers.

41 M Weekes to D Morris, 18 December 1962, Morris Papers.

42 '42', *Globe & Laurel*, vol. LXXI, no. 1, February/March 1963, 20.

43 '42', *Globe & Laurel*, vol. LXXI, no. 1, February/March 1963, 21.

44 Press Statement, undated, 2, Morris Papers.
45 District Officer Report, 26 April 1963, 5, Morris Papers.
46 Leslie Thomas Hyland, Interview (1998), IWM17994, Reel 1. Hyland was with Headquarters Troop, 42 Commando Royal Marines in Malaya (1950–51).
47 H Dalton, 'A Brunei Christmas (with apologies)', *Globe & Laurel*, vol. LXXI, no. 1, February/March 1963, 17.
48 '42', *Globe & Laurel*, vol. LXXI, no. 1, February/March 1963, 20.
49 *Globe & Laurel*, vol. LXXI, no. 1, February/March 1963, 19.
50 'The People we met', *Globe & Laurel*, vol. LXXI, no. 2, April/May 1963, 82.
51 'The People we met', *Globe & Laurel*, vol. LXXI, no. 2, April/May 1963, 82.
52 *Globe & Laurel*, vol. LXXI, no. 1, February/March 1963, 17.
53 'Commando Brigade HQ', *Globe & Laurel*, vol. LXXI, no. 3, June/July 1963, 146.
54 'The People we met', *Globe & Laurel*, vol. LXXI, no. 2, April/May 1963, 82.
55 D Morris to RH Morris, 19 December 1962, 5, Morris Papers.
56 RH Morris to D Morris, 19 December 1962, 1, Morris Papers.
57 RH Morris to D Morris, 19 December 1962, 2, Morris Papers.
58 Poett was succeeded by Sir John David Luce GCB, DSO & Bar, who became Commander-in-Chief of British Forces in the Far East and UK Military Adviser to the Southeast Asia Treaty Organization in November 1962. Luce subsequently became First Sea Lord and Chief of the Naval Staff in August 1963, and resisted government moves to cut spending.
59 'Tribute and Criticism', *The Sarawak Tribune*, 20 December 1962, 1.
60 'Brunei Coup Frustrated', *The Sarawak Tribune*, 22 December 1962, 3.
61 Armed rebels remaining in the immediate vicinity of Limbang made it difficult to achieve normality quickly: RH Morris to Chief Secretary, Confidential Report, 8 March 1963, 5, Morris Papers.
62 'Two Top Rebels Captured', *The Straits Times*, 20 December 1962, 1.
63 'Rebels "lose faith" in Azahari', *The Straits Times*, 21 December 1962, 24.
64 'The last day of the month, last day of the year ... report of Limbang being nearly back to normal', Radio Sarawak Transcript, *The Sarawak Tribune*.
65 RH Morris to D Morris, 19 December 1962, 2, Morris Papers.
66 The Indonesians sent 855 infiltrators against Malaysia and Singapore. See: '7 years' jail for having 3 home-made bombs', *The Straits Times*, 23 June 1964, 9; 'Behind the Bombs', *The Straits Times*, 23 April 1964, 10; Lieut. Colonel JP Craw RA, 'Indonesian Military Incursions into West Malaysia and Singapore between August 1964 and 30th September 1965', *Royal United Services Institution Journal*, vol. 11, no. 642 (1966), 219.
67 At the time the Indonesian Air Force was patrolling the border between Indonesia and British Borneo. Indonesia alleged that foreign planes were conducting surveillance on Indonesian air force bases in Borneo, thus violating Indonesian air space. Indonesia warned against 'an unexpected thing' happening unless such 'black flights' were stopped. See: 'Jakarta puts off decision on intervention in Brunei', *New York Times*, 9 January 1963, 3; 'Air Patrol Over Border', *The Sarawak Tribune*, 11 January 1963, 1. Moreover,

Indonesian forces had shot down an American plane flying over Ambon in support of rebels in Sulawesi in May 1958, and captured its pilot. Indonesia held him under house arrest for just over four years. In 1960 an Indonesian court condemned him to death but in 1962 President Sukarno released him. On this, see: 'U. S. Aide sees captive: Flier shot down in Indonesia …', *New York Times*, 5 June 1958, 12; 'Sukarno adds pardons: US pilot may be freed …', *New York Times*, 22 October 1961, 10.

68   Kenneth Toft, 'Transportation in Singapore', National Archives Singapore 002579, Reel 5–6; Toft was a senior pilot with Malayan Airways, flying in Borneo, then later with Singapore Airlines. Toft does not specify the exact date of the incident. The Indonesian policy of Confrontation was first expressed by Foreign Minister Subandrio on 19 December 1961 to the Indonesian House of Representatives over moves in West Irian, coinciding with President Sukarno's Command for the Liberation of West Irian. It would continue to be expressed in relation to North Borneo through 1963, and later, as when Sukarno proclaimed *Konfrontasi* in his *Dwi Komando Rakjat* (DWIKORA) speech in Jakarta on 3 May 1964.

69   Captain GF Daniels, *The Brunei Rebellion* (1995), IWM09/53A.

70   David Walder Esq. ERD, MP, 'Malaysia', *Royal United Services Institution Journal*, vol. 110, no. 638 (1965), 107.

10   Aftermath

1   '40 – Sergeant's Mess', *Globe & Laurel*, vol. LXXI, no. 1, February/March 1963, 18.

2   RH Morris to DJ Morris, 30 December 1962, 1, Morris Papers.

3   This was CJ Gillingham, RM: 'Obituary', *Globe & Laurel*, vol. LXXI, no. 1, February/March 1963, 59.

4   '40', *Globe & Laurel*, vol. LXXI, no. 1, February/March 1963, 18.

5   '42', *Globe & Laurel*, vol. LXXI, no. 1, February/March 1963, 21.

6   'Commando Brigade HQ', *Globe & Laurel*, vol. LXXI, no. 1, February/March 1963, 16.

7   Maj Gen WC Walker, Undated Press Statement, 20 February 1963, Morris Papers; Colonel IG Wellstead to RH Morris, Morris Papers.

8   PERINTREP No. 4 7/20/11 Item 8, 7 Sarawak–Lawas District, TNKU a, Royal Marines Museum Archives.

9   Zaini Haji Ahmad, *The People's Party of Brunei: Selected Documents*, Petaling Jaya, Selangor: Institute of Social Analysis, 1987, 40; It was incorrectly reported that he was killed: 'Gurkha soldier lunge, Helping Malaysia Facing RPKAD', <menarainformasi.blogspot.com.au/2012/04/gurkha-soldier-lunge-helping-malaysia.html>, accessed 30 July 2012; AVM Horton, *A Biographical Dictionary of Negara Brunei Darussalam 1841–1998*, vol. 2, 4th edn, Bordesley, Worcestershire: AVM Horton, 1999, 942.

10   '42', *Globe & Laurel*, vol. LXXI, no. 2, April/May 1963, 81.

11   KL inward telegram to Commonwealth Relations Office, 21 December 1962.

12   Richard Brooks, *The Royal Marines*, London: Constable, 2002, 282.

13   Julian Thompson, Interview (2005), IWM28361, Reel 18.

14   *The Times* (London), 17 September, 2007; '42 Commando Casualties in Brunei', *Globe & Laurel*, vol. LXXI, no. 1, February/March 1963, 59.

15   Jeremy Black, Interview (1983), IWM9005, Reel 4: Black had come to notice after the counter-insurgency operation in Brunei Town's floating village. One of the small outboard dugouts used on that raid remained on Black's minesweeper. It had been 'borrowed' because it was ideally suited for use in the local conditions.

16   *London Gazette*, issue 43010 (31 May 1963), 6; Supplement to the *London Gazette* (8 June 1963), 4798.

17   Philip Ziegler, *Mountbatten: The official biography*, London: Collins, 1985, 629, cited in Philip Ziegler, 'Mountbatten, Louis Francis Albert Victor Nicholas, first Earl Mountbatten of Burma (1900–1979)', *Oxford Dictionary of National Biography*, Oxford University Press, 2004; online edition, January 2011, online at <www.oxforddnb.com/view/article/31480>, accessed 10 August 2012.

18   Tom Pocock, *Fighting General: The public and private campaigns of General Sir Walter Walker*, London: Collins, 1973, 241.

19   Zaini, *The People's Party of Brunei*, 38–39.

20   Capt JJ Moore to RH Morris, 28 December 1962, Morris Papers.

21   'B' Coy to RH Morris, 28 December 1963, Morris Papers; '42', *Globe & Laurel*, vol. LXXI, no. 1, February–March 1963, 21.

22   Teng to RH Morris, 18 December 1963, Morris Papers.

23   RH Morris, 'Abang Omar bin Abang Samaudin', 4, Morris Papers; Cutfield was awarded the Military Cross: *The London Gazette*, Third Supplement, no. 42188, 17 December 1963. The difficulty of the operation is described by an officer who served with the 2/7th Gurkha Rifles, and also gave his blood: Mike Allen, Interview (1992), IWM11129, Creator Charles Allen.

24   'Brunei Rebel Leader Sentenced', *The Times*, 31 May 1963. With good conduct remission, Sambas was released after ten years. He returned to live not far from Limbang.

25   *The Times* (London), 31 May 1963, 10.

26   RH Morris to DJ Morris, 30 December 1962, 4, Morris Papers.

27   RH Morris to Major General WC Walker, 27 April 1963, Morris Papers.

28   RH Morris to Brigadier AG Patterson, OBE, MC, 29 April 1963, Morris Papers.

29   Brigadier AG Patterson to RH Morris, 2 May 1963, Morris Papers.

30   Maj Gen WC Walker to RH Morris, 5 May 1963, Morris Papers.

31   'The Limbang Memorial Parade' in Inst Lt Ll Evans, RN (ed), *42 1962–1963, The Magazine of the 42 Commando Royal Marines*, Singapore, 1963, 66. RH Morris to D Morris, 8 March 1963, 2. Today the memorial is frequently visited by Royal Marines and maintained by them.

32   RH Morris, 'Limbang – An Inside Story', in Inst Lt Ll Evans, RN (ed), *42 1962–1963, The Magazine of the 42 Commando Royal Marines*, Singapore, 1963, 10.

33   Maj Gen WC Walker to RH Morris, n.d., Morris Papers.

34 Dato Abang Openg to RH Morris, 12 March, 1964, Morris Papers.

35 The annual Limbang commemoration is now replaced by commemoration of the Mount Kent Skirmish, Falkland Islands in May 1982.

36 'The Tercentenary of the Royal Marines: Parades and Celebrations', *Illustrated London News*, 1 August 1964, 146–47.

37 *Commonwealth Gazette*, 23 July 1970.

38 Lee Kuan Yew, 'The Legacy of Sultan Haji Omar Ali Saifuddien', 25 February 2009, online at <www.docstoc.com/docs/31476468/DRAFT-FOR-SULTAN-SIR-HAJI-OMAR-ALI-SAIFUDDIN-MEMORIAL-LECTURE-I>, accessed 3 March 2012. On maintaining the government of Brunei as a family business, see GMF Drower, *Britain's dependent territories: A fistful of islands*, Aldershot: Ashgate, 1992, 152–53.

39 Zaini, *The People's Party of Brunei*, 41.

40 Roger Kershaw, 'The Last Brunei Revolt? A Case Study of Microstate' (In-) Security *Internationales Asien Forum, International Quarterly for Asian Studies*, vol. 42 no. 1/2, May 2011, 117.

41 Thaine H Allison, Jr RPCV, 'Observations Limbang 40th Reunion, Lima Company 42 Commando Royal Marines', online at <peacecorpsonline.org/messages/messages/2629/2019318.html>, accessed 3 August 2012.

42 Martin Spirit, *Return to Limbang*, Dallas: Brushfire Films, 2006. The film is one in the series, Britain's Small Wars. See <www.britainssmallwars.com/Borneo/Limbang.html>, accessed 10 August 2012.

43 'Deaths In Memoriam', *The Times* (London), 12 December 1963, 1; Richard Hargreaves, 'Green Berets Forgotten Mission', *The News* (Portsmouth), 17 December 2002, 8.

BIBLIOGRAPHY

Unpublished material

Allison, Thaine H Jr. 'Reflections of Fifty Years of Peace Corps Service North Borneo/Sarawak 1962–64', unpublished manuscript, Morris Papers
—— Interview with the author, 8 May 2012, Morris Papers
Bell, Mike. Interview with the author, 2 April 2012, Morris Papers
Down, Lt Peter. Document for 50th Reunion (2012), unpublished manuscript, Morris Papers
—— Interview with the author, 9 July 2012, Morris Papers
Morris, Dorothy. 'V.A.D. Concerning certain activities of the Sarawak Branch of the British Red Cross and Limbang', unpublished manuscript, Morris Papers
Morris, Richard. *Sarawak Memoirs*, unpublished manuscript, Morris Papers
—— 'Abang Omar bin Abang Samaudin', unpublished manuscript, Morris Papers
Oakley, Capt Derek. Interview with the author, 3 April 2012, Morris Papers
Rawlinson, Cpl Bob. Interview with the author, 4 July 2012, Morris Papers
Samaudin, Abang Omar bin Abang. 'I declare …', unpublished manuscript, Morris Papers
Thompson, Maj Gen Julian. Interview with the author, 10 July 2012, Morris Papers
Walden, Col Bengie. Interview with the author, 11 July 2012, Morris Papers

Imperial War Museum, London

Burlison, Major JJ. *A Longest Day – Twenty Years After An Account of the Opening of the Brunei Revolt*, IWM96/555
Daniels, Captain GF. *The Brunei Rebellion* (1995), Private Papers of Captain GF Daniels, IWM09/53A

Sound Archives
Allen, Mike (1992) IWM11129, Creator Charles Allen
Black, John Jeremy (1983) IWM9005, Recorder Henry Raynham
Daker, Tony (2012) IWM33246, Creator Imperial War Museum
Downey, Brian (2012) IWM33244, Creator Imperial War Museum
Genge, John (2012) IWM33210, Creator Imperial War Museum
Greenhough, David (1992) IWM11144, Creator Charles Allen
Hyland, Leslie Thomas (1998) IWM17994, Recorder Conrad Wood
Jackman, Bruce (1990) IWM11125, Creator Charles Allen
Jenkins, Colonel Alan Middleton (2001) IWM21065, Recorder Conrad Wood
Moore, Jeremy (1999) IWM31692, Recorder Helen Arthy
Richards, Daphne (1983) IWM8450, Creator Charles Allen
Russell, Laurie (2012) IWM33214, Creator Imperial War Museum

Thompson, Julian Howard Atherden (2005) IWM28361, Recorder Nigel de Lee
Walker, General Sir Walter (1989) IWM11120, Creator Charles Allen

Mill Hill Missionaries Archive
BOR62-Miri 1962 Papers

Morris Family, Sydney
Morris, Dorothy Joan. Papers
Morris, Richard Holywell. Papers

National Archives, UK
ADM202/460 Commanders Diaries, Operations in Sarawak, April 1963
ADM202/461 Commanders Diaries, Operations in Sarawak, May 1963
ADM202/462 Commanders Diaries, Operations in Sarawak, June 1963
ADM202/463 Commanders Diaries, Operations in Sarawak, July 1963
ADM202/464 Commanders Diaries, Operations in Sarawak, August 1963
ADM202/465 Commanders Diaries, Operations in Sarawak, September 1963
ADM202/466 Commanders Diaries, Operations in Sarawak, October 1963
ADM202/467 Commanders Diaries, Operations in Sarawak,
    November 1963
ADM202/468 Commanders Diaries, Operations in Sarawak,
    December to January 1964
ADM202/469 Commanders Diaries, Operations in Sarawak, April 1963
ADM202/470 Commanders Diaries, Operations in Sarawak, May 1963
ADM202/471 Commanders Diaries, Operations in Sarawak, June 1963
ADM202/472 Commanders Diaries, Operations in Sarawak, July 1963
ADM202/474 40 Commando Royal Marines November 1963
ADM202/475 40 Commando Royal Marines December 1963
ADM202/476 40 Commando January to February 1964
ADM202/477 Commanders Diaries, Operations in Sarawak, July 10–31, 1963
ADM202/478 Commanders Diaries, Operations in Sarawak, August 1963
ADM202/478 Commanders Diaries, Operations in Sarawak, September 1963
ADM202/480 Commanders Diaries, Operations in Sarawak, October 1963
ADM202/583 42Cdo 1962
ADM301/1 42Cdo 1960–1963
ADM301/13 42Cdo 1962–1963
C01030/1068 Brunei disturbances 1962
C01030/1069 Brunei disturbances 1962
C01030/1070 Brunei disturbances 1962
C01030/1071 Brunei disturbances 1962
C01030/1072 Brunei disturbances 1962
C01030/1073 Brunei disturbances 1962
C01030/1075 Brunei disturbances 1962–1963
C01030/1076 Brunei disturbances 1962–1963
C01030/1077 Brunei disturbances 1962

CO1030/1125 Visit to Australia of Mr. R. H. Morris, Administrative Officer in Sarawak 1959–1960

CO1030/1241 Secretariat newsletter, Sarawak 1960–1962

CO1030/1296 Annexation of Limbang area 1960–1963

CO1030/1490 Brunei disturbances 1963

CO1030/1491 Brunei disturbances 1963

WO181/358 Borneo and Sarawak 1961–1965

WO32/19266 Borneo/Sarawak battalions 1963

WO32/20364 Comments on Chiefs of Staff report on measures to counter Indonesian action against Sarawak and Sabah 1963

National Archives, Singapore

Abraham, Ambassador Thomas (1999). 'Political History in Singapore 1945–1965', Oral History Interview, 02163

Bogaars, George Edwin (1981). 'The Civil Service – A Retrospection', Oral History Interview, 000032

Lee, Khoon Choy (1981). 'Political History in Singapore 1945–1965', Oral History Interview, 000022

Toft, Kenneth Edward (2002). 'Transportation in Singapore', Oral History Interview, 002579

Tregonning, Dr Kennedy Gordon (2003). 'Education in Singapore', Oral History Interview, 002783

Royal Marines Museum Archives

Bridges, Lt Col ER. Report, '42 Commando Operations in Brunei and Sarawak 11th December to 3rd January. Ref. Map Brunei FARELF MISC 1069 (Attached) Annex: The Assault on Limbang'

HQ British Forces Joint PERINTREP No. 1, Part lll Army Intelligence No. 4 (7/20/11)

Oakley, Captain DA. Chronology, 42 Codo Confrontation 1962–66 Borneo Campaign, Prepared for J D Ladd, April 1980, HR7/20/9

'Operations in the Temburong District by 42 Commando, Royal Marines 13th December 1962–5th February 1963', HR7/20/11

'The Assault on Limbang, Sarawak by "L" Company Group 42 Commando Royal Marines on 12th December 1962', HR7/20/11

Newspapers and journals

Brunei Times, The

Commonwealth Gazette

Daily Mirror (Sydney)

Daily Telegraph, The (UK)

Economist, The

Evening Standard, The (London)

42 1962–1963, The Magazine of 42 Commando Royal Marines

Globe & Laurel, Journal of the Royal Marines

Guardian, The
Highlife Magazine
Illustrated London News
Independent, The (UK)
Izvestiya
London Gazette, The
National Geographic Magazine
New Sunday Times
New York Times
News, The (Portsmouth)
North Borneo News and Sabah Times
Proceedings of the Royal Air Force Historical Society, The
Royal United Services Institution Journal
Sarawak by the Week
Sarawak Tribune, The
Scotsman, The
Star, The (Malaysia)
Straits Times, The
Sydney Morning Herald
Telegraph, The (London)
Times, The (London)
West Australian, The

Published material

Al-Sufri, Mohd. Jamil & Masni b. Ali. *Royal Poet al-marhum Sultan Haji Omar 'Ali Saifuddien Sa'adul Khairi Waddien*, Bandar Seri Begawan: Brunei History Centre, 2010

Amnesty International. *The Amnesty International Report, January to December 1984*, London: Amnesty International Publications, 1985

Andaya, BW & Y Leonard. *A History of Malaysia*, 2nd edn, Honolulu: University of Hawaii Press, 2001

Bayne, Alan. *Tuan in the Morning You Hang and other stories*, Lewes: Book Guild, 1996

Beaver, Paul. *Today's Royal Marines*, Wellingsborough, Northamptonshire: Patrick Stephens, 1988

Benjamin, Geoffrey & Cynthia Chou (eds). *Tribal Communities in the Malay World: Historical, Cultural and Social Perspectives*, Leiden: International Institute for Asian Studies; Singapore: Institute of Southeast Asian Studies, 2002

Bolkiah, Mohamed. *Remember, Remember, the Eight of December: A Journey to 1962*, Bandar Seri Begawan: Brunei Press, 2007

British Commonwealth Year Book, The. 10th Edition, London: MacGibbon & Kee, 1963

Brooks, Richard. *The Royal Marines*, London: Constable, 2002

Brown, Donald E. 'Mechanisms for the maintenance of traditional elites in Brunei to the eve of independence', in VT King & AVM Horton, *From Buckfast to Borneo: Essays Presented to Father Robert Nicholl on the 85th Anniversary of his Birth*,

27 March 1995, University of Hull: Centre for South-East Asian Studies, 1995

Burgess, Anthony. *Devil of a State*, London: William Heinemann, 1961

—— *Little Wilson and Big God*, London: William Heinemann, 1987

Calvocoressi, P. *World Politics since 1945*, 9th edn, Harlow, England; New York: Pearson Longman, 2008

Carey, Robert G with foreword by Joseph H Blatchford. *The Peace Corps*, New York: Praeger, 1970

Chang, Pat Foh. *Legends & History of Sarawak*, Kuching: Chang Pat Foh, 1999

Clodfelter, Michael. *Warfare and Armed Conflicts: A Statistical Encyclopedia of Casualty and Other Figures, 1494–2007*, 3rd edn, Jefferson, NC: McFarland, 2008

Clutterbuck, Richard. *The Long Long War: The Emergency in Malaya 1948–1960*, London: Cassell, 1966

—— *Living with Terrorism*, London: Faber & Faber, 1975

—— *Conflict and Violence in Singapore and Malaysia 1945–1983*, Singapore: Graham Brash, 1984, rev., updated and enlarged edn

Cobbs-Hoffman, Elizabeth. *All You Need Is Love: The Peace Corps and the Spirit of the 1960s*, Cambridge, Mass.: Harvard University Press, 1998

Cribb, Robert & Audrey Kahin. *Historical Dictionary of Indonesia*, 2nd edn, Lanham, Md.: Scarecrow Press, 2004

Dennis, Peter & Jeffery Grey. *Emergency and Confrontation: Australian Military Operations in Malaya and Borneo 1950–1966*, Sydney: Allen & Unwin and the Australian War Memorial, 1996

Dickson, Mora. *A Season in Sarawak*, London: Dennis Dobson, 1962

Drower, GMF. *Britain's Dependent Territories: A Fistful of Islands*, Aldershot: Ashgate, 1992

Easter, David. *Britain and the Confrontation with Indonesia 1960–1966*, London: IB Tauris, 2004

Edwards, Lt Col Brian. *After Limbang: A Royal Marines Anthology of Experiences of the Confrontation with Indonesia December 1962 to September 1966*, Eastney, UK: Royal Marines Historical Society, 2010

Empire Economic Union. *The British Commonwealth Year Book*, 10th edn, London: MacGibbon & Kee, 1963

Esposito, John L (ed). *The Oxford Encyclopedia of the Modern Islamic World*, New York: Oxford University Press, 1995

—— *The Oxford Encyclopedia of the Islamic World*, New York, NY: Oxford University Press, 2009

Fowler, Will. *Royal Marine Commando 1950–1982*, London: Osprey, 2009

Geddes, WR. *Nine Dyak Nights*, Melbourne: Oxford University Press, 1957

Gin, Ooi Keat. *Historical Dictionary of Malaysia*, Lanham, Md.; Plymouth: Scarecrow Press, 2009

Great Britain Colonial Office. *Sarawak Annual Report 1959*, Kuching: Sarawak Government Printing Office 1959

—— *Colonial Reports: Sarawak*, London: Great Britain Stationery Office, 1961–1962

—— *North Borneo Annual Report 1962*, London: HM Stationery Office, 1963

Harris, George Lawrence. *North Borneo, Brunei, Sarawak (British Borneo)*, New
Haven, Conn.: Human Relations Area Files, 1956

Harrisson, Tom DSO, OBE. *The Borneans*, Singapore: The Straits Times Press,
1963

—— *Background to a Revolt: Brunei and the Surrounding Territory*, Wellington, NZ:
Government Printer, 1965

Ho Ah Chon (comp.). *Kuching, 1950–1959: Sir Anthony Foster Abell's era*, Kuching:
Ho Ah Chon, 1960

Hoffman, Elizabeth Cobbs. *All You Need Is Love: The Peace Corps and the Spirit of
the 1960s*, Cambridge, Mass.: Harvard University Press, 1998

Horton, AVM. *The British Residency in Brunei, 1906–1959*, Hull, Yorkshire: Centre
for South-East Asian Studies, 1984

—— *A Biographical Dictionary of Negara Brunei Darussalam (1821–1998)*, 4th edn,
Bordesley, Worcestershire: AVM Horton, 1999

—— 'Brunei Rebellion (December 1962)', in Keat Gin Ooi (ed), *Southeast Asia:
A Historical Encyclopedia, from Angkor Wat to East Timor*, vol. 2, Santa Barbara,
Calif.: ABC–Clio, 2004

Hussainmiya, Bachamiya Abdul. *Sultan Omar Ali Saifuddin III and Britain*, Kuala
Lumpur: Oxford University Press, 1995

—— & Nicholas Tarling. *Brunei: Traditions of Monarchic Culture and History, R. H.
Hickling's Memorandum upon Brunei Constitutional History and Practice*, Bandar
Seri Begawan: Yayasan Sultan Haji Hassanal Bolkiah, 2011

James, Harold & D. Sheil-Small. *The Undeclared War: The Story of Indonesian
Confrontation, 1962–1966*, London: Leo Cooper, 1971

—— *The Undeclared War*, Kuala Lumpur: University of Malaya Cooperative
Bookshop Ltd, 1979

Jones, LW. *Report on the Housing Census Held in Eight Towns, March–June 1960*,
Kuching, Sarawak: Govt. Print Office, 1960

Jones, Matthew. *Conflict and Confrontation in South East Asia, 1961–1965: Britain,
the United States, Indonesia and the Creation of Malaysia*, Cambridge; New York:
Cambridge University Press, 2001

Kirk-Greene, Anthony HM. *A Biographical Dictionary of the British Colonial
Governor, Vol. 1: Africa*, Brighton, Sussex: The Harvester Press, 1980

Krause, Gerald H. 'Brunei and the sea: Transformation of a maritime state', in
Victor T King & AVM Horton (eds), *From Buckfast to Borneo: Essays Presented
to Father Robert Nicholl on the 85th Anniversary of his Birth, 27 March 1995*,
University of Hull, Yorkshire: Centre for South-East Asian Studies, 1995

Ladd, James D. *The Royal Marines 1919–1980: An Authorised History*, London;
New York; Sydney: Jane's, 1980

Latta, Robert & Alexander Macbeath. *The Elements of Logic*, London: Macmillan,
1929

Lee, Edwin. *Sarawak in the Early Sixties*, Singapore: University of Singapore, 1964

Leigh, Michael. *Brunei Darussalam: The Price of Consent*, Canberra: Department of
the Parliamentary Library, 1985

—— *The Rising Moon: Political Change in Sarawak*, Sydney: Sydney University
Press, 1974

Long, Gavin. *The Final Campaigns*, Canberra: Australian War Memorial, 1963

Macadam, Ivison (ed). *Annual Register of World Events, vol. 205, 1963*, London; New York: Longmans, Green & Co., 1964

Mackie, JAC. *Konfrontasi: The Indonesia–Malaysia Dispute, 1963–1966*, Kuala Lumpur: Oxford University Press, 1974

Majid, Harun Abdul. *Rebellion in Brunei: The 1962 Revolt, Imperialism, Confrontation and Oil*, London: IB Tauris, 2007

McDonald, Malcolm. *Borneo People*, London: Jonathan Cape, 1956

Meisler, Stanley. *When the World Calls: The Inside Story of the Peace Corps and its First Fifty Years*, Boston: Beacon Press, 2011

Meyer, PHR. *The Royal Brunei Yacht Club: The First Thirty Five Years*, Brunei: PHR Meyer, 1988

Morrison, Alastair. *Fair Land Sarawak: Some Recollections of an Expatriate Official*, Ithaca, NY: Cornell University, 1993

Moulton, Major-General JL CB, DSO, OBE. *The Royal Marines*, London: Leo Cooper, 1972

Murphy, Philip. *Alan Lennox-Boyd: A Biography*, London; New York: IB Tauris, 1999

Parker, John. *Commandos: The Inside Story of Britain's Most Elite Fighting Force*, London: Headline, 2000

Parker, Thomas & Douglas Nelson. *Day by Day: The Sixties vol. 1 1960–1964*, New York, NY: Facts on File, 1983

Payne, Junaidi with photographs by Gerald Cubitt & Dennis Lau. *This Is Borneo*, London: New Holland, 1994

Pluvier, Jan M. *Confrontations: A Study in Indonesian Politics*, Kuala Lumpur: Oxford University Press, 1965

Pocock, Tom. *Fighting General: The Public and Private Campaigns of General Sir Walter Walker*, London: Collins, 1973

Poett, General Sir Nigel. *Pure Poett: The Autobiography of General Sir Nigel Poett*, London: Leo Cooper, 1991

Porritt, Vernon L. *The Rise and Fall of Communism in Sarawak, 1940–1990*, Clayton, Vic.: Monash Asia Institute, 2004

Poulgrain, Gregory John. *The Genesis of 'Konfrontasi': Malyasia, Borneo and Indonesia 1945–1965*, London: C Hurst & Co., 1998

Rahman, Zariani binti Abdul. *Escape from Berakas! 1962 Brunei Revolt*, Selangor, Malaysia: Al-Ahad Enterprise, 1992

Reece, Bob. *Masa Jepun: Sarawak under the Japanese 1941–1945*, Kuching, Sarawak: Sarawak Literary Society, 1998

Roff, William R. 'Islam obscured? Some Reflections on Studies of Islam and Society in Southeast Asia', in *Studies on Islam and Society in Southeast Asia*, Singapore: NUS Press, 2009

Russell, Ronald (ed). *British Commonwealth Year Book vol. 10 1962–63*, London: MacGibbon & Kee, 1962–63

St John, Spenser. *The life of Sir James Brooke, Rajah of Sarawak from his Personal Papers and Correspondence*, London; Edinburgh: Blackwood & Sons, 1879

Samuels, Marwyn S. *Contest for the South China Seas*, London and New York:

Routledge, 2005

SarDesai, DR. *Southeast Asia Past & Present*, 2nd edn, Boulder; San Francisco: Westview Press, 1989

Saunders, Graham E. *A History of Brunei*, Kuala Lumpur; New York: Oxford University Press, 1994

Singh, Ranjit DS. *Brunei 1839–1983: The Problems of Political Survival*, Kuala Lumpur, Malaysia: Oxford University Press, 1991

——& Jatswan S Sidhu. *Historical Dictionary of Brunei Darussalam: (Asian/ Oceanian Historical Dictionaries, No. 25)*, Lanham, Md.: Scarecrow Press, 1997

Speller, Ian & Christopher Tuck. *Amphibious Warfare Strategy and Tactics: The Theory and Practice of Amphibious Operations in the 20th Century*, St Paul, MN: MBI Publishing, 2001

State of Brunei. *Annual Report*, London: HMSO, 1962

Sukarno, *An Autobiography as told to Cindy Adams*, Indianapolis; New York: The Bobbs-Merrill Company Inc., 1965

Thompson, Julian. *The Lifeblood of War: Logistics in Armed Conflict*, London; Washington: Brassey's (UK); New York, NY: Distributed in North America by Macmillan, 1991

—— *The Royal Marines: From Sea Soldiers to a Special Force*, London: Sidgwick & Jackson, 2000

Troubridge, Laura. *Etiquette and Entertaining*, London: Amalgamated Press, 1940

Tucci, Sandro. *Gurhkas*, London: Hamish Hamilton, 1985

United Nations General Assembly, Delegation from Malaysia. *United Nations Malaysia Mission: Report*, Kuala Lumpur: Department of Information Malaysia, 1963

Van der Bijl, Nick. *Confrontation: The War with Indonesia 1962–1966*, Barnsley, South Yorkshire: Pen & Sword Military, 2007

Walker, Sir Walter Colyear. *Fighting On*, London: New Millennium, 1997

Willard, Hanna A. *Eight Nation Makers: Southeast Asia's Charismatic Statesmen*, New York: St Martin's Press, 1964

Wilson, Hugh D. *The Year of the Hornbill: A Volunteer's Service in Sarawak*, Wellington: AH & AW Reed, 1966

Wright, LR. *The Origins of British Borneo*, Hong Kong: Hong Kong University Press; distributed outside Hong Kong by Oxford University Press, 1970

Zaini Haji Ahmad, Haji. *The People's Party of Brunei: Selected Documents*, Petaling Jaya, Selangor: Institute of Social Analysis, 1987

Ziegler, P. *Mountbatten: The Official Biography*, London: Collins, 1985

Journal articles

Ashton, Chris. 'Dick Morris, OBE', Obituary, *Sydney Morning Herald*, 28 October 2000

—— 'From the Highlands', *Highlife Magazine*, vol. 7. no. 1 (October 2002), 184–5

Cheah, Boon-Kheng. 'The left-wing movement in Malaya, Singapore and Borneo in the 1960s: "an era of hope or devil's decade"?', *Inter-Asia Cultural Studies*, vol. 7, no. 4 (2006), 634–49

Craw, Lt Col JP. 'Indonesian Military Incursions into West Malaysia and Singapore between August 1964 and 30th September 1965', *Royal United Services Institution Journal*, vol. 11, no. 643 (1966), 208–219

Darling, Major PH. 'Operations in Brunei 1962–3' in Inst W Ll Evans (ed), *42 1962-1963 The Magazine of 42 Commando Royal Marines*, Singapore, 1963, 4–5

Evans, Inst Lt W Ll. 'Rebel in Captivity' in Inst W Ll Evans (ed), *42 1962-1963 The Magazine of 42 Commando Royal Marines*, Singapore, 1963, 12–14

Francis, Simon. 'Brunei Darussalam: Stresses and uncertainty 50 years on from the 1959 agreement with Britain', Asian Affairs, vol. 40, no. 2 (2009), 196–209

Freer, Air Chief Marshall Sir Robert. 'A Station Commander's view', *The Proceedings of the Royal Air Force Historical Society*, no. 13 (1994), 50

Fulton, SJ. 'Brunei: Past and present', *Asian Affairs*, vol. 15, no. 1 (1984), 5–14

Jones, Matthew. 'Creating Malaysia: Singapore security, the Borneo territories, and the contours of British policy, 1961–63', *The Journal of Imperial and Commonwealth History*, vol. 28, no. 2 (2000), 85–109

Kershaw, Roger. 'Constraints of history: The eliciting of modern Brunei', *Asian Affairs*, vol. 29, no. 3 (1998), 312–17

—— 'Challenges of historiography: Interpreting the decolonisation of Brunei', *Asian Affairs*, vol. 31, no. 3 (2000), 314–23

—— 'The last Brunei Revolt? A case study of microstate (in-)security', *Internationales Asien Forum, International Quarterly for Asian Studies*, vol. 42, no. 1/2 May (2011), 107–34

Lee, YL. 'The port towns of British Borneo', *Australian Geographer*, vol. 8, no. 4 (1962), 161–72

Legge, John. 'Review: The Genesis of Konfrontasi. Malaysia, Brunei, Indonesia 1945–1965 by Greg Poulgrain', *Journal of Southeast Asian Studies*, vol. 30, no. 2 (September 1999), 393–96

Leigh, Michael. 'Party Formation in Sarawak', *Indonesia*, no. 9 (April 1970), 189–224

Moore, Sir Jeremy. 'Limbang 1962 – Again!', *The Globe & Laurel*, September/October 2003, 319

Morris, RH. 'Limbang – An inside story', in Inst W Ll Evans (ed), *42 1962-1963 The Magazine of 42 Commando Royal Marines*, Singapore, 1963, 8–10

Morris, Mrs RH. 'Etiquette and Alka Seltzers', *Globe & Laurel: Journal of the Royal Marines*, vol. LXXll (March/April 1964), 102–104

Morrison, Hedda. 'Jungle journeys in Sarawak', *The National Geographic Magazine*, no. 109 (May 1956), 710–36

Reece, Bob. 'Review: Alastair Morrison "Fair land Sarawak: some recollections of an expatriate official"', *Crossroads*, vol. 9, no. 1 (1995), 153–54

—— 'An interview with Dr. H. J. Zaini Ahmad, Kuala Lumpur, 1985', *Borneo Research Bulletin*, vol. 39 (2008), 91–103

Sarawak Information Service. 'Limbang, a story of courage and kindness', *Sarawak by the Week*, no. 51/62 (16–22 December 1962), 5–6

Shriver, Sargent. 'Ambassadors of Good Will: The Peace Corps', *National Geographic Magazine*, vol. 126, no. 3 (1 September 1964), 297

Stockwell, AJ. 'The historiography of Malaysia: Recent writings in English on the history of the area since 1874', *The Journal of Imperial and Commonwealth*

History, vol. 5, no. 1 (1976), 82–110

—— 'Malaysia: The making of a neo-colony?', *The Journal of Imperial and Commonwealth History*, vol. 26, no. 2 (1998), 138–56

Van der Kroef, Justus M. 'Indonesia, Malaya and the North Borneo Crisis', *Asian Survey*, vol. 3, no. 4 (April 1963), 173–181

Walder, David Esq. ERD, MP. 'Malaysia', *Royal United Services Institution Journal*, vol. 110, no. 638 (1965), 105–11

Wells, Mike. 'Training young officers of the Royal Marines', *Marine Corps Gazette*, vol. 81, no. 4 (April 1997), 56–61

Electronic resources

Allison, Thaine H Jr RPCV. 'Observations Limbang 40th Reunion, Lima Company 42 Commando Royal Marines', <peacecorpsonline.org/messages/messages/2629/2019318.html>, accessed 3 August 2012

Affendi, Tengku Reza. 'Vintage Malaya', online at <www.vintagemalaya.com/Kuching.html>, accessed 31 May 2012

Anonymous. 'Gurkha soldier lunge: Helping Malaysia facing RPKAD', <menara-informasi.blogspot.com.au/2012/04/gurkha-soldier-lunge-helping-malaysia.html>, accessed 30 July 2012

Anonymous. 'Malaysia and Brunei carry out border demarcation, new disputes arise over Limbang', Singapore Institute of International Affairs, 23 March 2009, online at <www.siionline.org/?9=programmes/insights/malaysia-and-brunei-carry-out-border-demarcation-new-disputes-arise-over-limbang>, accessed 12 August 2012

Anonymous. Obituary General Sir Walter Walker, *The Telegraph*, 13 August 2001, <www.telegraph.co.uk/news/obituaries/military-obituaries/gurkha-obituaries/1337219/General-Sir-Walter-Walker.html>, accessed 30 July 2012

Anonymous. 'Sarawak seeks out missing link', *The Brunei Times*, 1 March 2012, <www.bt.com.bn/news-asia/2012/03/01/sarawak-seeks-out-missing-link>, accessed 5 August 2012

Anonymous. 'Wanted poster: Yassin Affandy Rahman', Sea Your History <www.seayourhistory.org.uk/component/option/com_gallery2/Itemid,811/?g2_itemid=14762>, accessed 27 May 2012

Aspinall, Terry. 'Burma Camp for the 3rd time, February 1964 to July 1964', 1998, <www.terryaspinall.com/autobiographychapters/chapter09.html>, accessed 6 June 2012

——'Royal Marine Commandos April 1962–February 1963', online at <www.terryaspinall.com/autobiography-chapters/chapter04.html>, accessed 27 July 2012

——'Active Service February 1963–July 1963', online at <www.terryaspinall.com/autobiography-chapters/chapter05.html>, accessed 27 July 2012

Awang, Nela. 'Malay words Awang, Abang have similar meaning and origins', *The Brunei Times*, 21 November 2007, <www.bt.com.bn/node/25805/print>, accessed 29 May 2012

Bain, Kenneth. 'Obituary: Sir Derek Jakeway', *The Independent*, 13 November 1993, <www.independent.co.uk/news/people/obituary-sir-derek-jakeway-1503935.html>, accessed 1 June 2012

Bridgland, Fred. 'Field Marshall Sam Manekshaw', *The Scotsman*, 3 July
    2008, <www.scotsman.com/news/obituaries/field-marshal-sam-
    manekshaw-1-1078732>, accessed 29 May 2012

Britain's Small Wars, <www.britains-smallwars.com/Borneo/units.html>, accessed
    17 May 2012

—— <www.britains-smallwars.com/Borneo/Chawton.htm>, accessed 17 May 2012

—— <www.britains-smallwars.com/Borneo/index.html>, accessed 17 May 2012

Cotterell, Arthur. *A Dictionary of World Mythology*, Oxford University
    Press, 1997, online at <www.oxfordreference.com/views/ENTRY.
    html?subview=Main&entry=t 73.e118>, accessed 25 June 2012

Dennis, Peter & Jeffrey Grey, Ewan Morris, Robin Prior & Jean Bou (eds). *The
    Oxford Companion Australian Military History*, Oxford University Press, 2009,
    Oxford Reference Online, 27 November 2011 <www.oxfordreference.com/
    views/ENTRy.html?subview=Main&entry=t271.e653>, accessed 27 May 2012

Everett-Heath, John. 'Borneo', *Concise Dictionary of World Place-Names*, 2005, 2nd
    edn, Oxford University Press, 2010, online at <www.oxfordreference.com/
    views/ENTRY.html?subview=Main&entry=t209.e941>, accessed 25 June 2012

Farrar-Hockley, Anthony. 'Poett, Sir (Joseph Howard) Nigel (1907–1991)',
    Oxford Dictionary of National Biography, Oxford University Press, 2004 <www.
    oxforddnb.com/view/article/49929>, accessed 27 February 2012

Fyffe, Sgt KD. 'Bullets and Bumboats: Recollections of the Limbang Raid', online
    at <www.britains-smallwars.com/Borneo/Bullets-Bumboats.htm>, accessed
    8 October 2012.

Hamdan, Nurbaiti. 'Limbang border to be set', *The Star*, 20 March 2009 <thestar.
    com.my/news/story.asp?file=/2009/3/20/nation/3518846&sec=nation>,
    accessed 10 February 2012

Horton, AVM. 'Omar Ali Saifuddin III (1914–1986)', *Oxford Dictionary of
    National Biography*, Oxford University Press, 2004, online edition, January 2008
    <www.oxforddnb.com/view/article/66336>, accessed 27 February 2012

Hunter, Alex. 'Maj Gen A. G. Patterson CB DSO OBE MC – My grandfather',
    <www.haebc.com/2011/11/maj-gen-a-g-patterson-my-grandfather/>, accessed,
    11 November 2011

Johnson, Laurie AB. 'HMS *Chawton*, 1961–1963', <britains-smallwars.com/
    Borneo/Chawton.htm>, accessed 4 August 2012

Lee, David. 'A Year in 42 Commando, November 1963–1964 Singapore and
    Borneo', <file://localhost/Volumes/42CommandoBorneo/RM_42 Cdo
    Folder/A Year in 42 Commando.htm>, accessed 25 February 2012

Lee, Kuan Yew. 'The legacy of Sultan Haji Omar Ali Saifuddien', 25 February
    2009, <www.docstoc.com/docs/31476468/DRAFT-FOR-SULTAN-SIR-
    HAJI-OMAR-ALI-SAIFUDDIN-MEMORIAL-LECTURE-I>, accessed
    3 March 2012

Ling, Sharon. 'James Wong dies', *The Star* online, 19 July 2011, <thestar.com.my/
    news/story.asp?file=/2011/7/19/sarawak/9126319&sec=sarawak>, accessed 3
    March 2012

Little, Matthew G. 'The Victoria Cross and the Royal Marines', online at <www.
    royalmarinesmuseum.co.uk/item/researching-family-and-royal-marine-history/

the-victoria-cross-the-royal-marin>, accessed 8 October 2012

Manansala, Paul Kekai. 'Quests of the Dragon and Bird Clan', 13 March 2009 <sambali.blogspot.com.au/2009/03/on-title-dayang.html>, accessed 23 February 2012

Norbrook, Donald. 'Remembering Winston Churchill: Someone in particular, Sir John Martin', 11 November 1973, BBC Archive <www.bbc.co.uk/archive/churchill/11020.shtml>, accessed 1 June 2012

Pocock, Tom. 'Walker, Sir Walter Colyear (1912–2001)', *Oxford Dictionary of National Biography*, Oxford University Press, January 2005; online edition, January 2011 <www.oxforddnb.com/view/article/76147>, accessed 27 February 2012

Reece, Bob. 'An interview with Dr. Hj. Zaini Ahmad, Kuala Lumpur', 1985, <www.thefreelibrary.com/An+interview+with+D.+Hj.+Zaini+Ah,ad,+Kuala+Lumpur>, accessed 27 May 2012

Shirley, John. 'Major General Sir Jeremy Moore', *The Guardian*, 18 September 2007, <www.guardian.co.uk/news/2007/sep/18/guardianobituaries.military>, accessed 12 August 2012

Singapore Institute of International Affairs. 'Malaysia and Brunei carry out border demarcation, new disputes arise over Limbang', 23 March 2009, <www.siiaonline.org/?q=programmes/insights/malaysia-and-brunei-carry-out-border-demarcation-new-disputes-arise-over-limbang>, accessed 12 August 2012

Spirit, Martin & Nick van der Bijl. *Return to Limbang*, Dallas: Brushfire Films, 2006

Stephen, Martin. 'Obituary: Alec Dickson', *The Independent*, 10 October 1994, <www.independent.co.uk/news/people/obituary-alec-dickson-1442037.html>, accessed 8 August 2012

Thompson, Julian. 'Moore, Sir (John) Jeremy (1928–2007)', *Oxford Dictionary of National Biography*, Oxford University Press, January 2011, <www.oxforddnb.com/view/article/99104>, accessed 25 July 2012

Thomson, Mike. 'The stabbed governor of Sarawak', *BBC News Magazine*, 12 March 2012, <www.bbc.co.uk/news/magazine-17299633>, accessed 14 March 2012

Wong, Dennis. 'I led a bloody revolt in Limbang', *New Sunday Times*, 1 May 2100, <imageshack.us/f/685/TheLimbangRaidfromthere.jpg/>, accessed 12 August 2012

Yunos, Rozan. 'An abridged history of modern Brunei', *The Brunei Times*, 24 February 2008, <www.bt.com.bn/life/2008/02/24/an_abridged_history_of_modern_brunei>, accessed 6 May 2012

—— 'Birth of Brunei Administrative Service', *The Brunei Times*, 7 June 2010, <www.bt.com.bn/art-culture/2010/06/07/birth-brunei- administrative-service>, accessed 28 February 2012

Ziegler, Philip. 'Mountbatten, Louis Francis Albert Victor Nicholas, first Earl Mountbatten of Burma (1900–1979)', *Oxford Dictionary of National Biography*, Oxford University Press, 2004; online edition, January 2011, <www.oxforddnb.com/view/article/31480>, accessed 10 August 2012

INDEX